MAR 3 1 2023

S0-AZE-212

"*Fool Me Once* is a lively, relatable, and pragmatic approach to the subject of 'everyday fraud'—the quotidian scams that don't always make headlines but that do always take their toll in human misery, economic disruption, and social mistrust. Intimate stories of victims, perpetrators, and whistleblowers deepen the impact of Kelly Richmond Pope's research, giving us uncommon insights into these all-too-common crimes."

> —**DIANA B. HENRIQUES**, author, *New York Times* bestseller
> *The Wizard of Lies*

"*Fool Me Once* is insightful, educational, and highly entertaining. Based on hundreds of hours of direct personal contact with fraudsters, Kelly Richmond Pope offers a riveting take on the human side of fraud. A must-read!"

> —**BETHANY MCLEAN**, coauthor, *New York Times* bestseller
> *All the Devils Are Here*

"As someone who has been a certified fraud examiner for most of my career, I have long been fascinated with the psychology of human behavior. I have lived through the WorldCom fraud and have witnessed the devastating impact that fraud can have on the lives of so many people. *Fool Me Once* is required reading for anyone who wants to better understand perpetrators, victims, and whistleblowers and how to better prevent, detect, and investigate fraud."

> —**CYNTHIA COOPER**, international speaker; author,
> *Extraordinary Circumstances*

"Accessible, humorous, and engaging, *Fool Me Once* includes fascinating stories from the perspective of one of the nation's foremost fraud research experts. I recommend this book for corporate and academic discussion or for anyone interested in understanding and preventing fraud. I do *not* recommend it for potential fraudsters!"

—**PAULA A. PRICE**, former Chief Financial Officer, Macy's; senior lecturer, Harvard Business School

FOOL ME ONCE

FOOL

SCAMS, STORIES, AND SECRETS

ME

FROM THE TRILLION-DOLLAR

KELLY RICHMOND POPE

ONCE

FRAUD INDUSTRY

Harvard Business Review Press

Boston, Massachusetts

The web addresses referenced in this book were live and correct at the time of the book's publication but may be subject to change.

Library of Congress Cataloging-in-Publication Data

Names: Pope, Kelly R., 1974- author.
Title: Fool me once : scams, stories, and secrets from the trillion-dollar fraud industry / Kelly Richmond Pope.
Description: Boston, Massachusetts : Harvard Business Review Press, [2022] | Includes index. |
Identifiers: LCCN 2022042885 (print) | LCCN 2022042886 (ebook) | ISBN 9781647823917 (hardcover) | ISBN 9781647823924 (epub)
Subjects: LCSH: Fraud. | Impostors and imposture. | Whistle blowers. | Business ethics. | Psychology, Industrial.
Classification: LCC HV6691 .P67 2022 (print) | LCC HV6691 (ebook) | DDC 364.16/3—dc23/eng/20221123
LC record available at https://lccn.loc.gov/2022042885
LC ebook record available at https://lccn.loc.gov/2022042886

ISBN: 978-1-64782-391-7
eISBN: 978-1-64782-392-4

The paper used in this publication meets the requirements of the American National Standard for Permanence of Paper for Publications and Documents in Libraries and Archives Z39.48-1992.

CONTENTS

FOOL
ME
ONCE

FOREWORD

"Fool me once, shame on you; fool me twice, shame on me."

This well-known proverb was made more famous when George W. Bush fumbled the saying during a September 17, 2002, speech given in Nashville, Tennessee. Mr. Bush said, "Fool me once, shame on—shame on you. Fool me—can't get fooled again." Although the gaffe went down in history, the sentiment still holds true.

This idea of taking personal ownership when being fooled a second time by an untrustworthy person was first found in *The Court and Character in King James* written by Anthony Weldon in 1651. As the proverb stands, if you get fooled more than once, it's totally your fault.

I thought this would be the perfect title for this book. Maybe you were deceived once, but the stories and lessons included in this book can help you never be fooled a second time. And if you do get fooled a second time, well . . . it actually may be your fault.

INTRODUCTION

Kathe Swanson arrived at the Dixon, Illinois, city hall and entered the redbrick building through the side door, the same way she had for the last three decades. She looked younger than her sixty-two years, wearing her hair short and feathered. She was usually very busy, and today was no different.

As was often the case, her boss, Rita Crundwell, was away. Rita was Dixon's city comptroller, but she was also a quarter-horse breeder with massive ranches in Dixon, Illinois, and Beloit, Wisconsin, eventually owning four hundred quarter horses on twenty-two farms across thirteen states. She had a $2.1 million motor home along with custom saddles, bedazzled riding jackets, and jewelry. She often took time off from work to do Lord knows what—something relating to horses. She had already won multiple national breeding championships.[1] Kathe wasn't sure what went on at these shows, but she knew that they were expensive and that Rita lived for them.

People wondered aloud how Rita managed to afford all of this. Rita was never consistent with her responses. She told some people that her money came from selling horses and winning championships. Others believed that her parents were investors in the Campbell's Soup Company. Still others thought she'd had an older boyfriend who left her money after he died. Kathe didn't know and didn't care. It wasn't her business.

Today, Kathe had to pull together a fiscal report for a city council meeting. That in itself wasn't a problem. The issue was that Rita had never set up the user ID for the online banking system, so Kathe couldn't access the statements digitally, and the city's bank hadn't mailed the statements.

Rita had always instructed Kathe to gather information on specific accounts. But for some reason, today Kathe didn't feel like following protocol. She's still not sure why. Maybe she was annoyed that her boss was out of the office yet again and that it fell on her to pick up the slack. Or maybe she was just listening to her gut. Whatever the case, she called the bank and asked them to fax over information on every single account for Dixon.

The pages arrived—reams of them—and her eyes began to film over. Kathe wasn't quite sure what she was seeing, but something didn't smell right. She noticed deposits of $200,000, $300,000, and $500,000 into "RSCDA—Reserve Fund, or Reserve Sewer Capital Development Account." Maybe it was a private account Rita had put under the city's name so she could buy and sell horses without the IRS catching on? But on closer inspection, Kathe realized she was wrong. This wasn't a city account. It was a private account. Rita's.

She didn't know it, but everything was about to change. For her. For Dixon. And for me.

• • •

Rita Crundwell had been tiptoeing, and then stomping, around my psyche since April 2012, when I opened the *Chicago Tribune* and a headline blasted out: "Dixon Comptroller Accused of Stealing $30 Million from City Coffers."[2] That was *before* they realized it was more like $53 million.

My heart jumped. How did a woman with a high school education pull off the largest city government fraud in US history? How did she steal over $37,000 *a day* from a town with an annual budget of $6 million? Rita was raised in Dixon, began working for the city right out of high school, and had no family wealth to speak of. How did her coworkers believe she financed such a luxurious lifestyle? And how did the city's auditor, a top-ten national accounting firm, miss all the evidence that fraud was occurring?

It was my kind of story.

I've been fascinated with fraud ever since I was a graduate student at Virginia Tech, where I earned my PhD in accounting. Part of my interest had to do with my father, Dr. Tyronza R. Richmond. He was the chancellor of North Carolina Central University in Durham from 1986 until 1991, and he was forced to resign when one of his employees was caught embezzling money.[3] My father had nothing to do with it, but he took the rap. The specter of that debacle loomed over him for the rest of his life. And, I guess, mine too.

I teach forensic accounting at DePaul University in Chicago and research white-collar crime. For the last ten years, I've been traveling the country and have talked with countless whistleblowers, victims, and offenders, inviting them to my classes. All of these cases—from my former colleague who went to prison for mortgage fraud to the unsuspecting soccer mom who stole millions from her employer to the reformed cybercriminal who showed me how to access the dark web to the college counselor who blew the whistle on one of the largest academic fraud cases and was shunned by many—have shaped my thinking. All of these cases have impacted my views on how far people will push the envelope in any number of ways. Their stories are fascinating, scary, and also quite relatable. I want my students to get to know these people in the flesh; I want them to see themselves reflected in the fraud dilemmas. Because when you can imagine these issues happening to you, your judgment about the person facing the dilemma can change.

As I look back on the perpetrators, whistleblowers, and victims I've met over the years, I realize that every perp was different, every victim was different, and every whistleblower was different. Despite people lumping them all together, they're not the same. The only things they had in common were that they'd committed a crime, reported a crime, or were victims of a crime. But the reasons behind how they got there, and why, differed significantly. Some came from well-off families, while others never graduated from high school. Some were serial offenders, while others suffered lapses in judgment. Some people were simply minding their own business and were victimized, while some corporations had weak internal controls and became easy targets. So I devised categories to distinguish one from another—and also to help me figure out my own feelings toward each one. Why was I angry at one kind of perp but more forgiving of another? Why did one type of victim elicit pity in me and the other elicit condemnation?

I'm fixated on how people cheat, and even more by how they rationalize it. The media often focused on what happened in Dixon but rarely discussed *why* the fraud happened, why the townspeople were so trusting, and why it was discovered. I decided to conduct my own investigation, interviewing Rita's colleagues, the FBI, the US Marshals Service, and Kathe Swanson, Rita's employee-turned-whistleblower. I wanted to understand how the people who oversaw Rita's responsibilities overlooked her actions. Most importantly, I wanted to help other people, organizations, and cities learn how to protect themselves from similar predators.

So, I did what any good accounting professor would do: I made a documentary, *All the Queen's Horses*, about Rita and her crime.[4] It went surprisingly well, considering I had zero filmmaking experience. It appeared in thirteen international film festivals and was the number-one documentary on iTunes, Amazon Prime Video, Google Play, and Direct TV during its debut week in April 2018.[5] I began lecturing at companies, universities, and in towns around the country and abroad. The documentary opened to me a community of people outside of the classroom that I'd never met before.

Here's what I've learned: almost every organization has a potential Rita Crundwell in it—which is to say, a trusted colleague we'd never expect to betray us, which is why they can. No matter where I am in the world, every time I do a presentation, at least one person approaches me to share their own experience with fraud.

A Trillion-Dollar Problem

Fraud has become accepted as business-as-usual in our culture in a way that we've never seen before. Yes, hucksters, charlatans, and thieves have always existed, but nothing like today. Newspapers are filled with stories about major scams almost daily. There are the big stories we all know about—Bernie Madoff, Enron, or Volkswagen. Among companies with over $10 billion in global annual revenues, 52 percent experienced fraud during the past twenty-four months.[6] Within that group, nearly one in five reported that their most disruptive incident had a financial impact of more than $50 million.

The advent of Covid-19 has added a new opportunity for fraud. Since the pandemic began in 2020, scammers have taken full advantage. According to the Federal Trade Commission (FTC),

Americans have filed over half a million Covid-19 fraud reports and lost over $480 million.[7] Since the pandemic hit, global online fraud has increased by 46 percent.[8] "Fraudsters are always looking to take advantage of significant world events," Shai Cohen, Senior Vice President of Global Fraud Solutions at TransUnion, an American consumer reporting credit agency, noted in a March 2021 report.[9] "The pandemic and its corresponding rapid digital acceleration brought about by stay-at-home orders is a global event unrivaled in the online age."[10] That same report found that the countries with the highest rate of suspected fraudulent transactions between March 11, 2020, and March 10, 2021—the height of the pandemic— were the Seychelles, Kazakhstan, and Turkmenistan. Coincidentally, these three countries are located in the global regions where employer-related fraud losses are the highest (Eastern Europe, Western/Central Asia, and Middle East/North Africa).[11]

Then there are the smaller, gentler scams that fail to crack public consciousness. Some of the most common frauds don't even register as fraud. Have you ever fudged a timesheet or expense report? That's fraud. Have you ever accidentally-on-purpose failed to report all your earnings on your tax return? That's fraud, too.

By the end of 2020, there were 1,387,615 reports of identity theft in the United States.[12] Globally, more than 40 percent of consumers have been identity theft victims.[13] Not only does this type of fraud add up, but we also know that large-scale fraud often begins with small actions and nominal amounts of cash. According to the Association of Certified Fraud Examiners (ACFE), organizations worldwide lost an estimated $3.7 trillion to fraud in 2019.[14] Losses reached closer to $5 trillion in 2022.[15]

Governments, corporations, and nonprofits are equally susceptible to fraud. As a March 2021 article in the *Wall Street Journal* reported, the top 1 percent of households don't report about 21 percent of their income, "with six percentage points of that due to sophisticated strategies that random audits don't detect." Unreported income is almost twice as much for the top 0.1 percent.[16]

Remember: Rita Crundwell worked in a small town, where she had total control over city finances. She funneled taxpayer money into her own personal account, which went undetected for twenty years.

Unfortunately, the government is making it harder to curtail fraud. In May 2019, the Securities and Exchange Commission (SEC) voted to exempt small public companies—those with annual revenues of less than $100 million—from requiring an independent outside auditor to attest to the adequacy of the company's internal control auditing provisions.[17] The idea, the SEC said, was to reduce the "unnecessary burdens and compliance costs'" for smaller companies.[18] This was a modification to the Sarbanes Oxley Act of 2002 (SOX), a bipartisan federal law that was created to fix the way US public companies were audited. SOX was enacted in response to major corporate and accounting scandals, like Enron, Tyco, and WorldCom; essentially, it cracked down on corporate fraud. The act created new requirements for all public company boards, management, and public accounting firms in the United States, along with provisions for privately held companies. When he signed it into law, President George W. Bush said, "The era of low standards and false profit is over; no boardroom in America is above or beyond the law."[19]

This could have been true if SOX had stayed the way it was written. But the SEC's 2019 modifications made it easier for fraud to be ignored in companies with less than $100 million in annual revenues, because without independent audits, there was no one to challenge or monitor their accounting systems. The relaxation of SOX applies to most companies because companies with over $100 million in annual revenues are unicorns.[20] They're the exception rather than the rule. As a 2015 report from *Inc.* magazine noted, a mere .04 percent of companies reach $100 million in annual revenue.[21] So when the SEC relaxed rules for the under–$100 million group, it opened the opportunity for the overwhelming majority of US companies to behave however they want. With no independent audit, it's a free-for-all.

To me, this means one thing: that the onus is on employers—and employees—to understand what fraud looks and feels like. According to the 2022 PwC's Global Economic Crime and Fraud Survey, nearly half of reported incidents resulting in losses of $100 million or more were committed by insiders.[22] So insiders should know how to identify and prevent fraud.

Fraud Affects Us All

These are never victimless crimes. Fraud harms real people in virtually every scenario. Sometimes the effects are obvious, like the 1977 Ford Pinto scandal. The company knew that the placement of its gas tanks was potentially deadly, but the company didn't do anything to fix them. Dozens of people were killed when their gas tanks exploded in accidents.[23] Other times the fraud is subtle and difficult to untangle, like Rita Crundwell's. Nobody died, but people certainly suffered. Someone, somewhere, is always left holding the bill.

We've become accustomed to hearing about fraud; we accept it as part of the world we live in today—so much so that our abilities to identify it and speak about it are limited.

Based on survey responses from 2,550 executives from fifty-five countries and territories, an EY Global Fraud Survey found that respondents under thirty-five are more likely to justify fraud or corruption to meet financial targets or to help a business survive an economic downturn.[24] The study also found that this group would be more likely to act unethically to meet financial targets than older respondents.

That's why I teach fraud and why I'm compelled to write this book.

When I teach, I want my students to see themselves reflected in the stories we explore. They don't have millions of dollars like the late Bernie Madoff or the clients he duped, nor do they run an automobile enterprise. They can't relate to bigwig executives "rigging diesel-powered vehicles to cheat on government emissions tests" (the fraud for which Volkswagen was ordered to pay a $2.8 billion criminal fine 2021).[25]

But they can relate to an ambitious person with big dreams. Stories like Rita Crundwell's tap into the everyday people who find themselves entangled in a vicious lie.

Like Harriette Walters, a former civil servant and tax assessment manager for the District of Columbia, who stole $48 million from her employer and was sentenced to 17.5 years in prison in 2009.[26]

Or Randy Constant, a Missouri farmer who claimed his nonorganic crops were organic for over a decade, resulting in $142 million worth of fraudulent sales.[27] Rather than go to prison, Constant killed himself. (When white-collar crime results in murder or suicide, it's known as "red collar crime.")

Or Elizabeth Holmes, the charming young Theranos founder who duped luminaries like Henry Kissinger, former secretary of state George Schultz, and General James Mattis into investing millions of dollars in a bogus company. She was found guilty of lying to investors about her company's capabilities and convicted on three counts of wire fraud and one count of conspiracy to commit wire fraud.[28]

Fraud can happen anywhere, and to anyone.

The truth is, under the right circumstances and in the right environment, any one of us can be a Rita. And any organization, in any industry—real estate, government, health care, education, nonprofit, for-profit—can be a Dixon. Even the Covid-19 pandemic has had its own brand of fraud: People peddling fake vaccines or fake tests. People applying for PPP (Paycheck Protection Program) loans and using the money instead for jewelry, boats, or vacations. A spate of stories has cropped up about fraudulent vaccination cards.[29] According to the US Secret Service, criminals have stolen nearly $100 billion in Covid relief funds.[30]

* * *

So how do you protect yourself and your company from fraud? By understanding how fraud takes place and by not being afraid to speak up when it does.

I realize this is much easier said than done, especially if you grew up, as I did, being told to keep your nose out of other people's lives and "mind your own business." I vividly remember the first time I heard the phrase. I was twelve, and my eighteen-year-old brother had committed some kind of transgression. I don't recall what exactly. (Maybe he didn't clean his room? Or he ate crackers on the sofa with no plate?) All I know is that as the dutiful daughter, I marched straight over to my mother to tell her what had transpired. But instead of praising me for my honesty, my mom stared at me for a solid thirty seconds, her hand firmly placed on her hip. Then she turned back to the pot of soup simmering on the kitchen stove.

"Kelly, please let your dad and me handle this," she said. "It's best if you just mind your own business."

For real?

From that point on, I saw my brother do a lot of wrong things, but I never uttered a word. I just watched from the sidelines. It wasn't my business, right?

Fast forward to twenty years later when I became a parent and heard myself saying the same thing to my kids. My reasons varied over the years. Sometimes, I didn't want to be bothered with the mini-crisis at the time. Other times I felt that the child sharing the information with me was breaking some kind of sibling code. I say those three words, "Mind your business!" and I can picture my mother in her leopard housedress, a scarf tied around her head, and I laugh.

I didn't realize just how significant those words were until I became a business school professor and fraud researcher. I want everyone to mind their business, but in the *opposite* way to what my mother meant.

I want people to be vigilant, aware. I want people to stick their nose into other people's business, to say something if they see something. There are instances when you are simply going about your daily life, bothering no one and minding your own business, and *Boom!*—a fraud crisis throws your world into chaos. This is a scary situation to be in and very hard to predict and prevent. And it can happen personally and professionally, at the individual and organizational levels.

You just don't know what's lurking around the corner, and if you don't mind your business on a regular, if not daily, basis, you have no idea what might happen.

In fact, you need *other* people to mind your business. There are instances when someone else, like a whistleblower, is minding your business—maybe even better than you—and alerts you to unscrupulous activities. Every organization needs these types of people; they're the eyes in the back of your head.

We need whistleblowers because we regularly miss the red flags that are swatting us in the face. Look at Rita Crundwell. If she was so successful in the horse world, why did she keep working? Why didn't she just follow her passion and ride off into the sunset? Plenty of Dixon residents wondered the same thing.

Research shows that frauds are discovered most often by whistleblowers—those people who see something and say something. Forty-two percent of frauds are discovered by an internal tip.[31]

The Whistleblower Protection Act of 1989 protects federal employees who reveal "government illegality, waste, and corruption."[32] Although whistleblower laws vary from country to country, with some countries having no laws in place, many of the strongest US federal laws allow for non-US citizens to report fraud confidentially. Still, people are afraid to speak up for fear of retaliation. It's not surprising that so many people keep quiet. It takes a lot of courage to be a lone voice talking against the tide.

This is a tragedy because we *need* whistleblowers. Think about all the lifesaving information we know about thanks to those who blew the whistle.

Without Jeffrey Wigand, former Vice President for Research and Development at Brown & Williamson Tobacco Corporation, the public wouldn't know how deadly cigarettes really are. Wigand came forward and told the world that cigarette companies had intentionally sold products laden with addictive levels of nicotine, which led to a $368 billion settlement against the tobacco industry.[33]

Without Peter Buxtun, a former US Public Health Service employee, the Tuskegee syphilis study (official name, the Tuskegee Study of Untreated Syphilis in the Negro Male)—in which African American men were neither told they had the sexually transmitted disease nor treated for it—might still be taking place.[34]

Just as every organization has a potential Rita Crundwell in it, it also has a Kathe Swanson, the person who opens the door and exposes the fraud. Without Kathe, Rita Crundwell's crime may have never been discovered, and a small town in the Midwest would still be hemorrhaging money.

Behind most frauds that have been exposed, there's the voice of a whistleblower. I'm hoping to inspire more people to come forward when they know something isn't right.

Most people who study fraud are familiar with the "Fraud Triangle," a framework created by criminologist Donald Cressey in the 1950s.[35] Based on conversations with prison inmates, Cressey hypothesized that three elements are necessary to commit fraud: opportunity, pressure, and rationalization. All three elements are usually present on some level but to varying degrees. Many of us, whether in public or private entities, have access to tools that can allow us to commit fraud. Pressure is what often motivates people to engage in fraud and can include trying to meet Wall Street expectations, a sudden job loss, or even an addiction. And we can all rationalize why we deserve our ill-gotten gains, which can include entitlement or feelings of being overworked and underpaid.

Cressey's discussion about the actual people involved in fraud and their rationales was limited. Additionally, he interviewed only convicted embezzlers and not fraud perpetrators as a larger class. Although Cressey explored their schemes, he didn't fully analyze their rationale or the *why* behind what drove them to do what they did. All perpetrators are not the same, and to group them all into one category, as Cressey did, does not allow us to understand the nuances of why people commit fraud. The three key players involved in any fraudulent interaction are: those who perpetrate the fraud (perps), those who are victims of it (prey), and those who expose it (whistleblowers). He overlooked the most important component: the people. As I've learned over the years, fraud has many faces.

In order for most frauds to occur and be discovered, these three groups are typically present. Most books about fraud focus on the crime and how the perpetrator spent their money. But I'm taking it a step further by forcing you to understand that all perps, prey, and whistleblowers are *not* cookie-cutter. Some people hate all perpetrators of fraud, assuming they're the lowest form of humanity. But if you really dissect the perpetrator category and understand the different types of perps, you might be able to muster up some empathy for them. The same applies to the other two groups. All victims aren't gullible, and all whistleblowers aren't snitches.

I want readers to understand the motivations behind each group. How does understanding the different categories of perpetrators help you understand them better? Because it allows you to recognize that some perpetrators truly didn't mean to be there. For sure—some did. But not all. And understanding the difference will allow you to recognize areas of vulnerability in your organization.

Of course, my take is controversial. Because we live in a society where you're guilty until proven guilty—and if you happen to be innocent, well, good luck. Lots of people will always think you're guilty.

Victims of crimes are thought to be naive. Gullible. Stupid. Some are, certainly. But not all are. As for whistleblowers, I am adamantly, vehemently, fervently against the word *rat*, *snitch*, or any other pejorative. I believe whistleblowers are heroes.

There is a thin line, by the way, between whistleblowing and speaking up. Whistleblowers are intimately involved in whatever the issue is and have a lot to lose (or gain) by coming forward. Those who speak up typically have no dog in the fight. They're just voicing a concern or righting a wrong.

I am going to show you examples of how moving through the categories of perp, prey, and whistleblowers will challenge your preexisting notions about fraud. By the time you finish this book, you'll have a better understanding of—and perhaps more compassion for—perpetrators; a renewed connection to victims; and an appreciation for those who blow the whistle. This book will challenge your thinking. It will inspire you to question your own biases and commonly held beliefs about people. You'll find yourself asking, "What would I do if faced with this situation?" or "Why wouldn't I trust someone who's trying to expose something egregious?"

Fool Me Once is for anyone who manages money or thinks that fraud can never happen to them or their organization. Are you a middle manager at a regional bank? A clerk at a local supermarket? A highly paid realtor? An entrepreneur? A business executive? A lawyer? A doctor or nurse? No matter where you work, no matter where you live, no matter how much (or how little) money you make, your life could be tinged by fraud. It's to your benefit to understand how it works.

We all have to understand the cycle of fraud because at one point or another you're either impacted by it, you did it, or you were in a position to expose it. If you're not one of those people, you've certainly met one.

You never know where you're going to land. Sometimes an unassuming employee makes an error that unwittingly turns them into a perpetrator. Sometimes a frustrated coworker stumbles on information that can be used to expose a major fraud. And oftentimes victims don't know what's happened to them until it's too late.

This book will show everyday fraud in action, taking readers on a journey so they can think about their decisions while reading about these cases. I want you to explore your own behaviors and motivations. What would *you* do if you had access to a bank vault? Would you check to see if there are cameras? What would you do if you knew a quick flick of the pen could increase your profit margin by 40 percent, but there was a 10 percent chance that people would die because of this action? What if you controlled the bank statements in town and nobody else looked at them?

I will define the spectrum of perps (intentional, accidental, righteous), prey (innocent bystanders and organizational targets), and whistleblowers (accidental, noble, vigilante, crossover). Every perp is different, every victim is different, and every whistleblower is different. I will explore the necessary role whistleblowers play within the fraud cycle, the cost and necessity of speaking truth, and how to do it well.

Fool Me Once is designed to help you better navigate among the people who comprise your company and the decisions they make every day. The stories and cases in this book will help you understand the pitfalls of not paying enough attention, not installing the proper internal controls, and not empowering the right people to protect your organization. Mostly, I hope it motivates you to mind your business. Literally.

PERPETRATORS

'm pretty sure Rita Crundwell hates me. I don't know this for a fact, but I suspect it's true. I understand it. I—a mere accounting professor!—exposed her crimes to an international audience. I've made a career out of her. If I were her, I'd hate me too.

Rita and I have never actually spoken. I reached out once with a handwritten letter on beautiful stationery. I thought if I wrote it by hand, she might feel more compelled to respond. She must have told her brother because a few days later, on January 22, 2018, a text popped up on my phone. It was from a man named Richard Humphrey. He told me that he would be happy to get me an interview with his sister—provided I could get then-president Donald Trump to pardon her.

"If they are willing to pay her restitution and send the money tax-free to me so she has something when she gets out," he wrote. "Otherwise, it's off the board."

It stayed off the board.

One of the main reasons I wanted to talk to Rita when I was filming my documentary, *All the Queen's Horses*, is because I thought viewers would want to hear from her.[1] People wondered why she did what she did. Was it because no one was looking over her shoulder and it was just so easy? Was it because she derived enormous pleasure from having a secret life and deceiving an entire city? Or was she a sociopath or narcissist who didn't care who was hurt so long as she achieved her goals?

I'm not sure any of that matters. The truth is, I felt like I understood Rita even without ever uttering a word to her because I understood her *scheme*. I've spent years studying her life and her decisions around financial transactions, and I've interviewed dozens of people who knew and worked with her.

You can understand a ton about a person based on how they stole, how much they stole, the length of time the fraud lasted, and the whistleblower who reported it. You don't always need to talk to the perp. You just need to pay attention to the variables around the crime.

In Rita's case, there were seven City of Dixon accounts at Fifth Third Bank. She routinely moved funds from the six legitimate accounts into another legitimate account called the Capital Development Fund. Rita then set up a seventh account no one knew about. To get the fraud started, she created phony invoices to justify payment for imaginary capital projects such as fixing sidewalks and making street repairs. She then took the money from the city's capital development fund and funneled them straight into her secret account. Remember, no one knew about this account, and it had a similar-sounding name to a legitimate city account.

From her secret account, she wrote checks for spa visits, jewelry, real estate, a motorcoach, and of course, quarter horses, none of which benefited the city of Dixon. She made this choice 179 times.

This is really how I shaped my film. By the end of the seventy-one minutes, you feel like you know Rita Crundwell even though you never actually hear from her. Because by the end of the movie, you understand her scheme. You learn that Rita had complete control of the Dixon finances for a significant amount of time. You also learn that everyone trusted her. What Rita said is what everyone did. Also, the scheme showed that there were very few internal controls around Dixon's finances, making the heist simple. In this case, the scheme speaks for the schemer.

Chapter 1

Intentional Perps

Rita epitomizes a group I call *intentional perps*. Intentional perps set out to commit fraud. They're on a mission to enrich themselves at all costs. They rationalize why they can break the law, and that's largely because they don't believe the rules apply to them. If they're not causing physical harm to anyone, the thinking goes, what's the big deal? Intentional perps marinate over time. They're not born; they're made. Environment and circumstance allow them to commit their misdeeds.

Intentional perps are the most threatening category of perpetrators, and the most destructive. They're everywhere, in every industry; they blend well with others because they possess the traits we value so much in this culture. They're highly intelligent, confident risk-takers who work well with people. Though you may think you know them, you really don't. They push boundaries and are often rewarded for doing so. What makes them so powerful is that they're usually fully and totally in charge.

Unlike *accidental perps* or *righteous perps*, which we'll get to in chapters 2 and 3, intentional perps think they're smarter than others—and they often *do* have superior skill sets. They'll do anything to get ahead. They're dangerously arrogant and entitled, and it's their arrogance that makes them think they can get away with things that other people can't.

Movies are made about intentional perps; TV shows about them clog the airwaves. In the Netflix series *Ozarks*, for example, financial adviser Marty Byrde has secretly been working for years as a money launderer for the second-largest drug cartel in Mexico. The series highlights how a cash-based business can be susceptible to money laundering by illegitimate businesses. Marty and his business partner Bruce Liddell are both intentional perps.

Most of us are arrogant to some degree. If you're successful, you have to have some degree of arrogance. But intentional perps take it to another level. Because they're so charming, people tend to like them, often opening doors for them that might be closed to the rest of us.

Researchers at the University of Minnesota identified three kinds of arrogance: individual, comparative, and antagonistic.[1] Individual arrogance is when a person has a heightened sense of their own traits, abilities, or accomplishments. Comparative arrogance is when a person has an inflated ranking of their abilities compared with other people. Antagonistic arrogance, which is considered to be the worst type, is found in people who enjoy denigrating others based on an assumption of superiority.

Intentional perps fluctuate among these varying levels of arrogance depending on the severity of the crime.

Arrogance is also a component of narcissistic personality disorder (NPD), a clinical diagnosis in the DSM-5, the diagnostic bible of mental disorders. Along with psychopathy and Machiavellianism, narcissism is one of three characteristics in the "Dark Triad" of personality traits, a term used in a *Journal of Research in Personality* article published in 2002.[2]

Also known as *arrogant narcissists*, people with NPD tend to be obsessed with achievement and success. They have an enormous sense of entitlement. They're charming and often successful, but they desperately crave validation. They're very smart about a range of subjects and highly articulate. They're charismatic and appealing. And they'll pull the rug right from under you and then run away with it.

Again, most of us are narcissistic as well as arrogant. Narcissism has a negative connotation, but like everything, narcissism exists on a spectrum. Narcissism is a mental health diagnosis with a lot of variations. There are *vulnerable narcissists*—that is, people with fragile self-esteem—and, on the other end, *grandiose narcissists*, who have inordinately high confidence and a great sense of superiority.[3]

Grandiose narcissists need to be admired. They have an inflated sense of self and think they should receive special dispensations simply because they're so wonderful. They often appear conceited or arrogant. Overall, these narcissists are more assertive and extroverted than their counterparts with standard NPD.[4] In my experience, intentional perps typically exhibit traits of grandiose narcissism.

Grandiose narcissism is the traditional corporate form of narcissism that we see every day: those who have it are driven, dedicated, focused. While they may be exploitative and aggressive, I think this manifestation is more of the "good type."

Typical grandiose narcissists have super-high confidence and self-esteem. They, too, are entitled, and they're quick to anger and are often volatile.

Vulnerable narcissists, on the other hand, are much more in-troverted and less charismatic than their grandiose compatriots. Accidental and noble perps, whom I will discuss shortly, are usu-ally vulnerable narcissists.

Because He Could

Although I observed Rita's case only from afar, I've had several close interactions with other intentional peps. One of my favorites, and someone I consider a friend, is Jason Chez, who went to prison for fraud in 2008, when he was just twenty-eight years old.

I met Jason in 2018 when he came to speak to my graduate Prin-ciples of Forensic Accounting class. Jason grew up between Lake Forest and Highland Park, Illinois, wealthy Chicago suburbs. His parents were loaded. He didn't need the money, which he freely ad-mits. So why did he break the law? "Because we were young, stupid, and shot from the hip," he said.

In the early aughts, Jason started a radiology equipment com-pany. His company digitized X-rays, putting them on discs or DVDs. This was a big deal back then, before everything lived in the cloud. Jason serviced more than two thousand hospitals around the country, raking in an annual income of about $1.7 million. Take-home. Not bad for a guy who started his company in his twenties.

But then one day Sanju Abraham, the head of radiology at the University of Chicago Hospital, approached Jason with an offer.

"The hospital needs computer programming work and server maintenance," Abraham told him. "I can do the work, but the hos-pital won't hire me because I already work here and it's a conflict."

That conflict was the problem.

If you work in a company, you're probably familiar with its code of conduct policy (even if, ahem, you've never actually read it). That's the set of rules and regulations all employees must adhere to. In the event that you simply signed it without reading it, the code of conduct is essentially a pledge from all employees to act in the interest of their employer and not themselves. Both Jason and Sanju knew that starting their own company while Sanju was employed by the hospital would be in direct conflict with Sanju's employment agreement. But their work arrangement—Jason on the outside, Sanju on the inside—actually made them ideal partners in crime. In fact, nearly 70 percent of organizations experiencing fraud reported that the most disruptive incident came from an external attack or collusion between external and internal sources.[5] The federal Anti-Kickback Statute prohibits anyone from offering, paying, soliciting, or receiving money to induce or reward the referral of business reimbursable under any federal health care programs.[6] Yet they proceeded with the plan.

Sanju proposed that Jason's company outsource the work to him. "He wanted me to employ him on the side and split the profits," said Jason. He admitted that he thought "maybe this isn't a smart idea." He even brought up the business proposition to his lawyer. His lawyer told him it wasn't a criminal offense, but it was a civil one.

In typical intentional perp fashion, Jason didn't fret about a minor civil offense. As long as he wasn't going to be locked up in jail for the rest of his life, who cared? "If he had said it was criminal, I don't think we would have done it," he told me. "But once we were in it, we started to get greedier." If a problem arose, he figured they'd settle out of court and be done with it.

According to Dr. Nelson Cowan, a Curators' Distinguished Professor of Psychology at the University of Missouri-Columbia, "Humans overestimate what they know and underestimate the uncertainty, as well as underestimating what other people may know."[7] Jason and Sanju underestimated the risk involved in their scheme. Jason thought he could easily talk himself out of any problem that arose.

Jason's level of overconfidence is not unusual for an intentional perp. People often overestimate their abilities and underestimate the likelihood that they'll get caught committing a crime. In general, people tend to veer in the direction of optimism, a condition known as the "optimism bias."[8] A study by neuroscientist Tali Sharot found that most of us underestimate our chances of splitting from our partner, losing our job, or being diagnosed with a terminal illness.[9] We believe our children will be amazingly gifted, think we'll accomplish more than our peers, and expect to live twenty years longer than we most likely will.

Being super optimistic, however, can be detrimental. Research published in *Psychological Science* found that having a high perception of one's own expertise led people to anoint themselves with guru status, imagining they had financial expertise they didn't have or an understanding of biology they didn't know.[10]

Clearly, optimism can keep us motivated. "I wasn't smart enough to come up with a premeditated scheme and let it play out," Jason said. "Mine was just being stupid and getting caught and doing something dumb. But a Ponzi scheme takes planning. You don't just do it." In Jason's case, he simply overbilled the hospital and split the ill-gotten profits with Sanju. Since there was very little oversight of the invoices and Sanju had some authority to approve many of them, including Jason's fraudulent invoices, the overbilling scheme was a piece of cake.

But too much optimism can lead to disastrous miscalculations. Jason was working day and night and bringing in millions in sales. His business partner, on the other hand, was playing basketball and rolling into the office around 11 a.m. When Jason decided to fire him, his partner got angry and threatened to turn Jason in unless he paid him $1 million. Jason refused. Sanju made good on his word and exposed the multimillion-dollar billing scheme that Jason and Sanju were running. Turning Jason in meant that he also turned himself in since they were business partners. When Sanju heard that the scheme was exposed, Sanju figured he could blame Jason as the mastermind and talk his way into a lighter sentence. Ultimately, Jason was charged with mail fraud, ordered to pay $2,240,616 in restitution, and sentenced to thirty-seven months at Oxford Federal Prison Camp in Oxford, Wisconsin.[11] "That's where all the Chicago politicians and corrupt judges go," he said unironically.

The white-collar criminals he met were the worst of the worst, the sort of people who would "steal the gold teeth out of their mother's mouth." "They were all crazy narcissists," he said. "Maybe I am, too, but my crime was fairly straightforward: kickbacks."

A Fan Favorite

Jason Chez is one of my students' fan favorites. He's young, charismatic, and well-spoken. I think my students see a glimmer of themselves in him: a young professional pushing the envelope and hopefully not getting caught. He represents the risk-taking side of them. The adventurer.

That doesn't mean they *like* him. But they are intrigued.

Typically, after a speaker visits, I ask my students to write a reflection paper. I want them to break down the case into digestible nuggets.

One of the best responses about Jason came from my student Alexis, who wrote this:

> Jason Chez presented himself as an affable, charming neighborly narcissist. His privileged upbringing, coupled with the pervasive tone of toxic masculinity in the early 2000s, appears to have heralded his engagement in a kickback scheme. Mr. Chez exudes the confidence and intelligence that suggests he would have an easy time establishing relationships and finessing the sharper angles of coercion necessary to retain positive vendor rapport.

She nailed it!

Intentional perps like Jason could be classified as grandiose narcissists. And the business world is filled with them.

Again, most of us exist on a spectrum. We differ in how much or how little we have of any one trait. But based on my twenty-five years of teaching and my interviews with hundreds of intentional perp white-collar offenders, I can confidently say intentional perps are generally more narcissistic than most.

Some intentional perps are more intentional than others, and you can categorize them on a spectrum from 0 to 10, with 10 being the most intentional. Let's say that Jason is a grandiose narcissist, a 2 on the intentional perp spectrum. Rita Crundwell, also grandiose, would be a 6. Robert Courtney, whom you'll meet in a bit, is a 10.

If These Halls Could Talk

Not only does almost every organization have a Rita Crundwell in it—someone you trust implicitly who may not deserve that trust—but my own workplace did, too.

I'm talking about my friend and colleague Robert Lattas, who in 2015 was convicted in federal court on five counts of wire and mail fraud and sentenced to more than five years in prison.[12] He's a three on the intentional perp scale.

Bob was a lawyer and accountant who taught in DePaul's Driehaus College of Business, School of Accountancy and Management Information Systems. I liked him then, and I like him now. He was a family man. We taught together at the same institution for twelve years. Our desks were separated by a thin wall. But I had no idea that behind that wall, he was committing a crime.

I never in a million years expected Bob would be wanted by the Feds. He was a pillar of society, a high-powered real estate lawyer with lots of fancy clients. He lived in the suburbs in a big home with his wife, three kids, and a dog. He served on several boards, including his church, and several boards to help eradicate domestic violence and child abuse.

His life was moving along swimmingly, except for one minor detail: a few of his clients had taken advantage of the booming real estate market.

Between March 2007 and July 2012, Bob and his comrades allowed buyers to obtain mortgages to buy condos at a development called Vision on State by lying to lenders on loan applications, real estate contracts, and HUD-1 settlement statements about the sales price of the units. They also lied about the buyers' income, assets, liabilities, employment, and intention to occupy the condos. According to the lawsuit, Bob signed his name to mortgage loan applications despite knowing that they were filled with fake information that allowed unqualified buyers to get loans.[13]

As I read the indictment, my eyes nearly burst out of my head. I had so many questions for Bob, and I honestly didn't know where to start. How could my friend be part of a $22.9 million mortgage fraud scheme?

It was hard to imagine. But Bob and his two coconspirators, Aziz Aslam and Leonard Saunders, determined the minimum prices that their client, 13th & State, should receive for the condos and facilitated the sale of those units at inflated prices. The three men knew the difference between the two prices, or "the spread," would be paid to Aslam, Sanders, and others also hired to recruit buyers with incentives that were not disclosed in loan documents. All six defendants created fake documents that hid the fact that the buyers' down payments were actually provided by 13th & State. In reality, the buyers were contributing little or no equity, and the purchase prices were inflated.[14]

"This is really bad," I said to myself, tossing the indictment aside. I figured there must be a backstory that Bob would tell me about. Innocent until proven guilty. That's the law, right? He *could* be innocent. But deep down, I knew he wasn't.

I called Bob, and we spoke for hours. He had just been indicted so he could answer only some of my questions, not all. He thanked me for reaching out and I waited about a year to hear back from him.

I was devastated. How could I not have known that my trusted colleague was knowingly breaking the law to enrich himself? Of course, there was no way I would have known; we weren't in business together. Still, it was wrenching.

I went to his sentencing. I remember sitting in the courtroom, feeling like I was on the set of a *Law and Order* episode, only there was no ominous music and no district attorney Jack McCoy. Bob's brother and sister were there. His soon-to-be ex-wife was in the second row. This was real life. My friend was on trial.

Bob was found guilty on five counts, including wire and mail fraud, in October 2015.[15] He was sentenced to eighty-four months in federal prison. Bob was also convicted of bank fraud in a separate scheme. He pleaded guilty, admitting that he'd been recruited to help develop and sell condominiums in the South Loop area of Chicago and then hide the sales from the banks.[16]

He lost his law license, his teaching job, his house, his standing in the community, and his marriage.

As for me, I felt like someone had punched me in the kidney. Because as much as I liked him, he's an intentional perp. He didn't accidentally fall into fraud or do something bad to help a friend. He did this strictly for personal and professional gain. Like Jason Chez, he didn't think he'd get caught. He thought he was smarter than everyone else.

When he tried to get out of jail early during the pandemic, he said that his crime did not have a "widespread negative impact on communities."

The court disagreed. "When the mortgage loans Mr. Lattas facilitated ultimately were defaulted upon, the properties were foreclosed," the court wrote:

> The homes were then boarded up as a result, undoubtedly driving neighborhood property values down and crime up in a neighborhood already riddled with gangs, narcotics, and poverty. Mr. Lattas was not selling drugs, but his actions helped create an environment where it was easier to do so; his harm to the neighborhood was simply on a

grander scale. In addition, Mr. Lattas's actions resulted in a loss amount of over $6.7 million (and over $19 million when combined with his separate mortgage fraud scheme in the 2014 case). The seriousness of Mr. Lattas's actions cannot be overstated.[17]

Bob swears he's innocent and that he only made about $40,000 from the scheme. Still, the banks' losses hovered around $23 million. After Bob was convicted and before he reported to federal prison, we began speaking to students across the country about ethics and fraud.

After applying for compassionate release during Covid, his sentence was reduced to sixty-three months on January 11, 2021. He was released to home confinement, an ankle monitor tracking his every move.

Bad Blood

Robert Courtney is another intentional perpetrator who controlled the whole process. Courtney was a Kansas City, Missouri, compounding pharmacist. A compounding pharmacist makes drugs for patients who need specialty medicine that isn't available from regular pharmacists.[18] They typically work in a lab or in a medical facility. I heard about him from a speaker who came to one of my classes, a health care investigator named Dr. Susan Hayes.

In 1990, Courtney began buying pharmaceuticals on the gray market (an unauthorized distribution channel). He then used these drugs to fill prescriptions at the pharmacy he owned. Over time, he began watering down the prescriptions to save money.

Eight years later, an Eli Lilly sales rep named Darryl Ashley observed that Courtney was selling three times the amount he bought of Gemzar, a cancer drug. Ashley alerted his bosses, and they investigated. But they found nothing wrong.

Two years after that, a handful of nurses in the office of oncologist Verda Hunter noticed that many of her cancer patients weren't experiencing the debilitating side effects usually associated with chemotherapy. They brought their concerns to Ashley, who wondered if something was amiss. Maybe Hunter's patients weren't getting the full prescribed dose?

Ashley rifled through his records and discovered the same issue with Robert Courtney that he'd noticed in 1998.

Courtney seemed to be selling Gemzar for $20 per vial, *less* than what the drug was worth. On paper, anyway, he was taking a financial hit. The wheels started spinning in Ashley's head.

Hunter, too, noticed that many of her patients weren't suffering any side effects, like hair loss or nausea. Nor were they getting better. She decided to test the medication Courtney had given her. Her findings astonished her. The drug contained less than a third of the drug in it. She called the FBI.

The FBI and US Food and Drug Administration initially didn't believe that a pharmacist would do something so horrific. Nurses, doctors, and pharmacists are considered the most ethical and honest of all professions, along with grade-school teachers. (Members of Congress and car salespeople are considered the least.[19]) No one would ever suspect that a pharmacist, who was supposed to treat people, was slowly killing them.

In 2002, Courtney pleaded guilty to intentionally diluting ninety-eight thousand prescriptions for forty-two hundred patients.[20] He was sentenced to thirty years in federal prison.[21]

People were baffled by his behavior. He was an upstanding citizen—why did he do it? Because he was under the gun. Robert Courtney owed the IRS $600,000. Years earlier, he had pledged $1 million to his church, which was to be paid in three installments. Everything was coming due at the same time.

His whole world was crumbling. He was desperate. People will do almost anything when they're desperate.

He also had an opportunity. He worked alone and mixed drugs by himself; no one oversaw the final product. He was able to dilute the medication undetected. No one would think to check up on him, and no one was the wiser. Plus, he was giving drugs to terminally ill individuals who were at death's door! No one was surprised when they died.

He pleaded guilty to tampering and adulterating the chemotherapy drugs Taxol and Gemzar.[22]

As terrible as Courtney's crime was, when people's backs are against the wall and they have the opportunity to commit a crime, they see only the benefits and minimize the potential costs.

Most of us have faced seemingly impossible situations in our lives. But even if we haven't, it's not difficult to envision. When someone doesn't know how they'll pay a burdensome debt or how they'll face the humiliation of having feigned financial success, they're primed to make the most of any opportunity that becomes available. So what if it's illegal? When people are desperate, they'll do whatever they need to survive. And if they have access to a process that's not regulated, it's even easier. The Fraud Triangle is still in place: opportunity. rationalization. pressure.

. . .

Jason Chez and Robert Courtney are at the two ends of the fraud spectrum. Jason was a foolish rich kid; Robert Courtney was evil. Bob Lattas and Rita Crundwell are more similar to Jason.

So, what does this all mean for you? How do you spot an intentional perp in your midst? Look at your own life and the people who have complete control over financial processes. Does anything ever seem off? If your gut tells you that something's amiss, it probably is. Having stage 4 cancer, taking chemotherapy drugs, and not losing your hair is a red flag. A town hemorrhaging money for no good reason is another red flag. People looked the other way in both instances, and they paid the price.

Starting Early

I invited Tom Hughes to Chicago to do a class presentation.[23] Dressed in a blazer and bow tie, he had a soft and soothing voice that sounded like a cross between a therapist and a smooth jazz musician. His long, coiffed ponytail was hardly what I expected of a former accountant, but it worked for him. He had a kind, open face with a pleasant demeanor that motivates you to open up to him— you felt as though anything he did for you would be in your best interest. He exuded honesty and talked without filter in a way that you could practically see the thoughts and feelings he was wearing on his sleeve.

Tom started stealing money as a teenager in Danbury, Connecticut, and spent most of his adult life stealing money from his clients. "My first crime, and what I learned from that crime, is that I get away with stuff," he said.

Tom worked in a variety of financial roles, including accountant, banker, manager for touring musicians, and small-business CFO. All of these roles had one thing in common: busy clients who were laser-focused on their businesses and not remotely interested in accounting. Busyness is a victim hallmark, and victims, which I will discuss in a later chapter, often place their trust in a person who knows the ins and outs of their businesses. Therein lies the reason why they're such perfect targets.

"The more my clients liked and trusted me, the more I took," Tom said.

He was working at Hartford National Bank as a teller, and one day a coworker's till was short $200. When the shortage was noticed, all the employees dropped everything to look for the missing cash because at the end of the day, if someone is short, no one can leave until the money is found.

While they were scrambling to find the missing money, an armored car delivery came with the daily deposit for a local grocery store chain. The head teller signed for it and put it in a cabinet under his drawer to deal with later. They eventually found the missing $200, and everyone went home on time.

Two weeks later, the day before he took off on vacation, Tom went into the head teller's cabinet to get a roll of coins and discovered that the deposit bag was still there, uncounted and completely forgotten. He took a pack of twenties out of the bag, tucked it away, grabbed the roll of coins, and brought the cash home with him at the end of the day. He brought it with him on vacation, where he spent most of the $2,000.

It occurred to him that when someone inevitably realized the bag was still there, they would notice that the $2,000 was missing. Having spent most of it, he didn't have the money to replace it. Tom made a mental note to check if the bag was still under the cabinet when he returned from vacation.

So the day he got back, he bought some shirts during his lunch break, and when the head teller went on his lunch break, Tom put the cash bag underneath the shirts in the shopping bag and walked out at the end of the day. In other words, he took the remaining money. The amount totaled $11,600, which—adjusted for inflation—has the same buying power as $20,000 today. If he couldn't replace it, why not just steal the rest?

The money was eventually discovered missing, and the police questioned him about the crime. One of the officers told him that he knew he did it and detailed how it was done. Tom retrospectively said he might have confessed out of fear, but when the officer's details of the crime were totally inaccurate, Tom knew he was in the clear and could safely deny it. With the lack of evidence, it was written off as a loss, chalked up to having been mistakenly thrown away. Needless to say, Tom kept and spent the money.

What Tom learned from successfully fooling people with small lies to stealing that large amount of cash was that he was capable of getting away with pretty much anything. "I enjoyed being dishonest, and I loved getting a large amount of money without working for it," he said. And he didn't feel guilty about it.

Tom also helped entrepreneurs with their accounting. Because many small- to midsize business owners want to spend their time running and growing their businesses, they don't want to deal with the accounting side. Entrepreneurs mainly wanted to deal with the inner and outer workings of the company in terms of employee management, service, product quality, and other functions that make money come in.

Tom would step in and say, "Hey, while you're doing what you love, let me do what I love." His job was to make sure that the books were balanced and went to the right place.

His work with entrepreneurs expanded, and he started doing individual tax returns for them, building a strong reputation for balancing years' worth of back taxes as well as successfully filing old returns.

By his own admission, as often as not, Tom would figure out a way to steal from almost every one of the businesses he worked for. He recalled one client simply putting the unopened envelopes of bank statements on his desk, blatantly revealing that he wasn't looking at them. If the client had done something as simple as open the envelope, Tom might have thought twice, but, as he put it, he "would know in two bank cycles which clients were paying attention and which weren't."

And when they weren't, he would figure out a way to steal from them.

Tom worked as a part-time CFO for a company in Maine and another in Vermont, neither of which paid any attention to their finances. They both put all their trust in Tom's hands, and so there was very little oversight of Tom's activities.

Since Tom only had two primary clients, he wasn't making much money. To make the money he needed to maintain his frivolous lifestyle, he decided to steal from his clients. The schemes were varied, but the result was always the same: his pockets were lined.

He would pay his own bills with their checks if they shared the same vendor, pay his credit card bills if they shared the same credit card company, and do other simple schemes that were easily implemented when he had full control over their finances. At one point, the Vermont client asked him how much payroll tax exposure was going to be that month. It was $5,000, but without hesitating, Tom said $5,600 because he wanted $600 for himself. He put the full amount in his bank account on Friday, and by Monday, he had spent the $600, plus another $1,400. He decided he would try to make the money back by gambling in the stock market with risky and overvalued investments, which just made him lose more money and motivated him to steal more.

That was bad, but the most heinous crime was that he drove his Maine client to financial ruin. Tom instructed his client not to write a check to the IRS during tax season but to write it directly to him instead and *he* would pay taxes out of the firm's account. Nobody questioned him as he took the money meant for the federal government and deposited it directly into his bank account. Because of his actions, his client lost funding from their original investor and decided to ease out of business altogether, which was also when they realized that none of their unemployment taxes had been paid.

Overall, Tom stole money from the Maine client for a little under a year, and the Vermont client for a little more than a year.

"These were clients that trusted me to do a lot of work," he said. "They were my friends. One of these guys was my neighbor. I went to church with them. And I saw where the money was, and I knew they weren't paying attention."

Tom's crimes didn't come to a head until his Vermont client had a banner month. It was so good that the client had checks from one vendor for that month that equaled the previous year's sales. He asked Tom to pay off the credit line at the bank, which was $4,900. Tom figured that if he was writing a check for $4,900 to the bank, he might as well write one for himself too.

The bank made a mistake and ended up crediting one of the checks to the wrong account. The bank called the client while Tom was out of the office and asked him to look at the bank statements, which was when the company noticed that there were two checks deposited on the same day in the same amount. That made the client suspicious, and when he opened other bank statements and saw that the treasury tax and loan payments were higher than the company's payroll, he contacted the authorities.

Despite Tom's penchant for lying and stealing, he quickly confessed to his crimes. The local police ended up passing the case to the FBI because the federally insured bank had been cashing checks with Tom's clients' names on them but with Tom's signature despite Tom not being a signer on the account. In fact, the bank suffered a significant loss when it had to reimburse the client for a lot of the money Tom had stolen using his own signature.

The FBI came to Tom's house.

"Do you know who we are?" they asked.

"Yes," Tom replied.

"Do you know why we're here?" they asked.

"Yes," Tom replied.

"Did you do it?" they asked.

"Yes."

They asked him if there were any other financial crimes that they didn't know about, and he came clean about the Maine client. After years of lying, cheating, stealing, manipulating, and never getting caught, Tom felt something that he hadn't felt before: total and absolute relief.

Because Tom voluntarily disclosed all of his crimes—he even confessed to illegal activities the FBI probably wouldn't have uncovered—he received a downward departure in sentencing. Tom was sentenced to six months of house arrest, two hundred hours of community service, restitution to the embezzled clients in the amount of $50,000 without interest, and five years' probation.[24] He walked out of the courtroom feeling like he had gotten away with it . . . yet again.

And he still didn't learn his lesson.

Tom's probation officer didn't have the means to keep track of him. If she had looked at his bank statements, she would have noticed charges on his debit card in New York and New Jersey. Never mind that he wasn't allowed to leave Vermont. Using his charismatic personality, Tom managed to get another client who knew he was on probation. He had gotten away with pretty much everything he'd ever done his entire life, so why not cheat probation too? And heck, while he was at it, why not steal money from this new client?

So that's what he did, and when the new client noticed, they turned him in. This time, he was sentenced to eight years in prison. His wife at the time divorced him, but other than that, he didn't lose much else. He didn't have his own practice; whatever money he had, he had spent.

Tom looks back on prison as a blessing. It allowed him to let go of the things he had clung to, like the lavish lifestyle, an unhappy marriage, and not taking responsibility for his actions. In prison, he became much more religious, helped teach younger inmates to read, and met people from wildly disparate backgrounds. He was surrounded by people who had been given none of the opportunities he had, and it cut him to his core. "I've always been dishonest about something to someone," he said. "Not so much today, but certainly when I was doing whatever I wanted to whomever I wanted."

It's truly incredible that he got away with so many crimes, but his clients were sloppy. Basic accounting controls would have deterred his actions, and simply checking and reconciling the bank statement would have revealed the discrepancies early on. But as he said, he could tell if there was any oversight within two billing cycles of working for a client.

Since being released from prison, Tom has lived on the straight and narrow. He's been upfront about his past with every job he's been offered since then, none of which are in finance.

The single most important thing a business owner can do is pay attention. People go into business to do what they do, not to deal with things like learning Quickbooks Pro or doing administrative work. Someone like Tom can walk in and say, "Listen, you do what you love, I'll do what I love, and everyone's happy." It's a recipe for disaster.

CHAPTER TAKEAWAYS

- Intentional perps are the largest category of perps. You can find them in every industry, no matter how big or how small. They're typically the best employee on the team. This makes them both powerful and dangerous.

- Intentional perps are created in organizational cultures that lack sound internal controls. They usually believe they can talk their way out of anything because they always have. These are traits we typically praise, but in the wrong environment, these traits can be used destructively.

- Intentional perps' behavior tends to be praised and rewarded because they take risks that can often lead to success. However, this praise can send a confusing message because it can be in direct conflict with established organizational policies and procedures.

Intentional perp quick facts

Description	Characteristics
• Focus on enriching themselves	• Chameleons
• Operate as if rules don't apply to them	• Highly skilled
• Thrive in environments with lax internal controls	• Arrogant
	• Entitled
	• Likeable
	• Intelligent

Chapter 2

Accidental Perps

Not long ago, I ordered a handbag from one of my favorite designers, Calleen Cordero. Cordero makes timeless, supple, intricately beaded bags that are truly exquisite. She's also based in the United States, and I make it a point to buy handmade products from small US businesses whenever I can. I had been eyeing a new cross-body bag for a while and decided I'd splurge and get myself a new one for Mother's Day. The bag arrived, and I was thrilled.

The following day, I opened my door and found a box on my doorstep with the Calleen Cordero logo on it. I was surprised; I hadn't ordered anything. Had my beloved husband decided to buy me a post–Mother's Day gift from my favorite retailer?

Alas, he had not.

Instead, I got an even bigger surprise: there, buried under crisp wrapping paper, was the *exact same bag I had already received*. The company had sent me two handbags by mistake. *Ooops!*

What to do?

I asked a few friends and acquaintances, and their answers intrigued me. Most people said I should sell the second bag on eBay and pocket the cash. After all, as one friend pointed out, it wasn't *my* fault that the sales associate sent out an additional bag, right?

She was right. It wasn't my fault. So why should I have to take time out of my day to go to the post office, return the bag, and pay shipping costs myself? Who would know if I kept it?

And then the ethical side of my brain kicked in. What if someone *did* know, called me, and asked about the second bag? Or even worse—what if a sales associate was fired due to her error? Beyond that, I'm a fraud expert! I make my living teaching people how to conduct business ethically! What kind of hypocrite would I be if I kept something that wasn't mine? Shouldn't I practice what I preach?

So yes, I had a choice to make: *Do I take or do I tell?*

This might seem like a minor decision, and compared with a $53 million fraud like Rita Crundwell's, it is. On the other hand, it would catapult me into a category of fraud that is more common than you might think: the accidental perp.

Accidents Happen

An *accidental perp* is probably the most ubiquitous kind of perpetrator. Any of us—from a clerk at CVS to a bank teller to the average consumer—can become an accidental perp. It happens so quickly that you might not even realize it. You might not even know you're doing anything wrong.

Accidental perps are people who didn't originally set out to commit a crime but accidentally found themselves benefitting from someone else's mistake. They tend to exhibit vulnerable narcissistic traits such as introversion and neuroticism. They're also prone to feelings of shame and tend to blame others for their mistakes. Accidental perps are faced with the choice: *Do I take or do I tell?* We're all faced with these sorts of choices all the time. But we don't respond to them in the same ways.

Remember: all perps are not created equal. This variability is the reason why our reactions to some perpetrators differ from how we feel about others. Some perpetrators cause us to feel sympathy as we learn the details of their crimes; others leave us scratching our heads. But with accidental perps, we tend to understand their dilemma because we could easily be faced with (or have been faced with) a similar situation.

Accidental perps are unique because they're typically not motivated by money. Rather, they're presented with an *unsolicited* opportunity that can benefit them greatly should they choose to take it. The accidental perp doesn't seek out these opportunities in the same manner that an intentional perp does. It's as simple as opening your front door, finding an unexpected "present" that isn't intended for you, and hanging on to it. When presented with opportunities, accidental perps are skilled at shifting blame to others ("It's not my fault they sent me two handbags!").

In the workplace, the accidental perp is often the low person on the totem pole. They're usually a midlevel employee or new to the company and unsure of their place in it. They haven't found their voice yet and don't have an ally in the organization. So they follow orders, even if the orders feel wrong. They're often young, eager, and loyal. They're "people pleasers," obsessed with satisfying their bosses, teams, spouses, and—yes—even themselves.

People pleasers are everywhere. You might even be one. Also known as *social conformists*, these folks have a compulsive need to make other people feel good. There are many reasons why they feel this way: low self-worth, fear of rejection, and the desire to be well liked. Most people pleasers are women, who are taught to be less confrontational, more agreeable, and not make waves.[1]

The Asch conformity experiments were a series of studies in the 1950s named for social psychologist Solomon Asch, who researched if peers influence whether an individual goes along with or against the majority in a social group.[2] These studies found that many participants agreed with the majority about things that were nonconsequential simply to "fit in."[3] A network of brain regions lit up (indicating stress on the brain) during the few times the "people pleasers" disagreed.[4]

People pleasers are accidental perps in the making.

Oops! He Did It Again. And Again.

When I think of the prototypical accidental perps, I think of Andrew Johnson, the former VP of finance at Nicor Energy, a now-defunct startup gas company.[5] Andy came straight from central casting: nice guy, gingham shirts, khakis.[6] He worked in all aspects of the business, including meter reading, which exposed him to how the company worked. Within fifteen years, he had become director of cash management.

Between March 2001 and July 2002, Andy was responsible for Nicor Energy's finances, accounting, and back-office functions. This included billing and accounts receivable. Andy, then forty-two, enjoyed a business challenge and loved learning. The culture at Nicor was very sales-driven—the focus was on billing customers and finding more customers. Energy deals can be complicated (think: Enron).[7] Upper management never wanted to hear that the accounting people couldn't make the financials look the way they needed to look; they always had to figure out a way to get it done.

Andy was in way over his head, and he knew it. This was a new field for him. But he liked to solve problems, and he wanted to do right by the company. Andy felt that if he complained about the accounting systems Nicor had in place, he'd lose his job, so he kept quiet. Nicor Energy had no investment in infrastructure. Actually, there was no accounting system. Everything had to be built from scratch. He welcomed the challenge.

Here's where an understanding of accounting is helpful. (I know, it's super technical, but bear with me. You'll thank me.)

In some instances, customers aren't billed for services at the end of the month but rather in the middle of the month. This creates an accrual, which happens when a company delivers a product to someone who pays for it thirty days into the next fiscal year. In other words, the customer is *accruing* a bill until it's paid.

Even though the company won't get paid until the following accounting period, accounting rules allow revenue to be recognized in the current period. Accrued revenue is an account that appears on the balance sheet, and the revenue is recognized on the income statement—not too much accounting, I promise—but it is estimating the *accrual* piece of this equation that can be risky.

Say you've received gas for your home during the month of January, but the bill has not arrived yet, so you haven't paid for it. Your gas provider sends your bill on a different billing cycle than when you received the service. There's a window when your gas provider—let's say Nicor Energy—has to estimate if you (the Nicor customer) are going to pay the bill. Beyond that, natural gas prices often fluctuate. So you have to estimate if you are going to pay your bill using a fluctuating price. The company can either overstate how much money they think they'll make from you, the customer, or understate it. And herein lies the problem; Nicor Energy chose to overstate it.

Determining the amount of revenue to accrue created a real problem for Andy and his accounting group. Normally, he would have used historical models to calculate the accrued revenue. Once he knew the actual amount of revenue, he would have reversed the accrual and recorded the actual revenue earned. The goal is not to have big variants between the estimate and the actual cost.

In Nicor Energy's case, as it got more customers, the accrual process became more complicated. It was harder to estimate how much revenue it was going to earn. As the company grew, the accruals were off by a greater margin every month.

Andy's group paid attention to customers' past performances. The original premise was that when natural gas prices were low, consumers would use more energy because it was cheaper. When natural gas prices were high, consumers would use less gas because it was more expensive. But Mother Nature and human behavior had a different plan.

In December 2000, natural gas prices were extremely high and the weather was freezing in Chicago, where Andy was based. It was below zero every day. Natural gas prices quadrupled. All anyone could talk about was how high everyone's gas bill was going to be.

Rather than consumers using more gas, they used a lot less gas, which created a problem for Nicor Energy's revenue. Nicor's large industrial customers did the same. Some even shut down their plants, which again created a significant loss of revenue for Nicor Energy. The company didn't anticipate this. When Andy booked the accrual, Nicor overestimated how much gas customers were going to use. Remember: This was all just an estimate, "not a science," as Andy put it.

Regardless, Nicor Energy was facing a huge loss in revenue.

Andy had to explain all of these complex accounting rules to the higher-ups in his company, who didn't understand or care to understand accounting. They weren't interested in the details; they just wanted Andy to fix the problem. Make it go away. Andy had three kids, a mortgage, and a wife who didn't work. He didn't feel he had a choice but to make his bosses happy. Remember, Andy was a people pleaser.

Accounting standards require you to record an adjustment during the period in which you know about it. But while Andy knew about it in January—it was a $2 million loss—he didn't record it then.

Andy decided to spread the loss over a twelve-month period, even though he knew he was violating accounting rules. His bosses weren't concerned: they thought they could hide the losses since they were acquiring customers so fast. Because they were also earning a higher rate of revenue than they thought they would, they were actually able to create a surplus in some months, which allowed them to hide those losses. But when the market dipped, they weren't able to acquire customers as fast, and they weren't able to create enough of a surplus.

Andy knew that his days were numbered. He also knew that the company wouldn't survive an external audit. He was right on both counts. An external audit discovered the $2 million adjustment.

Andy got fired in May of 2002. About three months later, he found a job with a purchasing co-op for thirteen Catholic hospitals. "It had a kind of religious, spiritual feeling to the company, and it was very ethical, and the people were wonderful, and I went from this horrible environment to this really great environment," he told me. "I took a little bit of a pay cut, but I was so relieved and so happy, and I felt really good."

One morning, a few months into his new gig, as he was getting ready for work, his wife came upstairs to tell him that someone was at the front door: the FBI.

"I was like, 'What are they doing here?' I didn't think I had done anything wrong," he recalled. He thought they just needed information. "I had no idea that I was even a target."

He had no clue that he had done anything illegal.

This is common in the accidental perp world, at least in the early stages. Most accidental perps are generally unaware that they have committed any crime. Andy was just following orders, being a good employee. "I was doing everything I could to do the right thing," he said.

Based on my research on his case, I believe him. I empathize with him and can fully understand how and why he found himself in such a compromising situation. I could see myself or my friends in leadership positions face similar issues as Andy. His "tell versus take" decision centered around his ability to keep or lose his job, but never in Andy's wildest nightmares did he think his decision would lead him (along with Nicor Energy's president and CEO, former vice president, and an outside counsel) to federal prison.

In a study on financial statement fraud, researchers found that financial executives were often influenced by peer executives, controllers, and immediate supervisors as well as the CFO and CEO.[8] The subjectivity around accounting standards and problems with a company's internal information systems also impacted financial executives' involvement with financial statement fraud. The

TABLE 2-1

Selected rationalizations for accidental perps

"I never built up that moral conviction or whatever it is to [say no]. I don't know if that's just the blue-collar family background I come from but it's just the desire to please other people."	"I can't think of any time I said no to the CEO." "I was the sole bread earner."	"Could not afford to lose the job for the third time."*

Suh et al., "Boiling the Frog Slowly: The Immersion of C-Suite Financial Executives into Fraud," *Journal of Business Ethics* 162 (July 2020): 645–673. Retrieved February 15, 2022, from https://www.thecaq.org/wp-content/uploads/2018/03/Suh-et-al-Journal-of-Business-Ethics-published-20181.pdf.

executives were all working at companies experiencing rapid expansion, so they experienced the same pressures Andy did.

As I look back on the hundreds of interviews I've done, many accidental perps I've interacted with often use similar rationalizations as those in the study. Table 2-1 shows some of the ones that jumped out at me.

Not that we'll make the same decisions as these accidental perps, but I found that many students and business executives can at least empathize with the circumstances that led these accidental perps to commit fraud.

I never taught Andy's case in class. I was scared that it might turn my students off from accounting. A lot of responsibility falls on the shoulders of people in financial services. How many of us have sat in meetings and faced the same pressure Andy did—that is, the pressure to please our bosses by any means necessary? Most of us want to get a five-star rating on our performance evaluations, and we could never imagine that an earnest college graduate would end up in the slammer. Sometimes the desire to please can leave us in a tougher situation than we could have ever imagined.

The Unusual Suspect

Diann was also one of those ambitious college students who never imagined she would end up doing time.

Walt Pavlo, a former human resource consultant and convicted white-collar offender, introduced me to Diann when I was filming *Crossing the Line*, a documentary that chronicles the stories of five white-collar criminals.[9] Pavlo embezzled $6 million from MCI Telecommunications (later WorldCom) and was sentenced to forty-one months in prison. After his release, he became a fraud expert. Go figure.

I remember Diann's interview vividly.[10]

While working as a management consultant, Diann and her two young kids booked a trip to Utah to visit her parents. Her husband drove them to the airport and kissed them goodbye. Diann had two credit cards tied to her travel profile; rather than charge her personal credit card, the travel agent mistakenly charged the trip to Diann's company credit card. It was a mistake. When Diann noticed the credit card error, she had every intention of correcting it when she returned to the office. But she didn't. Instead of alerting the company immediately, she waited, and fell back into the normal cycle of life.

One day turned into one week, which turned into one month, which allowed Diann to rationalize making additional charges. Since she was responsible for automating the company's bookkeeping system, handling payroll, and interacting with outside vendors, she began indulging in a variety of fraud schemes, like claiming personal expenses as work expenses, giving herself an unauthorized raise, duplicating checks, and creating dummy vendors. Her life began a downward spiral. What started out as an accident became a habit.

"I never intended to defraud my employer," she said. Diann was a valued, trustworthy employee. She enjoyed her job, respected the company owners and was excited to be part of a growing company. As she said, "They treated me like family."[11]

"I was employee number 2, and they trusted me implicitly," she recalled. She was so upset about her transgressions that she made herself physically ill. She went to multiple doctors to figure out what was wrong with her. They found nothing.

According to Bill Sullivan, PhD, "dishonesty puts the brain in a state of heightened alert, and this stress increases with the magnitude of the lie."[12] Research from Leanne ten Brinke, assistant professor at the University of British Columbia and director of the school's Truth and Trust Lab, shows that constant lying is associated with a variety of health issues, including high blood pressure, increased heart rate, and elevated stress hormones in the blood although, over time, the brain adapts to dishonesty.[13] Diann experienced all of these health issues, but she couldn't properly put her finger on the source.

Diann's transgressions are common fraud schemes in today's business culture, with expense reimbursement one of the easiest ways to steal from an organization. This is largely because anything can be considered a "work expense," especially with so many of us working remotely.

A survey of over one thousand business travelers conducted by Chrome River, a provider of expense management and supplier invoice processing software, found that "expense fraud" cost US businesses more than $2.8 billion annually, with senior vice presidents having the highest rate of expense fraud. More than 1.1 million people submit fake expenses each year. Half of them attempt to get reimbursed for personal purchases; more than a third claim additional mileage while driving on company business. Three in ten say that they'd been giving larger tips than they really had been.[14]

The Association of Certified Fraud Examiners' 2022 *Report to the Nations* found that more than $4.7 trillion is lost each year to employer-related fraud globally. Of that, 11 percent is expense reimbursement fraud. That's a staggering $517 billion![15]

In the United Kingdom, estimated fraud losses in the first half of 2020 alone amounted to more than £374.3 million, according to UK Finance.[16] Much of that comes from employer-related fraud.

Lack of controls, little-to-no management review, and the ability to override existing controls are the most common reasons expense reimbursement schemes can occur. But in the end, it all boils down to trust. The minute you gain someone's trust, it's easy to exploit them.

What Diann did was wrong, but her company made it easy for her to do it because it lacked the proper segregation of duties and internal controls. This allowed her to manipulate the system and break the law. She was a company veteran. Everyone trusted her implicitly. *Boom.*

Diann did not get caught. She turned herself in. This was unusual. In general, only 17 percent of those who commit expense fraud get caught.[17]

"I couldn't live with myself emotionally or physically," she said. "I felt like such a disgrace to myself and my family."

When Diann confessed, she didn't plan out a speech or retain legal counsel. She wasn't sure what the next steps were going to be, but she knew she could no longer conceal the fraud. She confessed right before the start of the weekend with hopes of continuing the discussion on Monday morning. That Friday was her last day in the office.

She ultimately pleaded guilty to embezzling approximately $500,000 from her employer and spent 18 months in jail.[18] She and her husband divorced.

Since then, she's had a hard time finding work but has slowly been able to piece together a life for her children. When I asked her if she regretted her decision to ignore the credit card error, she responded immediately: "Absolutely."

I've been teaching Diann's crime story for more than ten years now, and everyone, both students and business professionals alike, see themselves in her story.

This relatability allows us to empathize with accidental perps. When you are able to see yourself in the perp (which often happens) when you hear the story of an accidental perp, you tend to judge it differently because this could be you.

· · ·

And what, you may wonder, happened to me and my beautiful bag? When I contacted the Los Angeles store and spoke to the sales associate, she was completely unaware of what had happened. None of their internal records showed that two bags had left the warehouse, so I easily could have gotten away with keeping the second bag. But I decided to tell. I returned the bag (on my dime, no less). The sales associate thanked me profusely and sent me a $75 gift card. I felt good about myself. Other people might call me stupid, but I call it smart.

What it showed me was that "return fraud" is common. Return fraud is just what it sounds like: something that occurs when customers use a store's return policy to defraud them.

According to a January 2021 report conducted by the National Retail Federation and Appriss Retail, consumers returned about $428 billion dollars in merchandise in 2020. About 5.9 percent—or $25.3 billion—of those were fraudulent.[19] That's a lot of socks.

Imagine I'm in a Walmart parking lot. I ask someone if I can borrow their receipt. I "lie" and tell them I'm doing a study on, say, the fonts used on paper receipts. I take their receipt and notice they purchased a big screen TV and a computer. I take the receipt, go inside the store, walk out with a big-screen TV or video camera, and then, the next day or so, "return" it. This is known as *shoplisting*, or shoplifting using found receipts. Scammers use a discarded or stolen receipt, and then return items for a "refund." This translates to extra cash in their pockets. If you've ever exited a store and they marked a line through your receipt, the line signals that your receipt has been seen and used before in order to prevent shoplisting.

Another scheme is "Keep the New/Return the Old," which is pretty much what it sounds like: you buy something new to replace a broken item (that you probably broke yourself). You purchase a new version, keep the receipt, and then return the broken item for cash or store credit. To make it easier, there are websites that duplicate or forge receipts in case you're unable to find a real-life receipt.

Return fraud is one of the most pervasive forms of retail and e-commerce fraud, and it's one of the hardest to stop.[20] If someone presents a receipt for a big-screen TV, why *wouldn't* the clerk assume they really bought it?

In my case, I could have kept the first bag and returned the second handbag—which, remember, I did not pay for—for a full refund and enjoyed the extra cash. The company would have never noticed the error.

However, had I kept the bag, not only would I have been an accidental perp, but I would also be contributing to the growing fraud epidemic. What started out as an accident would have catapulted me into intentional perp mode if I began to make a pattern of it. Not a good look for a forensic accountant.

CHAPTER TAKEAWAYS

Accidental perp quick facts

Description	Characteristics
• A mistake/oversight made by another person that opens the door for crime	• Affable
	• People pleasers
• Tend not to speak up and tend to avoid confrontation	• Unassuming
• Often follow the orders of a superior	• Insecure

Chapter 3

Righteous Perps

Not all perpetrators steal for personal gain. I've learned this lesson many times over the years and have tried to share it with my students. It might be hard to comprehend—how is it possible to not steal to benefit yourself? Quite easily.

Remember Robin Hood? He took from the rich and gave to the poor. He has since gotten his own syndrome, called, appropriately enough, the *Robin Hood effect*. The Robin Hood effect is the term used when less wealthy individuals make financial gains at the expense of the wealthier folks.[1] As Jason Gordon, an associate professor of legal studies and management at Georgia Gwinnett College in Lawrenceville, Georgia, said, "The Robin Hood effect entails the redistribution of wealth in the economy in which the poor acquire more financial stability at the expense of the rich."[2]

People like Robin Hood exist everywhere, including corporate America. Some of these folks—I call them *righteous perps*—rationalize their crimes because they're "helping someone else." They robbed Peter to pay their pal, Paul. (A new company, perhaps? PayPaul.)

For the Greater Good

Robert Smith, the billionaire CEO of Vista Equity Partners, is a righteous perp. In 2019, Smith paid down $34 million in student loan debt for more than four hundred graduates of Morehouse College in Atlanta. How generous! Alas, a year later, he was accused of failing to report $200 million of income.[3] If that's not a righteous perp, I don't know what is: rip off the government to give to the needy.

The righteous perp might sound a bit like the accidental perp, but there's a difference. An accidental perp's risky decisions impact the company they work for. Righteous perps, on the other hand, use company resources to help people *outside* of the workplace—say, a family member or friend in need. Righteous perps also exhibit similar vulnerable narcissist traits as accidental perps (introverted and neurotic personalities, prone to shame, tendency to blame others for their mistakes).

Consider *Breaking Bad* lead character Walter White (played by Bryan Cranston), a high school chemistry teacher diagnosed with stage 3 lung cancer. To secure his family's financial future before dying, White produces and sells crystallized methamphetamine. What I love about this series is how relatable White is. And it poses a serious question: If you only had a few months remaining to live, would you sell drugs to provide for your family? This series forces the viewer to witness a once-ethical citizen transform into a criminal to secure a future for noble reasons.

Righteous perps take a Kantian ethics approach to ethical decision making, which, you could argue, Walter White does. According to Prussian philosopher Immanuel Kant, "the only thing that is unconditionally good is a good will." To Kant, a person acts out of goodwill when they act from a sense of moral obligation. Kant maintains that a person is good or bad depending on the motivation of their actions and not on the goodness of the consequences of those actions. To Kant, we have moral worth *only* if we're motivated by morality. The motivation, or intention, outweighs the consequences.[4]

Imagine that you win the lottery and you're trying to figure out how to spend your newfound cash. You decide that it would be fun to either travel, go on a shopping spree, or give the money to the local food bank. You choose the latter, and you feel good about yourself for doing so. "I'm so awesome!" you think. "I just gave my winnings to charity!"

Immanuel Kant would beg to differ. Although you may *think* you're a morally worthy person, Kant would say you're not. The reason you gave the money to the charity was not that you were thinking about the people on the receiving end, but because you thought it would be a fun thing to do. Moral worthiness, in Kant's view, comes only when you do something out of obligation, not for fun.

Although Kant might not agree that what you do should land you in jail, he would argue that you're moral if your intention is to do good. So, in KantLand, righteous perps are moral. This may be a controversial way of looking at things, but my goal is to educate you about righteous perps. If there's any category of perp that you may be able to empathize with, it's a righteous one.

In his piece "Is Corruption Ever Ethically Permissible?" published in the *Arkansas Journal of Social Change and Public Service*, Chris Morgan sums up a righteous perp's dilemma—*Do I risk going to jail for doing something I believe is morally correct?*—and its relationship to Kantian Ethics:[5]

> Consider Bob who works for ABC corporation. Bob is an accounting executive in Seattle and through his subordinates has almost complete full control of ABC's cash flow and other assets. Dan is a secretary for ABC in Dallas. Due to the current economic recession, ABC has chosen to downsize its administrative staff in Dallas and Dan is the first and only secretary selected to be terminated. Dan is a single father raising five children in a Dallas suburb. He relies on government aid to provide food and health care for his family. Upon learning of the circumstances surrounding Dan's life and that Dan would be the first and only secretary terminated from ABC's affiliate office, Bob took action. After long and careful consideration of the illegal nature of his actions, Bob decided the duty to help another outweighed the possibility of future criminal sanctions. While he knew he was committing fraud and that he was engaging in corrupt practices, Bob manipulated ABC's accounting books to ensure that funds for Dan's position were available.
>
> Bob's decision was *corrupt and ethically permissible*. Bob's manipulation of ABC's accounting books was corrupt given that it was a fraudulent act and, while it may be a stretch, may also be considered embezzlement. Determining that his actions were ethically permissible, or moral, rests on the assumption that Bob acted only out of the duty to help others, not an inclination that would give him any sense of gratification or alleviate guilt. In this hypothetical situation, Bob

received no gratification and would have actually felt happy about losing an unnecessary secretary; he definitely would not have experienced guilt. Bob chose to help someone based on the duty to help. Therefore, his corrupt actions were moral and ethically permissible.

Based on this brief description of Kantian ethical theory, we can deduce that certain behaviors we consider "corrupt" may in fact be ethically permissible, depending on the intention. If the intent comes from a moral place and not for self-aggrandizement, then Kant would consider it ethically sound. So Kant would love righteous perps.

· · ·

I thought long and hard before using the term *righteous perp*. I even consulted my pastor. I wondered if it was blasphemous to call someone who does bad *righteous*? (He didn't respond, so I'll take that as a yes.)

But I believe that these perps *are* righteous and moral. It just depends on how you define righteousness and whose side you're on. As it says in Ezekiel 18:7b, "The righteous man does not steal, but instead feeds the hungry and clothes the naked."[6] Righteous perps steal to feed the hungry and clothe the naked.

When I think about the way righteous perps rationalize their decisions, *righteous* really is the best word to describe them. It's their righteousness that allows us to empathize with them and forgive them quicker. We root for the little guy; we love to see David beat Goliath. That's what righteous perps are doing. They're outwitting the Man in favor of the Little Guy.

That's the reason why we're often outraged when righteous perps receive a harsh prison sentence. *Haven't they been righting wrongs? Aren't they trying to do good? Why should they be punished for that?*

Think of Edward Snowden, the former contractor for the National Security Agency who leaked highly classified documents to the media.[7]

Snowden calls himself a whistleblower, but I consider him a righteous perp. His very existence inspires conflict. Some experts think he's a traitor because he violated the Espionage Act of 1917; others celebrate the fact that he did.[8] Still, others don't think he broke the law at all, believing he was morally obligated to do what he did and that his actions inspired various necessary legal reforms. As the *New York Times* put it, "he may have committed a crime . . . but he has done his country a great service."

The US government did not agree with that summary. Snowden was exiled to Russia, where he lives with his wife and child.

While he didn't set out to break the law to make money, his actions did serve him well financially. He rakes in about $1.8 million in speaking fees and got a $4 million advance for his book, *Permanent Record.*

. . .

When I introduce this category of perpetrator to my students or to employees at companies around the world, almost everyone leaps to their defense. It's because they connect with the person's inherent morality, even though they went to prison. We don't know what we're capable of until we're pushed, right? What would we do if our child was gravely ill and the only thing separating them from full recovery was stealing cash? *There but for the grace of God go I.*

The Rogue Secretary

I visited my first "behind bars" righteous perp about seven years ago in Bermuda, the sun-drenched tax haven in the North Atlantic Ocean.

I'd been invited to speak at a fraud conference on the island. While my colleagues went to the beach in their free time, I decided to visit a women's prison.

The place was nothing like Netflix's *Orange Is the New Black*. It looked like a college dorm. Minimum security. No bars on the windows. Peaceful. You'd never know the people on the inside couldn't leave.

I interviewed four women who had been charged with financial crimes, one of whom was named Elizabeth Rogers. Elizabeth was dressed in prison-issued khaki shirt and pants. She looked tired, her face worn, her shoulder-length hair matted and oily. She had been there for more than two years.

Elizabeth had been an office assistant for a construction company whose owner was a slumlord (a property owner who overcharges tenants and allows the property to deteriorate). She discovered that he was taking advantage of people in the community by increasing their rent and not giving them any of the amenities he promised them.

She was too scared to confront him—he was her boss, and she worried that he might blackball her so she couldn't get another job. But she believed that what he was doing was wrong, and she took it upon herself to fix it.

Since she had access to his accounts, she realized that she could create fake purchase orders and he'd be none the wiser. So she created, then approved, then paid, purchase orders for fictional broken pipes, electrical rewiring, and peeling paint. This, in turn, created "jobs" for plumbers, painters, electricians, all of whom lived in the community. It was a risk, but she felt that she had a moral obligation to take it. Besides, she wasn't personally benefiting. It was all for *other* people.

Her boss began asking questions when the money ran out. Elizabeth couldn't supply receipts for the purchase orders—understandable, since the jobs didn't really exist. Since there was no documentation to support many of the payments and the financial deficit was increasing, all roads led back to Elizabeth. The fraud was discovered; Elizabeth was arrested and sentenced to three years in prison.

Righteous perps always give me an inner conflict that I constantly wrestle with. I just couldn't understand why Elizabeth would risk so much. I later realized it was because I couldn't understand her cause. I understand wanting to do anything I can to protect my family. But she risked her family to save her *community*. Could I do that? Could *you*?

Understanding Immanuel Kant's approach to ethical decision-making helps me understand the Elizabeth Rogers's of the world.

Elizabeth didn't think she was behaving stupidly. She was proud of what she had done. She had kids and a husband, yet she had voluntarily risked their well-being in the name of "justice." She didn't even mind serving time. She felt like she had done the right thing.

There's also a distancing mechanism in place in this type of endeavor. When you do something questionable that benefits someone else, it alleviates any guilt you might have, even if it's illegal. That's how Elizabeth felt: guilt-free and at peace.

With a Little Help for My Friends

Although Elizabeth knew what she was doing, another woman I know was blindsided by her righteousness. Her name was Elise Dixon-Roper (no relation to Dixon, Illinois), and her pro bono legal team had reached out to me. They wanted me to conduct an on-camera interview with her to share with my students. They thought that by sharing her story, she could deter others from following in her footsteps.

By the time Elise and I met, I had already conducted many on-camera interviews with convicted white-collar offenders. Elise was the first offender I interviewed before their sentencing, which meant that I had to be very careful about the questions I asked her. She had to be careful how she responded, and her legal team would be present the entire time. I was nervous about this interview. I spent the next week carefully reading Elise's indictment and drafting questions.

We met at her attorney's office in a fancy downtown Chicago building with a lot of glass windows and long hallways. As I got off the elevator, I glimpsed a woman sitting in the conference room. Elise.

Wearing a beige turtleneck with a leopard-print scarf knotted around her throat, her black hair cropped close to her head, she looked like a librarian. Her smile was warm, and her handshake was soft and gentle. She felt familiar to me, like someone I'd met or seen before. I had to pinch myself from blurting out, "How did *you* end up in so much trouble?"

Elise was born and raised in Chicago. A straight-A student, she was involved in the yearbook committee and elected president of her senior class. She was also active in her church and sang in its choir. She got married, rose to the leadership ranks in her law firm, bought a house, and had kids.

Elise met a loan originator named Hakeem Rashid. They became friendly, and he started sending clients to her law firm. Before long, he was asking her to help him with some investments on a property, and she obliged.

One day Hakeem approached her about a sketchy mortgage deal. He wanted to use Elise's credit to obtain a mortgage, which is a form of identity theft and mortgage fraud. Mortgage fraud happens when there is some type of material misstatement, misrepresentation, or omission in the loan application.

Elise's gut reaction was nervousness—she knew it was illegal—but she thought she was being a good employee by helping her law firm make money. Hakeem offered her $10,000 for her role, and she took it. She also wanted to give Hakeem the benefit of the doubt. "If you're a friend of mine, I'm going to trust you and expect that you're going to treat me the way I treat you, so I'm going to look out for you," Elise told me. "I expected him to look out for me."

In hindsight, Elise should have followed her initial gut instinct. Science has shown that our guts are often pretty accurate. Our "second brain"—found in the walls of our digestive system—constantly sends us signals. This is known as the enteric nervous system, two thin layers of more than 100 million nerve cells lining your gastrointestinal tract from the esophagus to the rectum. This second brain can be responsible for huge emotional shifts and sends us frequent warning signals. We just need to pay attention to it.[9]

"Your gut is the collection of heuristics shortcuts," said Melody Wilding, a professor of human behavior at Hunter College in New York. "It holds insights that aren't immediately available to your conscious mind, but they're all things that you've learned and felt."[10]

Neuroscientist Antonio Damasio of the University of Southern California formulated a theory called the *somatic marker hypothesis*, which argues that emotional processes in the body can impact decision-making, both positively or negatively. Emotions play a huge role in our ability to make rational decisions. So, a heart beating like a metronome gone haywire might signal anxiety.[11] Goosebumps might indicate fear, and so on. The more attention we pay to those cues, the better our ability to make decisions.

Elise's gut was trying to tell her something. Unfortunately, she didn't listen.

The Fraud Triangle, which I discussed in the introduction, explains how opportunity, rationalization, and pressure can lead a person to commit fraud. Elise wanted to help her colleagues and friends, and the extra money was an added personal bonus. Things had changed at home, and she was under terrific pressure.

So when the opportunity to help her friend presented itself, she only needed to rationalize the decision to commit fraud. It was a small loan for a short period of time. Who would notice?

Together, Elise and Hakeem applied for a loan to buy a building. This would have been perfectly legal if the loan documents hadn't been altered. Hakeem told Elise that after a few months he would put the property in his name.

"He was getting money back from the properties, which he shouldn't have done, and we placed them in what we call a *possession: close of escrow*—and then after the closing, I would write him a check and give him the money," she said. (Possession: close of escrow occurs when a buyer takes ownership of a property after signing closing documents.)[12]

Essentially, Elise was acting as a straw buyer, someone who purchases a property on behalf of another person but who isn't actually going to own the property. The straw buyer usually has better credit; they pose as the buyer to get approved for the loan, but they're not going to live in the property. The straw buyer is usually given some kind of financial incentive to participate in the fraud.

In this scheme, Hakeem and a mortgage broker named Kareem Broughton recruited other straw buyers in addition to Elise and paid them to purchase properties. This allowed them to qualify for mortgages fraudulently. The payments the buyers received for their actions were hidden from lenders. The loan applications intentionally misrepresented information, as did the supporting documents that followed.[13]

Elise worked on the legal side, ensuring the HUD-1 settlement statements looked legitimate, and her firm accrued massive fees. She also represented the buyers and sellers at real estate closings, reporting possession: close of escrow to lenders that were being held by her or her law firm. After a closing, she would write Hakeem a check for the falsified escrow amount, which he would then pocket.

In order for the scheme to work, Elise had to approve many fraudulent documents, including loan applications and HUD-1 settlement statements. She and Hakeem fudged their income, employment, source of down payment, and intention to occupy the property.[14]

Not long afterward, Hakeem offered her another $10,000 to purchase another building. Then he bought a house and placed another $10,000 in her hand. Since all three properties were purchased within three months of each other, Elise was under the impression that they would all be put in Hakeem's name within the near future. She also believed that the buildings would be properly managed in accordance with codes and regulations. This made the unethical aspects of the transaction seem a little more palatable.

So, despite the fact that Elise was uncomfortable with the scheme, she rationalized her decision. The loans were short-term, her name was going to be removed from the mortgage, and most importantly, she was helping a friend.

Even if she remained the owner of the property, Elise reasoned that her family was building up assets. As long as the properties were taken care of and managed, nobody would notice the original fraudulent documents. She was hopeful that once Hakeem became the owner of the property, her name would eventually be removed and everything would be kosher.

While Hakeem and Broughton recruited the majority of the buyers, Elise did end up recruiting one herself: her husband. A personal friend of hers was about to lose their house, and Elise wanted to help them out by getting them a mortgage on another house. She believed she had a method that could offer the assistance they desperately needed. "I saw that as a way of helping, not hurting," she said.

She asked her husband to purchase the house, and Hakeem arranged the mortgage. (Her husband had no idea that his identity was being used fraudulently.)

Elise believed she was doing the right thing—or, at least, that she wasn't doing anything wrong. She assumed that the friend would get a job and be able to buy the house back from them. Instead, the property went into foreclosure.

About three years later, Hakeem left Chicago, and he and Elise lost contact. Their antics ground to a halt. Elise breathed a sigh of relief, happy to be done with it all.

One day she received a grand jury subpoena in the mail, asking for records for several properties, including the third property that was purchased under her name. That was just one of thirty-five fraudulent mortgage loans that were issued to Hakeem between 2005 and 2008, totaling $16.2 million.[15] Every single property had gone into foreclosure. Elise was concerned, but not overly so. "I was hoping that they'd go after him and leave me alone," she said.

They left her alone for about a month, when the FBI showed up at her doorstep and asked her husband questions regarding the case. He was oblivious. When he called Elise, her heart dropped. The weight of the potential consequences finally hit her.

Elise found an attorney and gave him all of the paperwork requested. She had never been in trouble before and had no criminal law experience, so she put her full faith in the attorney. She believed he'd do everything he could to try and work something out in her favor. Instead, she didn't hear back from him until the prosecution completed their investigation. She was indicted six months later.[16]

She spoke with the prosecution team after the indictment, hoping to plead her case by saying that she had learned her lesson and that she'd be more of a benefit to society by supporting her family rather than being locked up in jail. Plus, she hadn't been involved in any fraudulent activities prior to or after the scheme.

Elise faced six years in federal prison, but she was sentenced to only fifteen months. She stepped down from the law firm. The experience was shattering, and of course, she regretted it.

"If I could go back and relive the last ten years, I would've never gotten involved," she said. "I may have gotten $20,000 out of it, but it was for him. I would've never imagined myself being here today in this situation. I was always protecting other people from getting into trouble, but I guess I didn't have somebody to protect me from getting into trouble, so here we are."

Her attorneys could empathize with what she did and how it went down. They wanted to show that she was remorseful and had learned from her mistakes. My point is this: people wanted to help her. Her attorneys, who were working for free on her behalf, stood by her because she had such a good personal and professional reputation. They could see that she made a mistake and that anyone could do similarly, just trying to help a friend or colleague. Perhaps they could see themselves in Elise's story.

Law and Disorder

Keila Ravelo and I met on Twitter in mid-2021, when she DM'd me from the handle @ethicsanywhere.

"Ms. Pope," she wrote, *"I follow your career and passion for white-collar crime topics. Would you be interested in talking for a few minutes with a lawyer, now white-collar felon back from prison trying to do better? I hope so."*

By now, you probably know how I responded.

Because of Covid-19, Keila was released to home confinement after serving a little more than two years of a five-year sentence at Alderson Federal Prison Camp, a minimum-security facility in West Virginia.

I knew her story was fresh, as she was still serving her prison sentence. I also knew that this would be an amazing opportunity for my students to learn from someone who was still incarcerated how fraud, and a fall from grace, could happen. I'd never had a speaker like this before. It was also Keila's first time sharing her story with a group of students, so I wasn't sure how it would go.

I emailed my students the Department of Justice's (DOJ) indictment and instructed them to prepare questions for her.

Since it was during the pandemic, we met on Zoom. Keila appeared in a button-down shirt, her dark hair casually pulled back from her unlined face. She looked like one of my friends or colleagues, someone I could go out for a cocktail with. My students hung on to her every word.

$\bullet \quad \bullet \quad \bullet$

Keila was born in the Dominican Republic and went to a small liberal arts college in New Jersey, where she studied chemistry. Afterward, she attended Columbia University law school. She was the first person in her family to get an advanced degree. After graduating in 1991, she took a job as an associate at Sidley Austin, the same high-powered white-shoe law firm where Barack and Michele Obama met. Her goal was to pay down her student loans as quickly as possible.

"I was so gung-ho to make something out of myself, I was working really long hours," she said. She hobnobbed with general counsel from important corporations. Her cases were high-profile, splashed across the front pages of the *Wall Street Journal* and the *New York Times*.

Within a few years she was made partner. By this time, she was married and had two sons. The work/life balance was a struggle. Her husband, Melvin Feliz, had a criminal record for a state drug offense, which hindered his ability to find work. So Keila was the breadwinner.

She managed to "do it all," sort of. But she was always worried that she was failing at one part of her life.

"It seems like I got the brass ring. I achieved what everybody else was going after," she said. "But I always thought I was one mistake away from getting canned at work."

While she leaped from rung to rung, her husband wasn't even on the ladder. He was unemployed, depressed, and broke. Keila vowed to do whatever she could to help him. She didn't need money; she was a multimillion-dollar equity partner in a prestigious law firm. But she did need to lift up her downtrodden husband. Suddenly, an opportunity fell into her lap.

The Scheme

In 2005, Keila took a job at Hunton & Williams, a law firm where she was put in charge of hiring contractors to help out on a huge litigation case.

Her law firm was spending millions of dollars copying documents, and it occurred to Keila that her husband could do the work himself if he established a copying business. Melvin agreed and created an LLC.

This didn't scream fraud to Keila. Nepotism, yes, but her company didn't have an anti-nepotism clause in place. Still, a voice in her head told her not to let anyone at work know that the person she hired for the copying job happened to be her husband. She told herself it was because he had a criminal past and that she was protecting him. Or maybe she knew subconsciously that what she was doing wasn't completely legit.

For a few years in the early to mid-aughts, Melvin's company did some copying projects for Keila's law firm, earning about half a million dollars.

In 2006, another big case came up, which Keila was also in charge of. Once again, her husband got the contract to do copying and other litigation support work, which was fine. But problems arose when he—with Keila's blessing—started submitting invoices before the work was completed. Since she was in charge, she had the power to approve some of those invoices, and approve she did. This was illegal.

Still, it was all running like a well-oiled machine until her husband flaked out on the work. The invoices were being turned in on time, but the work wasn't. It turns out he was devoting his energy to other ventures. In 2014, the DOJ accused him of being part of a drug-trafficking organization. Keila was sure the DOJ had it wrong. But no. Not only was he trafficking drugs, he also had a whole other family. While Keila had been going out of her mind trying to save her marriage, her husband was leading a double life.

As soon as Keila discovered that the work wasn't getting done, she was faced with a dilemma. Should she tell on her husband and let down her firm (and him)? Should she let down her client? What kind of blight would this place on her own professional character?

She decided to let him continue to submit the inaccurate invoices for work that hadn't yet happened. She was trapped between a rock and, well, a rock. She wanted to please her company and the client, but also keep her husband happy and save her family. But both impulses were in direct conflict with each other.

So what started out as a legitimate business helping her husband turned into a multimillion-dollar mess.

"None of this happens consciously," she said. "It's sort of like you just kind of get comfortable with the lie."

If Melvin hadn't gotten busted for another drug offense in 2014, they would never have been caught. But the authorities began investigating him, and while doing so, they discovered his copying business and hence, the phony invoices.

Keila was arrested at the end of 2014 and pleaded guilty to a $7.8 million wire fraud conspiracy and tax evasion, admitting her role in approving invoices from two LLCs the DOJ called "fake vendors" who did no work.[17] She did twenty-seven months in jail and lost everything: her property, her bank accounts, all her savings, her career. This from a woman who had been earning seven figures.

"Most people don't wake up one morning and say, 'Today I'm going to start a scheme that's going to net me $8 million over the next six years,'" she said.

Keila wanted my students to know that "scheme" wasn't even the right word to describe what she did. That sounds way too intentional and preplanned, and hers wasn't. Rather—and this is important—it was a series of "small ideas, opportunities, and transgressions."

Translation: *It could happen in the blink of an eye. To anyone.*

She also had lots of people backing her up, including a former colleague, Andrew Jacobs. "After Keila's arrest in 2014, her former colleagues and I surmised that she was inherently criminal, stupid, or that we hadn't known her well enough," Jacobs said. "I can't tell you that it's not something that still crossed my mind when I reached out to Keila in jail in 2019. But I'd learned enough in the time since to understand that most of the bad in our world is explained by well-intentioned people, to paraphrase T. S. Eliot."

"I was pretty sure she didn't wake up one day and say, 'I'm going to commit a felony and gamble away my career,'" he continued. "I'd moved into a role where I'm trying to stop things like what Keila did from happening, and there is nuance. Beyond that, I knew her personally. If I didn't extend some trust, compassion, and the possibility of a second chance, who would?"

CHAPTER TAKEAWAYS

- Some perps are fueled by the desire to help others. They'll do whatever—even break the law—in order to support the person or organization they're trying to help.

- Righteous perps typically have trust, power, and privilege within their organizations. These components make it easier for others to overlook their fraud.

- Righteous perps use their company to help someone externally, like a family member or friend. In contrast, Accidental Perps' decisions negatively impact their organization.

- Don't be surprised when people rally around and support a righteous perp.

Righteous perp quick facts

Description	Characteristics
• Follow the Robin Hood syndrome	• Driven
• Use company resources to aid those outside the workplace	• Strong sense of morality
	• Empathetic
	• Justice oriented

PREY

I had been doing on-camera white-collar interviews for a few years when I realized that something was missing. I knew all about how people commit fraud and how people discover fraud, but I didn't really understand it from the *victim's* perspective.

Most people, academics and civilians alike, devote a lot of energy to understanding the perps, and understandably so. We want to know how perps do it, why they do it, and how we can stop them from doing it again. Obviously, that's important. But what about those on the receiving end? How do people deal with their victimization? How do they move on with their lives? And how do they become victims in the first place?

We pay little attention to victims. And when we do, we malign them. Those who were scammed by Bernie Madoff? "Greedy." Those who were deceived by Enron? "Gullible." Wiring money to a stranger overseas? "Stupid."

But not every victim simply leaves their door unlocked so someone can enter and steal their grandmother's china. Secretly, we all think we can't be duped. We're smarter than the next guy, right? But we all get scammed: doctors, lawyers, and even professors.

Back in 2018, renowned University of Chicago economics professor Roman Weil was lured into an investment scheme. Unbeknownst to him, his investment dollars were mixed up in a $5 million ticket-reselling scheme by a high school dropout. That's how the nameless perp was referred to in a *Chicago Sun-Times* article: a "high school dropout."[1]

The headline in the *Chicago Sun-Times* stopped me: "$5M Ticket Reselling Scheme's Victims Included an Economist at U. of C."!

What struck me about the headline was how the victim and perpetrator were described. The implication was that a high school dropout isn't capable of committing a ticket-reselling scheme and that a world-famous economist professor can't be a victim. But of course, that's ridiculous. Anyone can be scammed, just as anyone can commit a scam.

But just as there are different kinds of perpetrators, there are also different kinds of victims: some are individuals who were at the wrong place at the wrong time, whom I call *innocent bystanders*, and companies that were deliberately victimized, or *organizational targets*.

When *All the Queen's Horses* was released in August 2017, the film was screened in festivals and movie theaters worldwide.[2] But the most important screening I did was in Dixon, Illinois, before the very community that Rita Crundwell deceived. I was excited and nervous. How many people get to show their movie at the scene of the crime, before the innocent bystanders who had no idea their local official was robbing them blind?

It was a warm summer evening, and fifty invited residents gathered at Rita's former home to watch the film. I'd met the new owners during shooting, and they'd graciously offered to host a private screening once the film was complete. They'd bought the house from Rita in the government auction, and it was pretty much the way it was when she left it. It had a Western vibe, with leather furniture and lots of wood. It looked as if someone had plopped the Grand Ole Opry in the middle of Illinois. We had a popcorn machine, an inflatable movie screen, and an outstanding sound system that allowed you to hear the movie from miles away. People brought lawn chairs and blankets. It was a real Happening.

Kathe Swanson, the woman who discovered Rita's crime, was there with her family. I thanked her publicly, and everyone began clapping and cheering, raising cups and popcorn containers in her honor.

Before the film began, I fielded questions:

"What made you interested in this story?" (I study and teach about fraud.)

"Has Rita seen the film?" (No.)

"Will any of the film proceeds go to Rita?" (Emphatically no!)

"Will you make another film?" (Unclear.)

Once the movie started, you could only hear the crickets and the cars in the distance. All eyes were glued to the screen. When it ended, the audience was quiet. Then it erupted into applause.

Once word got out that only a select group of people had been invited to see the film, other residents began calling the Dixon Historic Theater to see if they would show the movie to a wider audience. We decided to hold a screening along with a daylong town hall session, where thousands of residents could ask questions about the status of the fraud investigation. My cohosts were Jason Wojdylo, a retired deputy marshal in the Asset Forfeiture Division of the US Marshals Service who was assigned to Rita's case, and Paula Meyer, who took over Rita Crundwell's job after Rita was arrested. The crowd had lots of questions. Some people were armed with thick files they'd assembled during the investigation.

These residents—the *innocent bystanders*—were fuming, and understandably so. They didn't comprehend what had hit them. And they had more questions.

"Did she do it alone?" (Yes.)

"Did you find any hidden assets?" (No.)

"Was all the money recovered?" (No.)

"Will she have to serve the full sentence?" (In theory, yes.)

"Did Rita show any remorse when you visited her in jail?" a man asked Jason.

"I think she was sorry she got caught," Jason replied. "I'm not sure she was sorry for the fraud."

"Was any money stashed away?" someone else asked.

"Most of the money went into the horses and came out as fertilizer," said Jason.

It's good to have a sense of humor sometimes.

"I noticed that the release date for Rita was 2030," a woman asked. "Could she get out earlier?"

"There's no parole in the federal system," said Jason. "And there's no opportunity for early release."

The crowd breathed a collective sigh of relief.

There was one lone voice I met during my five-year filming odyssey: Gene, the town complainer. He was That Guy, the one who attends city council meetings and writes letters to the editor. He was a permanent fixture in Dixon's City Hall. He had been very vocal that something seemed off in Dixon.

Gene tried to warm the other innocent bystanders for years, but no one listened. But Gene was right. Something was off with the city's finances.

When Rita finally got caught, but before she went to prison, he wrote a poem about it—a snippet:

Where oh where is Rita Crundwell?

She should be in a jail cell.

Instead she's free to roam the countryside

Have you heard of such restriction?

In Between Beloit and Dixon?

That's sixty miles and I don't know how wide.

People may have snickered at Gene for being so suspicious and overdramatic. But in the end, he got the last laugh.

Chapter 4

Innocent Bystanders

Innocent bystanders are the largest group in the victim category because everyone is a potential innocent bystander. By definition, a *bystander* is someone who's present when something happens, who sees an event but does not take part in it. For purposes of the *Fool Me Once* archetypes, bystanders are present when fraud happens but don't necessarily realize that a fraud is taking place. They're just living their daily lives, placing trust in their elected officials, airplane and car manufacturers, farmers who sell them food, and so on. Innocent bystanders are clueless to the potential danger lurking around them. They're *us*.

Innocent bystanders don't always notice red flags; they wouldn't even know what to look for. That's what makes them so vulnerable: it's hard to protect yourself against a threat that you cannot envision. We're all so vulnerable because we expect the system to work, and we trust that it will. We've been programmed to protect ourselves from some dangers, but not all. We wear seatbelts because we can foresee a potential car accident. We stop at a red light because we can imagine a car slamming into us. Those are specific, tangible hazards. But how do you protect yourself from someone tampering with your medicine or tainting your food? When we give our credit or debit card to a waiter to pay a bill, we assume they won't steal our identity. When we turn on our faucets, we assume the water isn't contaminated. When we get into our car, we assume that the manufacturer went through the appropriate quality controls, so the airbag works when it has to be deployed. You don't check it. And even if you thought to, whom would you call?

Most of us are, or will be, innocent bystanders at some point. I've been one.

I thought I would know the signs, but I didn't. And so, when I received a call from the Internal Revenue Service, I panicked.

I had just finished recording an interview for John Garrett's *Green Apple* podcast when I noticed a strange number on my cell phone. The number was 224-200-0078. As I suspiciously moved to put the phone to my ear, I heard a recorded voice say, "This is the Internal Revenue Service. Please stay on hold to learn more information about a lawsuit that has been filed against you by the federal government." My first reaction was sheer panic.

A call from the IRS is nothing to take lightly, so I stayed on the line to listen to the instructions. The recorded voice said to call the 224 number to receive information about a lawsuit. I hesitantly dialed the number, and a representative with an Indian accent picked up. The background noise sounded like a call center. I did think it sounded a bit loud for such a government office, but the fear of a lawsuit from the IRS outweighed any rational thought process at the time. I always remember Grandma Kelly, my mother's mother, telling me that you never mess with the IRS, so this wasn't an easy phone call to disregard.

The representative told me that the IRS had made a calculation error on my taxes from the years 2006 through 2015, and as a result of this error, I had an unpaid balance of $7,500 that had resulted in a federal lawsuit.

"Why haven't I received any notification from the IRS in writing about this?" I asked.

The representative said that she was only able to read me the federal code and if I had specific questions, she would need to forward my call to her supervisor. She then rattled off a very official-sounding federal code.

"This *must* be official," I thought.

She told me that a warrant had been issued for my arrest and that all of my assets would be seized, including my house, bank accounts, passport, and driver's license. Luckily, she assured me, I had two ways to handle this matter: either come to the federal courthouse in DC or settle it right away using a third-party provider. Obviously, going to a federal courthouse in DC was not an option, so I told the representative that I wanted to discuss how to settle the matter using a third party.

By this time, we were about seven minutes into the call. My heart was pounding, and my mind was racing. I was trying to think back to all of the red flags I've spent my life lecturing about, and so far, most everything had checked out. She told me that if I hung up, the police would be at my doorstep to arrest me. This sounded quite odd for a potential $7,500 debt, but I still wasn't convinced that this was a fraud. I immediately sent a text message to my Helios business partner, Ivy Walker, and asked her if she could listen to a phone call and tell me what she thought. Within thirty seconds, Ivy was on the phone listening to the call.

Five seconds later, I received a text from her. "This is not real!" she said. "I read a story about this fraud in the *Wall Street Journal* a few weeks back." I'd never seen the article she was talking about, but I started to feel less nervous. Still, I wasn't totally convinced. The folks on the call had a good amount of information about me, so part of me still believed that it could be real. Remember, I'm supposed to know all of the fraud signs. I'm an *expert*.

Ivy decided that she would role-play, telling the "IRS" representative that she was my attorney, that she knew this was a fraud scheme, and never to call me again. The representative became very angry and immediately disconnected. The call was over, but the impact lasted.

I study fraud all day (and sometimes all night), and I almost fell victim to this scheme.

In recent years, the IRS, state tax agencies, and tax-prep firms have faced a growing attack from cyber thieves who steal information, file false returns, and collect refunds in the names of legitimate taxpayers. According to the Government Accountability Office, thieves stole $3.1 billion in fraudulent refunds in 2014.[1] The IRS provides extensive resources on how to prevent tax fraud on its website, but the one piece of advice that I received as I shared this story with a few friends who had a similar experience is that the IRS does not call you.

A few things stuck out as odd:

- The noisy "call center" atmosphere

- The inability to provide an address for the Washington, DC, federal courthouse

- The failure of the "IRS" agent to state her name and numerical ID at the beginning of the call

- The $7,500 potential debt

- The caller ID identifying the number as being from Arlington Heights, Ilinois

- The caller's foreign accent

- The lack of receiving a notice in the mail

- The request for payment information

All of those things had gnawed at me, and I didn't take the bait. But I'm unusual. An international fraud survey conducted by KPMG found that 38 percent of red flags were ignored in major fraud cases.[2]

Unfortunately, this tax fraud scheme is very common. The Treasury Inspector General for the Tax Administration (TIGTA) announced that it received reports of roughly 896,000 contacts since October 2013 and has become aware of over five thousand victims who have collectively paid over $26.5 million as a result of the scam.[3] I am happy to report that I was not victim number 5,001.

But in 2017, I was the victim of a StubHub ticket scam. It was summer, and I was excited to get my hands on two Bruno Mars tickets. I was so focused on hitting "buy" on the StubHub website that perhaps I missed the red flags that would have alerted me to the fraud. However, when I reached the front of the line at the United Center in Chicago and handed my tickets over to the ticket handler and an "invalid" sign appeared on the scanner, I was despondent. The reseller had obviously sold the same ticket seats to multiple buyers, and the lucky person who stepped into the United Center first had the valid ticket. By the time my $250 ticket was scanned, it was deemed invalid.

The problem with this type of ticket scam is there's no way the buyer would ever know the reseller had sold the same ticket to multiple people. There is a lack of internal controls in the reseller process, which creates the opportunity for anyone to get duped. Thanks to my tweet to StubHub while at the United Center, Stub-Hub resolved the ticket debacle. I was issued new tickets immediately (and they were better seats than I originally purchased), just in time to see Bruno.

A classic study by Norbert Schwarz, an expert in consumer judgment, and psychology professor Rolf Reber found that people are more likely to think a statement is true when it is written in high color contrast (blue words on white) as opposed to low contrast (yellow words on white).[4] In my StubHub situation, the site had high-contrast colors so I thought it looked legitimate. In my defense, when purchasing concert tickets on a third-party website like StubHub and text is coupled with colorful imagery, everything seems fine. There were no indicators alerting me to a ruse.

. . .

A few years ago, two of my accounting professor colleagues were duped in an iTunes gift card scam, which resulted in one professor sending $1,000 to a con artist rather than our colleague.[5]

One colleague (let's call him Joe) received a text from another colleague (let's call him Allen) asking him to purchase an iTunes gift card. Allen explained to Joe that he was in a meeting and unable to purchase the gift card and asked Joe to get it. Joe did not think this was odd, so he purchased the gift card and sent back a text telling Allen the card was purchased. Since Joe didn't know Allen's cell phone number, it was not suspicious that he was unfamiliar with the cell phone number. Then Allen asked Joe to take a picture of the back of the card showing the gift card number. Joe followed Allen's instructions and did not think anything of it. After fifteen minutes passed, Allen sent another text asking Joe to purchase eight additional gift cards, and Joe said that he needed time because he was at dinner with friends. Once the dinner was over, Joe went to two different stores to pick up the additional gift cards. Then he received a rather aggressive text from the person he thought was Allen asking for pictures of the back of the additional gift cards. Although Joe was more suspicious now, he took the pictures and sent the images to Allen. Joe then received a call from his wife, and he explained to her what was going on. She told him that it sounded like a scam. By this time, Joe had received another text from "Allen" demanding the pictures of the additional cards, and Joe confronted the caller telling him that he was calling the police. Unfortunately, Joe was duped out of $1,000, the money on the gift cards was spent, and the imposter "Allen" moved on to the next victim.

As shocking as this may sound, it is so very common. According to Oracle and KPMG 2018 Cloud Threat Report, 55 percent of survey respondents say they fell victim to one (or both) of the two types of phishing emails, messages with malicious links, or malware-bearing attachments.[6] Organizations should also be mindful of other types of phishing techniques, such as vishing and smishing. *Vishing* is the use of voicemail to solicit a return call in which a user is convinced to share personal information. *Smishing* (which is similar to what my colleagues fell victim to) is the use of SMS text messages intended to lure recipients into clicking on a link to a webpage designed to steal credentials. With my colleagues, the duper was able to send an email that appeared to be from another university colleague, request assistance purchasing a gift card, and follow up with a text message from a cell phone number.

. . .

My family and I were also innocent bystanders.

While renovating our home in 2019, we stayed in a variety of Airbnbs (seven in seven weeks, to be exact). We could have gone to a hotel, but there were five of us, including our dog, Nigel. We needed space.

The apartment was advertised as a spacious two-bedroom, one-and-a-half-bath in close walking distance to the library, gym, cute restaurants, and one of my kid's schools. We were excited that we found a place that welcomed dogs, and something told me that it was too good to be true.

The first red flag: it was cheap.

As Grandmother Kelly always told me, there's no such thing as free money. Boy, was she right.

On our first evening at the apartment, we decided to walk to dinner. It was a beautiful Chicago summer evening, and we enjoyed a meal at one of our favorite local spots. When we returned, I knew it was my turn to take Nigel for his night walk.

To our surprise, the key didn't open the lock. We tried multiple times to get in, but we couldn't. And Nigel was trapped inside.

We called the emergency building maintenance and explained the situation. We waited for about two hours, and finally, they came. Because the door lock was so old and worn, it had to be severed.

Nigel was finally free. But we had no door lock.

Maintenance rushed to a hardware store to install a lock. Unfortunately, when the lock was severed, so was the doorknob. And when maintenance replaced the lock, they failed to replace the knob.

For the next two weeks, the only way to open the door from the inside was to slide a butter knife between the frame of the door and the door opening.

On the morning of day 2, we awoke to the kitchen sink shooting water (along with food and other debris) from the garbage disposal, creating a huge flood in the kitchen that made its way into the living room. After cleaning up this disgusting mess, my husband and I noticed that the kitchen baseboards had water damage. I then started to notice that the countertops around the sink had similar warping from water.

This was not the first time this kitchen had flooded.

I knew I should have read more reviews than the top four, which were all positive. Now I did. As I began scrolling down, the serious complaints began—complaint after complaint about kitchen water issues, nonresponsive maintenance, and unclean conditions. I felt completely bamboozled.

The kitchen floods continued into the next day, so I contacted the Airbnb hosts and demanded a refund. I also contacted Airbnb and questioned why they continued to allow these particular hosts to remain on their platform, given all the complaints. (They didn't really have an answer.)

I made such a fuss that the host moved us into another unit the following week and issued a full refund. I was relieved but not satisfied.

How could I have missed *this*? It was my fault for not getting proper intel.

The accountant in me reared her head. I decided to make a spreadsheet of the positive versus negative reviews because I wanted to

JUST FOR FUN!

I made a vow to myself long ago that I would only be fooled once. On the next page is my red flag list that sometimes keeps me from becoming an innocent bystander. I decided to do some soul searching and think about red flags that often make me pause when I'm meeting people, reading emails, or just thinking about my day. Not to say all of my red flags mean that there's fraud, but these things typically make me stop and wonder.

Do you know what your triggers are?

see if I noticed any pattern. The positive reviews were short, vague, and appeared after every fifth negative review. The negative reviews were very long, full of details and emotion. The writer never recommended the unit.

Google "Airbnb horror stories," and you'll find pages of examples of innocent bystanders victimized by hosts who know they can take advantage of people in need of a place to stay. From hosts with fake identities (which I believe mine were) to guests who have their apartments vandalized and burglarized when they're out, bystanders seem to always find themselves minding their own business yet falling victim to those who see them as prey.

This doesn't just happen on the ground, but also in the sky.

Airplane passengers became innocent bystanders in 2018 and 2019, when two Boeing 737 MAX's went down, killing nearly 350 people.[7] Boeing initially blamed both disasters on "pilot error." But it turned out that the accidents were not caused by a person, but the plane's Maneuvering Characteristics Augmentation System

Red flag triggers

Red flag	Reason
Never trust anyone who doesn't like dogs.	Didn't you watch Benji movies as a kid? Or *Lassie*? And what about *A Dog's Way Home*? Tears.
Never trust anyone who refers to themselves in the third person.	Why distance yourself in a conversation when you're actually participating in it?
Never trust anyone who doesn't say please and thank you.	Manners matter. If someone can't utter these two simple words, then there are probably more words they can't say (like, "My mistake" and "I'm sorry").
Never trust anyone who doesn't have a streaming account.	Is there any other option?
Never trust anyone with a Hotmail account.	Hotmail screams *Phishing Scheme!*
Never trust anyone over thirty whose mail still goes to their parents' house.	Even if you still live with them, at least get a PO box.
Never, ever trust someone who doesn't like Beyoncé.	'Nuff said.
Never trust anyone who doesn't have a photo on LinkedIn.	It's a social network for business. What are you trying to hide?
Never trust people who talk about themselves incessantly.	Just stop. Narcissist.
If you don't agree that Whitney Houston is one of the greatest singers of all time, I don't trust you.	She's the G.O.A.T. Hands down.
Never trust anyone who says they only check their emails once a day.	Research shows that the average person checks their email fifteen times a day. So these people who say they don't are *liars*.
Never trust anyone who can't take a day off work—for anything.	What are you trying to prove, and to whom?

(MCAS), which impacted the flight control system of the Boeing 737 MAX.[8]

There are more than ten thousand Boeing commercial airplanes in use.[9] Millions of passengers boarded an airplane and had no idea of the error that might cause the plane to crash. (An exposé about

the subject, *Downfall: The Case Against Boeing*, aired on Netflix.[10])
But if a crime isn't exposed or an accident doesn't come to light,
we might never know anything is amiss. Which is to say, we don't
know when—or if—we're being preyed on.

So how do you safeguard yourself against the medicine you take,
the food you eat, the plane you fly on, or the place you live? You
can't. You just have to trust that other people have the same sen-
sibilities as you do and are doing their job. But they don't always.
And therein lies the rub.

You Don't Know What You Don't Know

When I was thinking of a name for the largest category of victims, I began seeing the relationships between this group and the
bystander effect, a theory coined in 1964 after the death of Kitty
Genovese.

Genovese was a twenty-eight-year-old bartender who was
stabbed outside her apartment building in in Queens, New York,
when she was coming home from work at 2:30 a.m. Two weeks
after her murder, the *New York Times* reported that thirty-eight
witnesses had seen or heard the attack, but no one had called the
police or helped her.[11]

The story was later proven false; it turns out that only two neighbors refused to help. But the bystander effect still holds.

The theory (aka the "Genovese Syndrome") describes how
people fail to react to something they actually should respond to—
like a woman screaming for her life. It also applies to the workplace.
An *Academy of Management* study investigated how "information
redundancy" affects people's desire to keep quiet when they see

something wrong. In other words, the more people know the same information, the less likely they are to speak up. Instead, they tend to "stand by" and say nothing because they believe someone else will.[12] So if we all think the water is contaminated and no one says anything, then we're all innocent bystanders. Innocent victims.

I liken it to the parable of the emperor's new clothes. The entire village—the bystander—notices that the emperor is prancing around in the buff, but no one trusts their own eyes. Since no one else is saying anything, they rationalize, they must be imagining it. So they all keep quiet until an especially vocal neighbor calls him out.

The emperor, by the way, was also an innocent bystander. He was swindled by two con men who offered to weave him spectacular clothing that was invisible to foolish people. The emperor bites, and the weavers set up a loom in town. Various officials, along with the emperor, check in on them as they're working. They see nothing, no thread or yarn, but they pretend otherwise rather than risk looking stupid. Eventually, the weavers tell the emperor that they're finished, and they "dress" him in the lavish new garb. The villagers watch silently as the emperor parades around in the nude. Finally, a child blurts out that the emperor is naked. That's when everyone realizes that they've been duped. The emperor, to his credit, continues to march proudly (if not comfortably).

You saw a similar story in Dixon, albeit with Western garb. Some residents were aware that Rita Crundwell owned over four hundred horses spread between her two ranches. Her colleagues were aware that she took four months—*four months*—of unpaid vacation annually. And yet, with the exception of Gene, the "town crier," no one raised any concerns, largely because they weren't sure that what they were seeing was a problem. Maybe Rita had simply amassed a lot of vacation days. Maybe a rich investor paid for her ranch. By keeping the information to themselves, everyone became an innocent bystander.

History is filled with innocent bystanders, like the men who took part in a 1932 study, officially named the "Tuskegee Study of Untreated Syphilis in the Negro Male." The United States Health Service used six hundred unwitting Black men to study the effects of syphilis on humans. Most of the men were poor; 399 had syphilis, and 201 did not. All were told that they were being treated for "bad blood," a euphemism for several ailments, including syphilis—an often-fatal disease. In exchange for their participation in the study, they were told they would receive free medical treatment, along with free transportation to and from appointments, free hot lunches, and free burial.[13]

What they did not know was that half the men with syphilis were given an arsenic-mercury treatment, but the other half received no treatment—not even ten years later when penicillin was discovered as an effective treatment for the venereal disease. Nor were they given any kind of informed consent.

The ruse was discovered in 1972—forty years later—by a reporter named Jean Heller, who published her story on the front page of the *New York Times*.[14] Surviving participants and their descendants filed a class-action lawsuit resulting in a $10 million settlement in 1974. President Bill Clinton issued a formal apology in 1997, but the damage lingers.[15] The Tuskegee syphilis study is one of the main reasons so many people in the Black community didn't want to get vaccinated for Covid. They didn't trust that the government really had their best interests at heart. Can you blame them?

"History has not been kind to African Americans," said Carmen Head Thornton, whose grandfather, Freddie Lee Tyson, was one of the men in the study. "It has not been kind, and because of misperceptions that are connected to what happened in the study . . . I think it helps to grow mistrust, and that's one of the things that we deal with."[16]

Dr. Death

Just as the men of Tuskegee trusted the medical process and the federal agency that was implementing the study, the people of Dixon trusted their government. They never anticipated the injustice coming their way. This is what makes them so vulnerable and so powerless.

Lola Bailey was victimized by pharmacist Robert Courtney, the intentional perp you met in chapter 1. Courtney, you may recall, was convicted of intentionally diluting ninety-eight thousand prescriptions given to forty-two hundred patients.[17] Lola Bailey was one of Courtney's victims.

Lola died at age sixty-eight. But her daughter, Glenda, is very much alive. I wanted to talk to her. I don't know what I expected her to say. Maybe I just wanted to know how she moved on with her life after such a horrific betrayal. I was grateful that she was open to discussing the case.

Glenda first heard that Courtney had been diluting cancer drugs in 2000. She was pulling into her garage at her home in Dallas when the phone rang. Her mother had died about a year earlier, and Glenda was still processing it.

She can't quite recall who was on the line—either her father or sister—but she remembers them saying something crazy about Robert Courtney and cancer drugs. Her mother had been diagnosed with lymphoma seven years earlier and was one of the more than four thousand cancer patients whose drugs Courtney had diluted. It was unfathomable. Who would *do* something like this?

After she got the news about Courtney, Glenda scoured her brain for clues that her mother may not have been getting the proper treatment. But she didn't really find any. Her mother didn't lose her hair from the chemo drugs, true. But so what? Different people react differently to chemotherapy. Was that really a flag?

Glenda was too upset to attend Courtney's trial. She never met him, never spoke to him, never laid eyes on the man. She fantasized about writing him a letter, but she didn't know what she would say. To cope with her trauma, she burned all the legal papers. "I had to go through a process of letting go, and that was my way to do that," she said.

The family received a settlement from a class-action lawsuit, which Glenda's father split between himself, Glenda's sister, and Glenda. Glenda's share was $20,000, a third of the $60,000 windfall. That's how much her mother's life was worth: $60,000.

Like other innocent bystanders, Glenda and her mother, Lola, would have never suspected that their pharmacist—a highly trusted position—was diluting chemo drugs.

It's terrifying to think that we're all *this close* to becoming an innocent bystander. How would you know to ask your compounding pharmacist—the person who makes the solution, not the nice person behind the counter at Walgreens—if they're adding the proper amount of medication? You can't. You don't know what you don't know.

Are You What You Eat?

Food is another area in which we're at the complete mercy of the powers that be.

We have little idea of what we're consuming, but we assume it's safe. Unless we're sitting in a barn, yanking on a cow's udders, do we really know where the milk comes from? Unless we pluck the eggs from under a hen, how do we know if it's cage-free or not?

Experts estimate that food fraud affects 1 percent of the global food industry, at the cost of about $10 to $15 billion a year. Some put the cost as high as $40 billion a year.[18]

The FDA calls it economically motivated adulteration, or EMA. It's also called food fraud, and it occurs when someone deliberately adds or removes or substitutes an important ingredient or part of a food. EMA also occurs when someone adds something to a food to make it seem better or more valuable or mislabels a product. Sometimes, what's labeled as organic isn't necessarily organic, and what's labeled as local comes from miles and miles away. Ditto for "GMO-free."

Did you know that about 75 to 80 percent of extra-virgin olive oil in the United States isn't properly labeled?[19] Often, Italian extra-virgin olive oil is mixed with low-quality olive oil—or it could be a totally different kind of oil that's been altered to smell and look like the real thing. (I know. Who thinks of this?) The cheaper the bottle, the greater the chance it's not made from olives. The public. Has. No. Idea.

And it can be deadly.

The Centers for Disease Control estimates that foodborne pathogens infect roughly one in six Americans annually, with about 128,000 hospitalizations and three thousand deaths.[20] The World Health Organization, which tracks foodborne diseases globally, reports that unsafe food causes 600 million cases of foodborne diseases and 420,000 deaths annually. Thirty percent of foodborne deaths around the world happen to children under five years old.[21]

Stewart Parnell, the former CEO of the now-defunct Peanut Corporation of America, was responsible for foodborne pathogen deaths in the United States. Parnell was convicted in 2015 of federal felony charges related to food poisoning—the first corporate executive in US history to receive this "honor."[22]

Parnell was sentenced to twenty-eight years in prison after he knowingly shipped salmonella-contaminated peanut butter across forty-six states. His brother, Michael, a food broker, was sentenced to twenty years.[23] Hundreds of people became sick as a result of their antics, and nine people died. Parnell knew that the products were contaminated, but he shipped them anyway. Why did he do this? Because it saved money.

Beech-Nut is another example. Beech-Nut Nutrition Corporation, owned by Swiss firm Hero Group, is an artificial-preservative-free baby food company headquartered in Amsterdam. In 1987, Beech-Nut paid a $2 million fine for deliberately filling its "100 percent apple juice" bottles—a product meant for babies—with sugary water containing mostly water, beet sugar, corn syrup, and cane syrup. The apple did not fall even close to the tree. But Beech-Nut didn't care. As the *New York Times* reported, the faux juice cost about 20 percent less to manufacture.[24] Those poor babies were innocent bystanders. So were their parents.

Then there was 2008's "Chinese milk scandal," in which milk was adulterated with melamine, a nitrogen-based compound that increases the likelihood of kidney problems. Companies like Nestlé were implicated in the fraud; by the end of that year, more than 300,000 people had gotten sick, more than 50,000 kids had been hospitalized, and six babies had died. The intentional perpetrators who carried out this scheme were arrested; two of them were executed.[25]

Never a Victimless Crime

A few months ago, my friend's octogenarian father received an email from his son. The son, who was in his late forties, had been robbed and his wallet stolen. "Can you please send me some money now?" the email asked. My friend's father was set to wire the money when the phone rang. It was his son, coincidentally calling to say hi. He had no idea what his father was talking about. He hadn't been robbed; he was perfectly fine. It was a giant ruse, and his elderly father nearly fell for it.

Older people epitomize innocent bystanders. They're trusting, they tend to have more money, they're not always as tech-savvy as they could be, and they may not be watching their finances as closely as they once may have.

According to a recent AARP report, people over 65 are swindled out of an estimated $4.8 billion each year. But this is just an estimate, since most crimes aren't reported. A study by the Consumer Financial Protection Bureau found that older adults lose an average of $34,200 to financial exploitation. The number rises to $83,600 if fiduciaries—lawyers, trustees, financial professionals—are involved.[26]

And that's how Mary West became a victim of elder fraud: through a trusted financial professional who shouldn't have been trusted.[27]

The West family owned a mountain farm property in Asheville, North Carolina, that had been passed down through four generations. After the Civil War, Mary's grandparents settled on the property, growing produce to support their family of six. The farm was profitable, so they purchased additional land in the 1930s and '40s. Over the years, they raised goats and cattle, farmed dairy, and grew corn. After her father died, Mary was next in line to take over the farm. She and her husband, Norris, built a home on the land and raised Black Angus cattle and buffalo. Their three children grew up there.

In 2000, Mary, who was over eighty at the time, attended a seminar on estate management. She was especially impressed by a presentation from Southern Financial Services, whose owner, James W. "Bill" Bailey, appeared trusting, courteous, and smart. Still, Mary did her due diligence and checked him out with the Better Business Bureau and local attorneys and accountants. Bailey and Southern Financial had a clean record and reputation, and Mary decided to invest with him. She suggested her children do the same, and they did.

Bailey promised to invest their money into a 1031 Exchange Services account.[28] The term comes from Section 1031 of the US Internal Revenue Code, and it allows real estate investors to save taxes by deferring payment on some of the capital gains at the time of the exchange. For the next several years, Southern Financial paid the Wests dividends and provided them quarterly financial statements.

Once Norris passed away, Mary sold the cattle and rented the land for farming. Later, Mary, her two daughters, and her son formed a partnership of ownership over the land. In 2007, they sold 123 acres for $6 million, which they divided evenly. It was a great reward for more than a century of the family's hard manual labor.

Everything changed in early 2011 when the Wests received a letter from the US government informing them that Bailey had been indicted on charges of securities fraud, mail fraud, and falsifying tax returns. The Wests were frozen with shock.

For over a decade, Bailey had been operating a $13 million Ponzi scheme involving 120 investors. Each one of them was an innocent bystander. The Wests racked their brains for red flags, but there weren't any. In fact, investigators and forensic accountants on the case said that the heavy card stock on which Southern Financial printed its financial statements was the only thing investors might have noticed as unusual. It looked more like a wedding invitation than an earnings report.

Bailey pleaded guilty to securities fraud, mail fraud, and filing false tax returns and was sentenced to thirty-two years in prison for operating a Ponzi scheme that defrauded investors of $13 million between 2000 and 2010.

The West family, and the other victims, sued. I was an expert witness, testifying on their behalf. I explained how they had done their due diligence and that the bank should have noticed that so much money was coming out of Bailey's accounts. The bank didn't. So why, I argued, should the victims be penalized?

The judge ruled in favor of the bank, claiming it had followed all the appropriate protocols. The Wests and the other families never recovered their losses.

I felt like I let the victims down.

Although victims of fraud are not alone, they often suffer their losses alone. Shame, guilt, embarrassment, and disbelief are among the reasons that only an estimated 15 percent of fraud victims in the United States report their plight to the police. Other reasons include victims' doubt about their own judgment, a sense of betrayal, and fears about how their family members, friends, and business associates will react. Some victims feel their losses are not significant enough to report, think law enforcement agencies won't take the crime seriously, or believe that nothing will result from reporting the crime. Many victims feel they only have themselves to blame when in reality, calculating, skilled perpetrators are at fault.

CHAPTER TAKEAWAYS

This is a tough category because it affects so many areas of our lives that we have no control over: Food. Medicine. Transportation. The elderly.

- Most innocent bystanders rationalize red flags away, if they notice them at all. But we tend to doubt ourselves and what we see. ("How can the emperor really not know he's naked? I must be seeing things!")

- It's critical to pay attention to what's around you. If you think the emperor is naked, he probably is. If there's smoke, there's fire. Don't assume that there's no fire if the smoke alarm goes off.

- But other times, there's not much an innocent bystander can do. Because sometimes there's nothing to see. Sometimes, the alarm doesn't go off. If a company, or a person, wants to prey on you, they can. Unless someone blows the whistle, you're screwed. Sad, but true.

Innocent bystander quick facts

Description	Characteristics
• Largest prey category	• Vulnerable
• Rationalize red flags away	• Unaware
• Targeted by every category of perpetrators	• Unguarded
	• Typical
	• Trusting

Chapter 5

Organizational Targets

While innocent bystanders are victimized at the individual level, *organizational targets* are victimized at the *organizational* level (hence the name). Whether an internal or external threat, organizational targets are usually dependent on the person victimizing them. Organizations must employ key people who have extreme decision-making power—just as the city of Dixon, Illinois, relied on the financial expertise of Rita Crundwell and believed they were better off because she worked for the town.

Perps (primarily intentional perps) watch and study organizational targets. They know the organization's habits, and they *specifically* target it. Organizational targets usually employ a person who holds a position of power, and this person (who could be an intentional perp, accidental perp, or righteous perp) has great access. They could be a clerk in accounts payable or a chief information officer. The perpetrators also have knowledge of the way systems work and understand the internal control weaknesses the organization may have.

According to a PwC Global Economic Crime and Fraud Survey, nearly half of reported fraud was committed by insiders.[1] Rita Crundwell knew Dixon's every move, so the town was an easy mark. It was like taking candy from a baby.

A Wolf in Sheep's Clothing

I met Pastor Suzanne Anderson-Hurdle one Sunday afternoon in early 2019. I had just finished a screening in Chicago, and as usual, the audience had questions.

A raspy female voice called out from the back of the theater. "Why does this keep happening to innocent people?"

Most questions I have answers for, but this one stumped me. "Well," I said after a few seconds, "if I knew that, I could solve world hunger!"

The audience laughed. The voice continued.

"I came last week to see this film and I was blown away," she said. "I had so many questions, so I came back so I could ask you directly." Instead of attending alone, she had brought a group from her church. "What happened to the residents of Dixon is the same thing that happened to my church," she said tearfully.

For nineteen years, Pastor Suzanne ran Good Shepherd Lutheran Church in Romeoville, Illinois, a small town about twenty-five miles from Chicago. Church finances and operations were handled by an outside governing body called the Council of Elders. Suzanne was focused on community building, preaching, and Bible study, not finance, and she knew she needed someone to help her with that area. Suzanne put out a call for volunteers, and Deborah Suchomel stepped up. Debbie, as they called her, pretty much had free rein. She became the Sunday school coordinator, and the two women grew close.

The Good Shepherd's Church's betrayal was fresh and hurtful, and no one ever saw it coming. Intentional perp Debbie knew the inner workings of the church (the organizational target). She knew that Pastor Suzanne didn't read the church's financial statements. She knew that the pastor actually didn't oversee the church's money at all; a governing council did that. The church's governance structure made it ripe for fraud.

In 2008, a letter arrived at the church office from the Illinois Department of Revenue saying that the church's wages weren't reported correctly. Suzanne asked Debbie to explain, and Debbie pieced together some response. Pastor Suzanne believed it. Debbie was the church treasurer. If anyone could be trusted, she could.

But another email came three years later, in June of 2011, along with a notice from the IRS stating that they had no record of receiving tax returns from fourth quarter 2009 through fourth quarter 2011. Again, the church council asked Debbie to deal with it. She said that she had sent the money they owed, but it had been credited to the wrong account.

This sounded fishy, so Pastor Suzanne went to the bank. She wanted to find out where this check from the IRS had gone. She told the bank manager what was going on, and he logged onto his computer. Since Suzanne was not listed on the account, the manager was hesitant to give her too much information. After a few moments of back and forth, the manager decided to help. "That was a personal check," he said.

Suzanne was stunned. She expected the check to be from the IRS, not from the treasurer's personal account. "From whom?"

He angled the computer screen toward her, and she could see in bold letters that it was a check from Debbie's account for $19,000.

Pastor Suzanne's initial thought was that there was some kind of accident. There *had* to be some explanation. "As a Christian, I wanted there to be a reason," she said.

Then they discovered that it was not just $19,000; it was almost $181,000.

Pastor Suzanne decided to launch her own investigation. She felt responsible and needed answers to her many questions.

Pastor Suzanne spent many months and sleepless nights reviewing hundreds of bank statements, credit card receipts, and internal church records. One of the many red flags she discovered was a financial discrepancy between the church's bank statement and the treasurer's report. Pastor Suzanne kicked herself as she read the documents. Had someone compared the two documents, they would have noticed that the bank statement had a lower balance than what was reported on the treasurer's report. But no one did that.

The church's internal audit committee decided to bring in an assistant to help with the finances. At the time, Debbie was in charge of both the church finances and the preschool finances, and the church decided that it was too much work for one person. But Debbie delayed training the new woman by almost a year. Whenever the council asked about the transition, Debbie always had an excuse.

In hindsight, Pastor Suzanne realized this was a brightly waving red flag. Debbie almost always said. "It's taking me longer to get the records in order."

Although it didn't seem odd at the time, Pastor Suzanne realized that Debbie had delayed the training because she wanted to be sure the fraud stayed hidden.

From January 31, 2011, to March 2011, Debbie deposited a total of $17,656.41 into the church's bank account.[2] Where in God's name did Debbie get $17,000 from? No one thought this was odd because no one realized the check was drawn from Debbie's personal account.

The church had multiple accounts, which made it easier to move and steal money without detection. Confusion is fraud's best friend. In order to detect Debbie's fraud, the council and the audit committee would have had to compare the bank statements to Debbie's treasurer's reports. But they rarely compared the two documents.

Once Pastor Suzanne started her research, she noticed dozens of checks made out to "Cash." This was odd.

"Besides being against church policy, the only time the church would have checks written to cash was during their annual rummage sale," Pastor Suzanne said. But there were no rummage sales on the horizon. Debbie was also running personal expenses through the church's books. Since no one was checking, it was easy for her to submit duplicate invoices for payment. The vendor would get paid from the legitimate invoice, and then the payment from the fraudulent duplicate invoice would go into Debbie's personal account. Yet another casualty of lax internal controls.

After almost a year of full-time investigating, Pastor Suzanne finally went to the police. Because she had no prior record, Debbie ended up getting sentenced to four years of probation and 480 hours of community service. That hurt even more.

"Justice doesn't always look like what we hope it's going to look like," Suzanne told me. "Somebody goes into a 7-11 and they steal a pack of gum, they get arrested." But not Debbie.

Pastor Suzanne beat herself up afterward. Why didn't she ask more questions over the years? Why was she so trusting?

TABLE 5-1

Types of nonprofit schemes

Scheme	Percent of cases
Corruption	41
Billing	30
Expense reimbursements	23
Cash on hand	17
Noncash	16
Skimming	15
Check and payment tampering	14
Cash larceny	12
Payroll	12
Financial statement fraud	11
Register disbursements	3

Source: Association of Certified Fraud Examiners, *ACFE Report to the Nations*, April 16, 2020, https://www.acfe.com/report-to-the-nations/2020/. Retrieved February 14, 2022, from https://www.acfe.com/press-release.aspx?id=42950105632020 ACFE Report to the Nations.

"One of the reasons why churches can be so vulnerable is because of the large percentage of volunteerism," she said. "You're trusting people with fiduciary responsibilities and in a religious organization, you may not feel comfortable saying, 'Let me do a background check or let me double-check what you say.' You may not feel comfortable doing that, like you might in a corporate job. We didn't learn about internal controls in seminary."

The average nonprofit doesn't have a lot of money to spend on internal controls. According to various ACFE's yearly *Reports to the Nations*, median nonprofit fraud loss has ranged from $60,000 to $75,000.[3] The average nonprofit loss reached $639,000 in 2020.[4] Table 5-1 shows the common schemes experienced by the 191 nonprofit cases included in the 2020 study.

I serve on the board of the Greater Chicago Food Depository, a nonprofit hub for seven hundred food pantries, soup kitchens, shelters, and other programs. One of the things we do as a board is to match our director's skill sets with the needs of the organization. It's no surprise that I'm also the chair of the audit committee. Making sure volunteers are paired with their skill sets is one key way to assist nonprofit management and provide a low-cost internal control strategy.

Inside Job

Nonprofits are easy targets, but for-profits can be, too. Banks are especially easy marks. The Association of Certified Fraud Examiners' 2020 *Report to the Nations* researched 2,504 cases of internal fraud from 125 countries and found that banking and financial services accounted for 15.4 percent of internal fraud cases, the largest share.[5] The ACFE's 2022 report found similarly.[6]

Although there are various types of banks, they mostly operate in the same way, and this level of predictability makes them easy organizational targets.

In 2019, I was invited to be the closing-bell speaker at the Willie A. Deese School of Business and Economics at North Carolina A&T State University in Greensboro, where I did my undergraduate studies. I typically try to hire a videographer when I do large speaking engagements, and I was referred to Ken B., who grew up nearby. (Because he has since reengineered his life, I'll refer to him as "Ken B." to protect his identity.)

I had just completed a keynote speech about fraud, and we were analyzing whether Rita Crundwell's nearly twenty-year prison sentence was fair. I noticed how uncomfortable Ken seemed. He stepped from behind the camera and appeared to want to join the discussion with me and 150 eager business students, all of whom thought her sentence should be longer. At the end of the gig, I thanked him and drove off. And that, I thought, was that.

Later that day, as I was driving from Greensboro to Blacksburg, Virginia, the phone rang.

"That was a very interesting presentation," a voice said. Ken's.

"Thank you," I replied, a little surprised that he had even been paying attention.

"I must admit, when I'm hired for these gigs, I rarely listen to the speaker," he said. "But you captured my attention."

After a ten-second awkward silence, he cleared his throat. "I was interested in what you were saying for a lot of personal reasons," he said. "There's a lot you don't know about me."

This was true. In general, I make it a point to properly vet everyone I work with, but Ken was a referral, so I didn't put him through my typical vetting process. Crazy scenarios raced through my mind. Was he an ax murderer? In the US Witness Protection Program?

"I was listening to the way the students responded to the different fraud scenarios you were giving them, and I started to think back to how I was when I was their age," he said. (See table 5-2.) "I didn't have a care in the world and actually thought I was on top of the world, until I wasn't."

Ken grew up lower middle class in Winston-Salem, North Carolina, and went to school at North Carolina A&T State University in Greensboro. He did really well the first semester. But by his second semester, he wanted to "play around a little bit and enjoy college life." He enjoyed it so much that his grades plummeted and he had to return to his parents' house.

One afternoon he was in a grocery store when he ran across a sharply dressed recruiter who happened to be a Marine. Ken was impressed with him, and in 2000 he signed up for a "two by six"

TABLE 5-2

"What would you do . . . ?" worksheet

How you respond could determine if you are an intentional perp (chapter 1) or accidental perp (chapter 2) in the making.

Scenario	Dilemma	What would you do?
1	Your cab driver gives you a blank reimbursement slip and the actual receipt for the ride. Instead of using the actual receipt, you could submit the blank receipt and add $2 to the fare price on your expense reimbursement.	a. Add the $2 and submit the receipt. b. Don't add the $2 and submit the fare price.
2	You invite a friend who works in the same industry to lunch and you spend fifteen minutes talking about work-related items and an hour talking about personal items. You could submit the receipt to your company as a work-related lunch for reimbursement.	a. It's a work lunch. Submit the expense. b. This is a personal lunch. Don't submit.
3	Your company sends you to a conference in Hawaii and instead of attending conference sessions, you could spend the majority of your time on the beach and touring the island.	a. I work hard and deserve some free time. b. I would attend every session and not take time away.
4	Your friend works for a tech that is about to go public. Your friend tells you about the pending IPO and you could buy shares based on this information.	a. No; this is illegal. b. Buying shares is fine.
5	It's time for you to complete your annual compliance training. Instead of taking the online course and reading each question per the instructions, you might barely read the questions and guess the correct answer until you get the needed score. Then, upon completion, you could simply sign the compliance certification form indicating you read and completed all sections of the training.	a. Yes; I will sign the certification. b. No; I will not sign the certification.

contract with the Marines, which meant he'd serve two years and be inactive for six.

For the two years that he was active, he lived in Twentynine Palms, California, where he repaired radio devices used in combat.

At the end of the two years, Ken found himself getting a little depressed. "I knew time was coming for me to go home and continue the lifestyle that I was living before I joined the Marine Corps," he said. He could have been a reservist, but he didn't want that. He tried to stay on active duty, but that wasn't possible.

Ken came home and looked for work while he tried to get back in school. And lo and behold, he found a position as an "electronics technician" for ATM machines.

He was only twenty and had no experience as an electronics technician, but he believes he got the job because of his experience in the Marine Corps. Military men *had* to be trustworthy.

He trained for about two months. "I was literally excited about being an electronics technician working on circuits and capacitors and current-voltage," he said. "I had no idea that I was going to be working with money."

If this were a TV show, right about now is when the *dum-dum-dum-dum* would kick in. Sounds ominous, doesn't it? And it was.

Ken was making good money. His father told him to save for a house. "But immediate gratification kicked in. Like, I had to have it *right now.*"

He rented an apartment. And then he needed furniture. But he was only earning about $800 a week, barely enough for a living room set and the things he wanted.

Many of his friends were in similar situations, with young children and financial obligations. They needed their cars repaired. They had mouths to feed. Ken grew frustrated that they were all in this situation. They were hardworking but didn't have health benefits and only made minimum wage.

After thinking about how he could make extra money fast, he came up with a solution. One day he went to work and grabbed "a pinch" from one of the ATMs he serviced. It was a small amount—about a half an inch of $20 bills, which amounts to about $2,000—but he knew it was wrong. Yet he couldn't help himself.

"I suppressed everything the Marines taught me," he said. "Everybody knows the consequence of stealing, so I don't think it's fair to say that I wasn't thinking about that. I thought in the back of my head, 'There is no way that they can be missing this money; there is no way that anybody could know $1,000 out of hundreds of thousand dollars is gone.'"

The average ATM machine holds anywhere from $250,000 to $300,000.[7] That money is held in something called cassettes, which hold anywhere from $1,000 to $2,000 each. Ken serviced six to ten ATMs a day.

On this particular day, Ken decided he was going to take (and definitely not tell, like I did with my beloved bag). Not only for himself but for others, too. This time when he went in to service the ATM machines, he opened the cassette filled with dollar bills and dropped it in his "little tool bag." Then he went on his merry way.

He did this almost daily for about two months, racking up nearly $40,000. Any time his close friends and family experienced hardship, he'd slip them $100 or $1,000 to catch up on a bill or to spend at Walmart to buy groceries. Or else he'd take his buddies out to expensive dinners and pay for them himself. He liked being flush.

"It felt good to take care of people," he said.

Plus, he didn't think the banks would miss the money. And they didn't, until they did.

●　●　●

One spring day in 2004, Ken got a call from human resources asking him to come in.

He knew right then the jig was up. He put all his equipment on the motorcycle he had purchased with stolen money and drove to company headquarters.

"They asked me how much I took at any given time, and I told him a 'pinch,' anywhere from $800 to $1,200, sometimes up to $2,000, from thirteen different ATMs," he said.

He didn't even try to talk his way out of it. He simply handed over his keys and walked away. And that was it until October, when he received a knock on the door. You guessed it: the Feds.

In 1934, it became a federal crime to rob any national bank or state member bank of the Federal Reserve System.[8] He went to jail for six months. Nothing happened to the friends he helped with stolen money.

After Ken got out, he had to find a job. He was a felon. Companies didn't look kindly on his method of giving.

In 2007, with no other options, he started his own video business, shooting weddings, birthdays, and corporate events and reconfigured his entire life.

The Pothole Queen

Ken's organizational target was his bank, but entrepreneurs' businesses are also prime organizational targets for fraud.

One day, I was looking to speak to entrepreneurs whose businesses were victimized by fraud. A friend introduced me to Cheryl Obermiller. My film team and I decided to fly and meet her at the company headquarters, Obermiller Construction Services, in Harrisonville, Missouri, outside of Kansas City.[9]

Small businesses face unique challenges in protecting themselves from fraud. Oftentimes, business founders are focused on building their product or service and less focused on the internal controls needed to secure their business from theft. According to the ACFE's 2022 *Report to the Nations on Occupational Fraud and Abuse*, private companies and small businesses rank highest in occupational fraud frequency at 42 percent, compared with large corporations, governments, and nonprofits. The biggest contributing factor is the lack of internal controls. The median loss is $164,000.[10]

The ACFE's global report also showed that businesses with fewer than one hundred employees had the highest median loss, at $150,000, while the largest organizations (more than ten thousand employees) had a median loss of $138,000. Of course, a small business will have a much harder time absorbing its fraud losses, if it can survive them at all.[11]

Billing schemes, wire transfers, expense reimbursement, payroll schemes, cash larceny, check tampering, inventory theft, financial statement fraud, and corruption schemes were among the most common schemes.[12] In other words, there's a lot for an entrepreneur to look out for. Cheryl couldn't look out for it all.

Trust is never an internal control.

• • •

"Good morning, everyone," Cheryl said, dressed in a black pencil skirt with a pink and black blazer, cradling a sweet ten-month-old.

"I'm proud of what I've built here," she told me as we zig-zagged around large machinery and oversized tools. "But I came close to losing it all because I placed my business in the hands of the wrong person."

To paraphrase Lily Tomlin, "The road to success is always under construction." There were lots of bumps, and even more potholes, on Cheryl's road.

Cheryl grew up in an entrepreneurial family in Grandview, Missouri (population twenty-five thousand). Her father and uncle owned a family-operated grocery store and meat market that her grandparents opened in 1919, and the family worked there too. In Cheryl's mind, business was an extension of family, built on trust and hard work.

Cheryl had been a successful model, but continuing in that field didn't feel practical with a large family. So she joined her husband's engineering firm in a supporting capacity but didn't take a salary. After a few years, she realized that she had no social security, no income of her own, and no credit of her own. This wasn't smart, so she decided to start her construction company.

Her business really took off after she rammed her Lincoln Navigator into a massive pothole in a Walmart parking lot in town. She made such a fuss with the Walmart regional manager that she won the deal to resurface the entire parking lot, a $750,000 project. Not only was this the start of a lucrative construction company, but she also became known as the "Pothole Queen."

In 1993, she started Obermiller Construction. Once the company really started to take off, its primary focus was making sure that its work exceeded expectations, its name and reputation were properly marketed, and its customer service was impeccable. Cheryl needed someone to take care of the accounting portion of the business, a facet of the company to which she could no longer give her attention.

Cheryl spoke with a CPA friend from church about the accounting position. The friend had recently interviewed an accountant for a job. The woman was overqualified for that position but could be the perfect candidate for Cheryl's needs. Her name was Tammie Lynn Cowell, and she nailed the interview. Cheryl dutifully checked her references. Tammie had no prior record of any criminal or suspicious activity. After everything checked out, Tammie was hired.

Tammie's responsibilities included accounting and general office management. She answered the phones, relayed messages, did all the invoicing, balanced the checkbook, and processed the accounts payable and payroll. Sometimes, she even cleaned the bathroom. She was the glue that held Obermiller Construction together.

Cheryl would be talking to a client about having paperwork to them within the next few days, and before the meeting was over, Tammie would come in with the paperwork, having overheard the conversation. Or Cheryl would call Tammie from the other room and ask her what they paid per cubic yard for a concrete project they did years earlier. Tammie would know the amount down to the cent off the top of her head.

In fact, Tammie was often so anal retentive about every last detail that it would annoy Cheryl (in an endearing way). She remembered the time Tammie entered her office, detailing and complaining for fifteen minutes about how, for the third time, receipts turned in didn't balance out. Cheryl was concerned, thinking that there was a serious and consistent problem she may need to worry about.

"How much was it off?" asked Cheryl.

"By 25 cents again."

The two became close friends, both inside and outside the work-place. Tammie was equally family oriented, totally devoted to her husband and daughter, even coaching her cheerleading team. Tammie and Cheryl grew to know each other's families well.

"Tammie was the most trusted person in the company," said Cheryl.

In January, a huge blizzard hit the area. Cheryl arrived at work early, but Tammie didn't make it in. A letter had arrived from the IRS. Normally Tammie would have gotten the mail, but she wasn't there, so Cheryl decided to open the letter. Inside was a final notice letter, saying that they had been trying to contact her for over six months, that every phone call and letter had been ignored. Because of this, the IRS would start levying Obermiller Construction accounts and seizing business assets.

Cheryl was baffled. She had assumed that all payments to the IRS went out on time and were squared away, that they were pre-pared and delivered immaculately.

She called Tammie immediately, who explained that the IRS had made legitimate errors on the account in years past. "The IRS screwed up again," Tammie said. "Don't worry about it." She said she'd take care of it the next day.

But Cheryl did worry about it. She called the IRS and told them that her accountant had assured her that all taxes had been paid on time. They told her that according to their records, no quarterly payments had been made in the first and second quarters of 2009. The IRS admitted that it was possible that it was an electronic error and that payments might have been credited to a different account.

The IRS said it would put the notice on hold for thirty days to give Cheryl a chance to sort things out on her end, but at this point,

Cheryl was annoyed. She was busy enough as it was without dealing with a government agency's negligence.

Then she called Tammie back. Tammie sounded nervous and upset.

Cheryl repeated what the IRS had told her. But Tammie didn't say much, which struck Cheryl as odd.

"The same person that could recall the price of a cubic yard of asphalt from a project they did over two years ago suddenly acted like she didn't remember exactly when and how much she paid the large—$35,000 plus each—quarterly payments of less than a year ago?" said Cheryl.

Cheryl began doing some digging. This was hard on her; she felt like she was rifling through someone's medicine cabinet. She hoped that she wouldn't find anything.

She went into Tammie's computer and saw that the quarterly payments the IRS said were missing weren't even recorded. Then she went into one of Tammie's desk drawers. Tucked into the far back corner was a file with every notice the IRS had sent over the past six months. Cheryl's mouth literally dropped open.

The business had two bank accounts, a local one for payroll and a large national bank used for everything else. At the end of that whirlwind of a day, Cheryl called both of her bankers and had them put a freeze on the accounts. "Let me know if anything else comes in," she said.

The following day, Cheryl told her son, who also worked at the company and usually arrived a couple of hours before she did, to refuse to let Tammie inside and to call Cheryl when she got there. At 7:15 a.m., her son called, and Cheryl zipped over. On the way, she got a phone call from the local bank, telling her that she had two checks come in overnight. The first was a small, routine utilities payment, and the other was a check to Tammie for $3,570 on a day when Cheryl wasn't even in the office. Knowing she didn't write the check and that there would be no good reason for Tammie to have written it, she asked the bank to pull her signature card. Thirty seconds later, it was confirmed: it was not Cheryl's signature. The bank told her they would pull every check on her account since she opened it and get back to her soon.

When Cheryl arrived at the office, Tammie was sitting in the foyer. Cheryl didn't confront her about the hidden folder with the IRS payments, but she did let her know that she saw that the two payments weren't made to the IRS and that Tammie couldn't come back to work until they got it all straightened out.

Tammie sputtered in desperate fright about how she had made a mistake and that she should have paid the taxes on time.

"Well," Cheryl thought, "why the heck didn't you?"

But she didn't say that. Instead, she said very matter-of-factly, "I'm going to have to investigate this further."

Tammie was close to tears. "I love my job," she said. "I love working here. I really want to keep my job."

"I understand that, and I hope you can come back, but for right now, I have to go and see what's happening with these taxes. I can't let you return to work until I know what's going on."

Cheryl kicked into gear. The branch manager at the local bank came in with six months' worth of check records. The two of them went through one by one, easily spotting when a signature was forged. They found more than $27,000 worth of forged checks.

"Cheryl, you've been embezzled," the bank manager said. "This is check fraud."

When Cheryl first started her business, the electronic revolution had not yet begun, so every check deposited was personally verified by matching the signature on the check to the signature on the signature card. She recalls a time when she had her husband sign a check for her for $80, and the bank called her and asked her about the mismatched signature. Cheryl wasn't aware that years later—with everything being done electronically—this was no longer the procedure, making it imperative that she check every bank statement to verify every signature. She points out that if she had done that, she would have caught the first instance of fraud, and the whole thing would have been avoided. The lack of oversight with each check was so bad that one was processed without a signature.

It took Cheryl a couple of sleepless weeks to finally admit that Tammie had stolen from her company.

For the insurance to pay and for the authorities to be willing to work with her, Cheryl had to sign a complaint, which opened a criminal investigation. Local detectives and the FBI got involved.

"It was sickening," Cheryl said. The more information came out, the sicker she felt, especially when she learned that Tammie had begun embezzling money from her *three months* into her employment. The level of betrayal was staggering.

It took Cheryl, the banks, CPAs, and the authorities months to figure out the extent of Tammie's fraud. She didn't just forge checks for hundreds of thousands of dollars; she also added her family members to the company's health insurance, totaling more than $85,000 in premiums. But the scheme didn't even stop there. Foremen were given debit cards that would be funded daily to ensure no one abused them, and when one of them quit, Cheryl had asked Tammie to cancel the account. Instead, Tammie used the account for personal expenses then hid the account statements that came in the mail. The fraud started as $100 to $200 checks every few months. By the end of the nine years she worked there, Tammie was cashing $3,000 to $5,000 checks once or twice a month. All told, Cheryl figured the total amount of Tammie's embezzlement was about $1.5 million.

Beyond the betrayal, Cheryl was truly bewildered. Why did Tammie do it? Cheryl and Tammie both earned six figures, and the cost of living in their area was very low. Often in fraud cases, people are motivated by a loved one being sick, their house being threatened by foreclosure or other desperate circumstances. In other cases, embezzlers will want to buy assets that will set them up for the future or simply live incredibly lavish lifestyles. But Tammie just spent her money on dinner and the movies.

"The FBI tried very, very hard to find some kind of a tangible asset, that maybe she'd been investing in something or bought a lake house or a cool car or something," said Cheryl. "There was nothing! She was living paycheck to paycheck. There were no savings. It was just frivolous spending."

The local authorities recommended that Cheryl get in touch with the FBI, which agreed to take on the case due to the massive extent of the fraud.

A year and three months after the embezzlement was discovered, Tammie's case went to trial. It was the first time she and Cheryl had seen each other since that morning in the lobby.

Tammie pleaded guilty to embezzling $400,000 and served four years in prison. She was ordered to pay Obermiller Construction 10 percent of her monthly gross income or $100, whichever was higher, for the rest of her life upon release.[13] Cheryl received the payments with a heavy heart. "Every time I opened an envelope with a court-ordered check from Tammie, I was reminded of the hell she put my business through," she said.

Cheryl was also reminded of the fact that she was getting reimbursed a fraction of the $1.5 million that Tammie actually stole, as well as the $1 million that it cost to clean everything up. While a $100 per month check was better than nothing, it was not something Cheryl relied on. At the same time, it was money that Tammie could use for groceries, to help her get back on her feet. Cheryl eventually decided to waive her right to restitution.

When I finished Cheryl's interview, I asked her what advice she would offer entrepreneurs so that they could protect their businesses from fraud. "If I only gave the impression that I was paying closer attention to the finances and less on growing my business, I think I could have stopped Tammie," she said. "She knew my weaknesses and took complete advantage of that."

Today, Cheryl is setting her company up for the future. While she's not yet ready to retire, she knows that someday soon it will be out of her hands. She's been training her staff to be accountable to each other, do small things like signing out equipment, even for family members, and request backups to all financial documentation. Cheryl emphasizes that these measures have to do with transparency.

"I tell people that you have to remember the three Fs. They are: friendship, faith, and family," she said. "Because we think that our friends and the people that we share faith and go to church with and are our family, we're safe with them. But you have to remember that friendship, faith, and family are not accounting controls. They are relationships, and you must never confuse the two."[14]

Cyber Monday

I was doing my morning reading before class, and a story about a reformed cybercriminal caught my attention.[15] I always wanted to learn more about cybercrime, but I'd never interacted with a convicted cyber offender. Here was my chance.

I did a quick Google search and found his personal website. I reached out, explained my interest in his story, and waited. By evening, I had an email from gollum@anglerphish.com. I was immediately suspicious, but it was a legit address of Brett Johnson, the man from the article.

After a few email exchanges, we got on a call. He was super friendly and had the voice of a radio DJ. I invited him to come speak to my class at DePaul.

"I teach on Monday nights for the next eight weeks, so whatever works for you will work for me," I said.

"How about I hop in my car and come visit your class this coming Monday?" he said.

I was a little shocked—Birmingham, Alabama was a long drive—but I immediately took him up on his offer.

Brett was born and raised in Hazard, Kentucky, "one of these areas like the Florida Panhandle and parts of Louisiana, where if you're not fortunate enough to have a job, you may be involved in some sort of scam, hustle, fraud, whatever you want to call it," he said.

Maybe there was something in the water because his entire family engaged in fraud. Insurance fraud, document forgery, drug trafficking, mining illegal coal. You name it, Brett's family did it.

Young Brett was a natural liar. As he grew up, he participated in the family scams.

Eventually, he branched out on his own. His first scam: in 1994, he faked his own car accident. Second scam: eBay fraud.

He reached his peak in the mid-'90s, during the Beanie Baby heyday. The Royal Blue Peanut, essentially a cobalt stuffed elephant toy, sold for as much as $1,700. Only five hundred of the dolls were manufactured, making it one of the most valuable Beanie Babies.

Brett was trying to earn some extra money. A Beanie Baby scam seemed easy and quick.

He advertised on eBay that he was selling Royal Blue Peanut for $1,500. Except he was actually selling a gray Beanie Baby that he dipped in blue dye to *look* like Royal Blue Peanut for $1,500.

He accepted a bid and instructed the winner to send a US postal money order. "It protects us both," he said via email. "As soon as I get that and it clears, I'll send you your elephant."

The bidder sent Brett the money order; Brett cashed it and sent her his version of the blue Beanie Baby. The phone rang almost immediately.

"This is not what I ordered!" yelled a voice on the other line.

Brett's response was swift. "Lady, you ordered a blue elephant. I sent you a blue-ish elephant."

Brett gave her the runaround for a few weeks until she finally disappeared.

This experience taught Brett two very important lessons about cybercrime:

- Delay the victim as long as possible.

- Victims rarely report the crime and eventually go away.

Brett continued to perfect his skills and graduated to selling pirated software. From pirated software, he moved to installing mod chips (a small electronic device used to disable artificial restrictions of computers or entertainment devices) into gaming systems so owners could play the pirated games. Then he began installing mod chips in the cable boxes that would turn on all the pay-per-view on clients' TV channels for free. Then it was programming satellite DSS cards (the satellite DSS card allows access to tv channels).

He was getting requests for his cable boxes from customers all over the United States and Canada. He was on a roll.

Finally, it occurred to him: Why even fulfill the cable box order? Just take the money and run. He knew that no customer would complain about losing money in an illegal transaction.

He stole even more money with this updated version of his cable box scam but soon worried that he'd get flagged for money laundering. He decided he needed a fake driver's license so he could open up a bank account and launder the money through cash taken out of the ATM.

He found a person online who sold fake licenses. He sent a picture, $200, and waited. He waited and waited. Then reality punched him in the face: He'd been scammed. The nerve!

No one hates being deceived more than someone who deceives for a living. Brett was so frustrated he started ShadowCrew.com, an online forum where people could learn the ins and outs of cybercrime. *Forbes* called it "a one-stop marketplace for identity theft."[16] The ShadowCrew operated from August 2002 through November 2004, attracting as many as four thousand criminals or aspiring criminals. It's considered the forerunner of today's cybercrime forums and marketplaces; Brett is known as the Godfather of Cybercrime.

"Before ShadowCrew, the only avenue you had to commit online crime was a rolling chat board," he told my students. "It's called an IRC chat session and stands for Internet Relay Chat." The problem with these rolling chat screens was that you had no idea if you were talking to a cop or a crook. Either was possible.

ShadowCrew gave criminals a trust mechanism. It was a large communication channel where people in different time zones could reference conversations. "By looking at someone's screen name, you could tell if you could trust that person, if you could network with that person, or if you could learn from that person," he said. The screen name on the dark web became the criminal's brand name. They keep this brand name throughout their entire criminal tenure and it helps establish trust with others, so the screen name matters.

When Brett was in class, he showed my students how information ended up on the dark web. "You can find social security numbers, home addresses, driver's license numbers, credit card numbers on the dark web for $3," he explained. All the information is there, practically begging to be taken.

In 2004, authorities arrested twenty-eight men in six countries, claiming they had swapped 1.7 million stolen card numbers and caused $4.3 million in losses. But Brett escaped. He was placed on the Secret Service's Most Wanted list. After four months on the run, he was arrested.[17]

Brett has been in and out of prison five times and spent 7.5 years in federal prison. Today he considers himself a reformed white-collar offender.

. . .

Brett has visited my class multiple times. He and I have also partnered to give lectures to banks on the origins of cybercrime. In September 2021, he joined me to discuss how organizations can protect themselves from cybercriminals during the pandemic.

Covid birthed an entirely new criminal who mainly targeted large organizations like businesses and governmental agencies. "Victims are really based on need," Brett explained. "My needs determined the scope of the crime. If I need a lot of money, I'm targeting an organization. I don't need to victimize someone for a few hundred dollars."

According to cybersecurity firm Purple Security (Purplesec. com), cybercrime increased 600 percent during the pandemic.[18] Cybercriminals exposed more than 40 billion records in 2021 alone, up from 22 billion in 2020.[19] Scammers stole the identities and social security numbers of dead, incarcerated, or out-of-state people and filed unemployment insurance benefit claims. An international Harris poll concluded that during the pandemic, nearly 330 million people across ten countries were victims of cybercrime and more than 55 million people were victims of identity theft worldwide.[20] Cybercrime victims collectively spent nearly 2.7 billion hours trying to resolve their issues.[21]

Cybercrime poses the biggest threat across organizations of all sizes, followed by customer fraud and asset misappropriation. The Convention on Cybercrime, also known as the Budapest Convention on Cybercrime or the Budapest Convention, was the first international treaty seeking to address internet and computer crime (i.e., cybercrime) by harmonizing national laws, improving investigative techniques, and increasing cooperation among nations.[22]

In the United States, the Payroll Protection Program (PPP) was created on March 4, 2020, under the Coronavirus Aid, Relief, and Economic Security (CARES) Act. The program has lent out $755 million to "struggling" American businesses.[23]

The program helped many people. But it was also a fraudster's playground. In an effort to quickly get money into the hands of entrepreneurs and businesses, the Small Business Administration (SBA) relaxed its internal controls. Normally, the SBA requires loan applicants to fill out a form allowing the agency to verify their tax information with the IRS. But the CARES Act removed this control. The SBA also approved loans in batches with little-to-no vetting and abandoned the rule requiring two SBA employees to approve each loan application.[24]

Along with the US government, banks were prime targets. Financial crime and corruption are major issues, not only for the law enforcement community but also for financial institutions, the private sector and other international stakeholders.

The perpetrators weren't underground criminals but doctors, nurses, entrepreneurs, and business owners. Many business owners inflated their payroll expenses to obtain larger loans than they would have otherwise qualified for. Fifty-seven-year-old Dana McIntyre, the former owner of Rasta Pasta Pizzeria in Beverly, Massachusetts, was one of the many business owners who abused the program.[25] The pizzeria was located in a sleepy suburban strip mall and had just ten employees. But he claimed that he had forty-seven employees and a monthly payroll of $265,000. He received more than $661,000 in PPP money.

The stolen funds were put to good use, depending on who you ask. Instead of using the funds in his business, McIntyre purchased an alpaca farm in Vermont. He also used the funds for weekly airtime for a cryptocurrency-themed radio show called *Cryptomania* on 104.9 FM.

Dinesh Shah, fifty-five, of Coppell, Texas, applied for fifteen different loans from eight different lenders using eleven different companies. He sought a total of $24.8 million. According to the indictment, Shah claimed that these businesses had numerous employees and hundreds of thousands of dollars in payroll expenses.[26]

It was all a lie.

Shah admitted that he had fabricated federal tax filings and bank statements, and also stolen other people's identities. He pleaded guilty to one count of wire fraud and one count of money laundering and was sentenced to eleven years in prison.[27]

Another type of Covid loan fraud centered around Economic Injury Disaster Loans (EIDLs). The loans were granted to small businesses, agricultural, and nonprofits that had lost revenue. EIDL money was supposed to be used to cover normal operating expenses like health-care benefits, rent, and utilities. If an applicant also obtained a PPP loan, the EIDL funds weren't supposed to be used for the same purpose. But criminals applied for EIDL advances and loans on behalf of shell companies that did not really exist.

Austin Hsu, the former owner of Back 2 Health Bellevue, a chiropractic franchise in Issaquah, Washington, joined the Covid fraud party. Hsu submitted nine fraudulent disaster loan applications. He used the names of Back 2 Health's current and former employees to apply for additional PPP loans under the names of four other companies he owned and controlled. He claimed that one of the companies, Blueline, had been in business since 2017, had nine employees, and took in gross receipts of over $1.5 million. He also submitted fake federal tax filings. According to the indictment, six of the nine fraudulent applications were approved, and he received more than $700,000 in Covid-19 relief funds. On August 10, 2021, Hsu was sentenced to two years in prison. Additionally, he was ordered to pay a $25,000 fine and $709,104.97 in restitution.[28]

When the pandemic hit, 36.5 million Americans applied for unemployment insurance (UI) in less than two months.[29] The unemployment rate soared to almost 15 percent, the highest since the Great Depression.[30] The sudden surge overwhelmed state employment departments. Many waived certification and work search requirements, making the $860 billion in federal funds appropri- ated for UI benefits ripe for the taking.

Domestic offenders, as well as international crime organizations, were committing UI fraud. As a result, the SBA established the National Unemployment Insurance Task Force, a prosecutor-led multi-agency task force with representatives from more than eight different federal law enforcement agencies.[31]

"Covid changed the way cybercriminals think," Brett told me. "Now, criminals are looking at areas within organizations they never thought to attack," like disability benefits, food stamps, even Zelle. This is dangerous because many of these areas never had ap- propriate controls in place before. They never needed to.

And though these types of claims start small, they can quickly escalate. "Criminals can use bots to register thousands of accounts at a time, allowing these dollar amounts to add up quickly," he said. "All organizations should beware."

CHAPTER TAKEAWAYS

- Every organization can be a target.

- Pay attention to the tones at the top, middle, and bottom (from the custodian to the CEO). All employees at all levels have access to sensitive information, making any employee an ideal path for your organization to get victimized.

- Never take your eye off your business operations. Perception can be a powerful and cost-efficient internal control that can protect your organization. Forty percent of an organization's fraud-related losses are tied to insider threats.

- Smaller businesses are especially vulnerable to fraud because they typically devote very little time or resources to internal controls.

Organizational target quick facts

Description	Characteristics
• Entities chosen by a perp to defraud • Entities that have vulnerabilities that can be exploited	• Entities with routine, predictable roles • Entities that instill trust in key employees with lax oversight • Internal control weaknesses can be present

---

WHISTLEBLOWERS

After my TEDx talk about whistleblowers ran on the TED website in October 2018, something odd happened.[1] At least it was odd to me, since I had never given a talk that reached such a wide audience.

Within less than an hour, my inbox was flooded with emails. Many thanked me for recognizing them and not berating them, as so many people had done. Others wanted to tell me about the fallout they'd experienced after "whistling." And then there were those people who told me that my talk had inspired them to come forward.

"Your talk was the last straw on the camel's back," Tricia Newbold wrote.

That name wasn't familiar to me at the time, though now it is. Tricia told the world about how senior officials in the Trump White House had granted security clearances to at least twenty-five people whose applications had been rejected because they could put national security at risk.[2]

I responded to every person who wrote. I thought it was important to acknowledge them, even if I didn't talk to them all. I did speak with Tricia.

She and I have been in communication ever since that initial email, and I've watched from the sidelines. Tricia went back to work, and she experienced isolation, bullying, and invalidation. All because she stood up for what was right. Or, I should say, she stood up for what *she* believed was right. But many people disagreed with her.

I've always had a soft spot for whistleblowers because they're good people who are treated really, really badly. I always save my whistleblower lecture for the end of the quarter because it's such a controversial area. My students get into heated debates about the topic, and I understand it. One person's hero is another person's rat, snitch, or tattletale. Whatever you call them, many think they're troublemakers. Meddlers. Busybodies who simply refuse to mind their own business.

Whistleblowers insert themselves into a situation, even if it has nothing to do with them. They get involved, usually because they couldn't live with themselves if they stayed silent. As often as not, they've experienced some kind of moral injury. The concept of *moral injury*, a cousin of PTSD, was introduced in 1994 by doctor and clinical psychologist Jonathan Shay. Shay was studying Vietnam veterans and noticed that many of them had experienced a "moral injury" when they witnessed or failed to prevent behavior that went against their moral, religious, or spiritual beliefs or values.[3] Whistleblowers usually feel this way.

It's worth noting that accusing someone of unethical behavior can actually make the accuser appear more trustworthy to other people—as long as the accusation seems to be motivated by morality and isn't frivolous and calculated. But often, the accuser is *not* perceived as more trustworthy because most people don't agree with bringing light to the unethical situation in the first place.

We like to think that all whistleblowers are the same, but of course, there's a continuum. Our reactions to them, however, are fairly similar: we hate them.

It takes such courage to stand up to a system. But when a person speaks out against an injustice, we usually mistrust them. We begin to think of every way possible to discredit them. Never mind that they're actually going out of their way to protect us all from harm— and we *need* them.

As no smaller a mind than Albert Einstein's put it, "The world will not be destroyed by those who do evil, but by those who watch them without doing anything."

Still, when an employee decides to come forward when they see something amiss, they're taking a huge risk. Instead of being praised and rewarded, they're often ostracized and ridiculed. I've spent over ten years interviewing whistleblowers. Though they all believe that they did the right thing and would do it again if they had to, they also said their lives were made miserable by the organizations they exposed. A *Harvard Business Review* study by behavioral scientist Nuala Walsh found that 82 percent of whistleblowers were harassed after making allegations against a company, and 60 percent lost their jobs.[4] Whistleblowers have also been blacklisted from future employment, face social ostracism from coworkers, and undergo severe psychological stress.[5]

One of the first whistlers in the United States was Benjamin Franklin, who blew the whistle in 1773 when he shared confidential letters showing that the governor of Massachusetts had deliberately misled Parliament to promote a military buildup in the Colonies.[6]

The Civil War was also rife with fraud, most notably with defense contractors who sold the Union Army rifles and ammunition that didn't work, mules that didn't move, and food that gave soldiers scurvy and dysentery.[7]

In response, on March 2, 1863, Congress passed the False Claims Act (FCA), which allowed "relators." Relators are people who sue a contractor on behalf of the United States if they had personal knowledge of the scam. If their lawsuits were successful, the relators (or whistleblowers) were allowed to receive half the money the government recouped.[8]

More than a century later, in 1986, Congress increased the financial incentives for whistleblowers to file lawsuits alleging false claims on the government's behalf, also known as a *qui tam* action. *Qui tam* allows private citizens to file suit on behalf of the government against anyone believed to be committing fraud against the government.[9] Most of these cases involve health care. Qui tam cases are controversial because the person filing suit—the whistleblower—is allowed to share some of the money that the government recoups. The reward provision was specifically created to motivate people, especially those whose hands may have a little dirt sprinkled on them, to come forward.

In July 2010, Congress passed the Dodd-Frank Wall Street Reform and Consumer Protection Act, which is designed to regulate financial markets and protect consumers by preventing a repeat of the 2008 financial crisis. With a nod to the FCA, Congress also created the Securities and Exchange Commission's Office of the Whistleblower.[10]

In fiscal year 2018, the US Department of Justice recovered $2.1 billion of the $2.8 billion total in settlements and judgments arising from lawsuits filed under the FCA's *qui tam* provisions.[11]

Whistleblower protection has been recognized as part of international law since 2003, when the United Nations adopted the Convention Against Corruption.[12] The Convention serves as the only universally legally binding anti-corruption instrument. It covers many different forms of corruption, such as bribery, abuse of function, and various acts included in the private sector. The Convention was subsequently signed by 140 nations and formally ratified, accepted, approved, or acceded by 137 nations, including the United States.[13]

Despite popular belief, whistleblowers aren't all disgruntled employees who have a problem with the company. Whistleblowers are hopeful, and their hopefulness drives them to come forward. They're also committed and passionate. And it's their commitment and passion for their organization that makes them want to come forward in the first place. They're also super ethical. They're not seeking fame; they're seeking justice.

The "Whistleblowing Triangle," which is modeled after the Fraud Triangle, outlines the decisions that confront most whistleblowers. Similar to perps, whistleblowers weigh the opportunity, pressure, and incentives to blow the whistle.[14]

As with perps and prey, whistleblowers come in different shapes and forms. The whistleblower categories—*accidental*, *noble*, and *vigilante*—emerged as I began to interact with more whistleblowers. I thought it was important not to lump all whistleblowers into one category because their motives are vastly different.

Vigilantes, for example, are the group that inspires the most ire. When we think of "snitches," "rats," and "tattletales," we're referring to vigilantes. They *could* have walked away and ignored whatever injustice they witnessed, but they chose to fight. They arguably experience the most moral injury of any group, which is why they can't just sit back and watch.

Accidental whistleblowers and noble whistleblowers, on the other hand, are far more confused when whistleblower shame comes their way because they are typically "just doing their job" when something comes up. They often don't know where to turn or who to talk to because they are ostracized from everything that is familiar to them.

My hope is that understanding these various categories will allow you to empathize more with those silent heroes in your organization and help create a supportive environment that allows and inspires them to come forward.

Chapter 6

Accidental Whistleblowers

Accidental whistleblowers don't set out to expose fraud. They're not looking to find what they found. They're terrified of what they discovered and don't know whom to turn to and whom to trust. At first, they may want to ignore their finding in the hopes it will just disappear. They don't want to get involved, but their inner voice tells them they must. They're good soldiers, even if they're not prepared for war.

Kathe Swanson (the Dixon fraud whistleblower) was simply doing her job and stumbled upon something that didn't look right. She reported it to her superior, as any good employee would. She certainly never expected to discover that her boss had stolen over $50 million from their small town.

After discovering the bank statement, Kathe slipped it into the sunglass container in her SUV. "I didn't know who to turn to," she recalled. "I didn't know if it was something I should go to our police department with. Honestly, I thought, 'Who can I trust?'"[1]

Several days later, she told Dixon mayor Jim Burke about the suspicious account that Rita controlled. She handed him a copy of the bank statement.

Burke was a beloved fixture in Dixon. He had a reputation for being honest and fair; he was elected to four terms—sixteen years— as mayor. He had done a lot of good things for Dixon (population 15,165), the boyhood hometown of President Ronald Reagan, who had been a lifeguard at the local park. Abraham Lincoln joined the militia in Dixon during the Black Hawk War. Charles Rudolph Walgreen, the founder of the eponymous drugstore chain, got his pharmacy started here. People came from around the globe to visit the historic town. They were charmed by the folksy vibe and friendly faces.

But over the last few years, the town had been suffering. Money seemed to disappear. Budgets were slashed. City employees had been laid off, and necessary town equipment hadn't been pur- chased. No one could understand why.

Burke looked over the bank statement pages and the acid in his gut started to churn. "Before we call the authorities, we need to make sure that what we think is true is true," he told Kathe.[2]

Kathe and Burke conducted their own research at night, on weekends, and in the early mornings. Eventually, Burke brought the information to the FBI in Rockford, Illinois, and agents began investigating.

For six months, Kathe had to pretend everything was fine. She couldn't let Rita know that anything was amiss. "I'd ask questions like, 'How are your dogs? How was your competition?'" she said.[3] Meaningless conversation.

The deception took a toll on Kathe. She and Rita Crundwell were very different people: Kathe Swanson was traditional and quiet, whereas Crundwell was brassy, jet-setting around the world and hobnobbing with horse folk. Still, they were friendly enough. Crundwell, who gave everyone nicknames, dubbed her "Swan." Kathe never thought her beloved boss—who returned from trips laden with gifts for the entire office—would do anything under-handed.[4] There was no reason *not* to trust her. No one ever suspected that Dixon's favorite daughter was robbing them blind.

Rita had been working at city hall since 1970 when she was a sixteen-year-old high school kid. She was an honor roll student, a homecoming attendant, and a regular participant in the town's 4-H club.

The investigation took six months, during which time Kathe developed stomach ulcers and a heart murmur. Her hair started to fall out. She told no one what was really going on—not her boyfriend or her adult children. Everyone wondered if she was ill. "I said it was a work thing, but that I was OK," she said.

April 17, 2012 was sunny and brisk. Mayor Burke's mood was grim. Instead of cracking his usual jokes, he peered wordlessly into his coffee cup. His two visitors, men in dark suits and red ties, sat silently, their backs as straight as number 2 pencils, waiting for him to make his move. Finally, the mayor picked up the phone.[5]

"Can you come in here?" he said.

Two minutes later, Rita knocked on the door.

"Rita, these two gentlemen want to talk to you," he said as he walked out. Rita sat down.

On Feb. 14, 2013, Rita Crundwell was sentenced to nineteen years and seven months in prison. In March 2020, she requested compassionate release from prison because of the Covid crisis—nearly ten years before her sentence was up. She ultimately withdrew the request; I suspect it had to do with public outcry.

But in August 2021, she was released to home confinement.

The town was furious, and I was confused. Tons of people sitting in jails and prisons all over the country hadn't been released during the pandemic. So why was Rita Crundwell let go?

It sent a very mixed message to those of us who train people around fraud prevention and detection. She still has restitution to pay back, but she's no longer incarcerated. She went from a halfway house to her brother's house.

It's shocking that someone can commit such an egregious crime and not have to serve the full sentence. It sends a really odd message: crime DOES pay. Rita lived like a queen for twenty years and only served eight and a half behind bars. The residents of Dixon became victims for a second time: once by Rita and once by the justice system.

It took me over three years to track Kathe down and convince her to do the interview for my documentary.

Interestingly, unlike other kinds of whistleblowers, which we'll hear about later, Kathe wasn't ostracized for speaking out. This makes sense when you think about it. Often, when accidental whistleblowers notice something off and speak up about it, they're *celebrated*. They weren't trying to be troublemakers, and people respect that. (As my Dad would say, they were "keeping their head down and their nose clean.")

At my Dixon movie premiere, Kathe received an Ethical Courage award from the National Association of State Boards of Accountancy (NASBA) Center for the Public Trust in front of thousands of residents.[6] She had no idea it was coming. In fact, she was sitting smack in the middle of the balcony and had to make her way down to the stage. She received a standing ovation. Kathe was in tears.

More Money, More Problems

Accidental whistleblowers are the secret internal weapons that sniff out fraud. In Nathan Mueller's case, an accidental whistleblower actually saved him from himself. In fact, Nathan credits an accidental whistleblower's courage and tenacity with helping him turn his life around. I've been studying and co-presenting at conferences with Nathan for years, and I'm always fascinated when he shares the accidental whistleblower's role in his fraud case.

I thought my students would be, too, and so I arranged for them (and me) to meet him in person.

"Who's available tomorrow at 6 a.m. to meet me at Midway Airport to go to Minneapolis for a fraud field trip?" I asked. Everyone raised their hand. There was genuine excitement in their eyes.

My fifteen students and I boarded a Southwest flight ($60 round trip!) to Minneapolis–Saint Paul. We landed, rented a white panel van and drove to Nathan's sister's house in the suburbs. He was living above the garage, just like Fonzie from the '80s sitcom *Happy Days*. The sixteen of us quickly filled up his studio apartment.

Dressed in a checked button-down shirt and khakis, Nathan looked unassuming. As we began to take off our coats and place book bags in the corner of the futon sofa, he offered us food and drink.

"Such a pleasure to put a face to an email," I said, trying to make him feel at ease. "This will be the most important fraud class experience my students will probably ever have."

Nathan chuckled uncomfortably. "Well," he said. "I hope I can say something that will help you all not make the same mistakes I made when I was your age."

A former CPA at ING Insurance in Minneapolis, Nathan mas-terminded an $8.5 million fraud scheme that lasted four years.[7] Nathan was nothing if not self-aware. "There was a period in my life, a very long period, where literally every situation I was faced with I did the wrong thing," he said. "Not the wrong thing, probably the *worst* thing. Like, if I was given a number of choices, I would choose the worst one."[8]

Let's rewind to 2003, when Nathan was an accountant in ING Reinsurance's Minneapolis office. ING Reinsurance was a subsidiary of Amsterdam-based global financial services company ING Group and it folded in February 2012.[9] Nathan was used to working with high dollar amounts. It wasn't uncommon for him to issue a transaction of $50 million in a single workday. With high-dollar transactions come high-dollar write-offs, the perfect opportunity for him to write his first fraudulent check. His wife was pregnant, and he was "obsessed about being the breadwinner in my family because that's what a successful person does," he recalled.[10]

He knew that it was customary for a payment in the hundreds of thousands to be sent, yet no one in his department could identify where it came from. He used the overt oversight to his advantage, knowing full well that with no one looking closely, he could write off an incorrect amount.

It was just so . . . easy. And his debt made him feel like 50-pound weights were attached to each ankle. "I thought, 'If I just didn't have those school loans anymore' and 'If I paid off those credit cards, then everything would just be, you know, fine.' And I was making good money. Supporting a family wouldn't have been that big of a deal. So, that was the 'I'm going to do it. I'm just going to pay off this debt, and that's going to be it.'"[11]

With intense internal pressure and endless opportunities to embezzle right at his fingertips, he took the plunge, writing his first fraudulent check for $1,100. He logged into the system using one of his coworkers' passwords, requesting that a check for $1,100 be sent to one of his credit card companies. He chose this particular credit card because it had a name similar to a legitimate company that they worked with (a common scheme among embezzlers). Nathan confirmed that the check was mailed to the credit card company, and his bill was paid.[12] Easy like Sunday morning. Although he felt worried and a bit guilty, it was irresistible. Of course, he rationalized it. What he was doing was for the good of his family. Two weeks later, Nathan applied $1,800 to his credit card balance. By the end of the summer, he had pretty effortlessly stolen $88,000.[13] He was finally free of credit card and school loan debt.

Nathan was fraud-free for six months, and during that time no one suspected anything untoward. Why not continue? And this time, why not do something *fun* with the money?

"All I did was pay off debt with it," he said. "And I thought, 'There's probably a way where I could do this and probably have some fun.'"[14]

He quickly made good on his wishes. The new scheme involved creating his own company and writing checks to himself through a shell corporation (a company that exists only on paper). Nathan gave his "consulting" firm a name similar to one of the legitimate ING insurance brokers. Once again, he took advantage of an organizational loophole. He logged into the company's system using his coworkers' passwords and requested checks.

This is not uncommon. Everyone shares passwords, professionally and personally. (And yes, this includes Netflix and Amazon.)

This time, blinded by confidence, Nathan upped the dollar amounts, approving the checks and making sure he was the one assigned to pick them up. Instead of refunding unidentifiable payments, he directed them into his fake company.

Check fraud isn't new or even rare. In 2018, check fraud accounted for 47 percent of industry losses—$1.3 billion—according to the American Bankers Association's 2019 Deposit Account Fraud Survey.[15] That's a 12 percent jump from 2016. Check fraud can include altered checks, counterfeit checks, or forged checks. Nathan's preferred method was counterfeit checks: false checks drawn on real accounts and checks obtained from opening a false account based on fraudulent identification.

His scams didn't stop there. Nathan was also responsible for reconciling a Canadian bank account, and he was the only person in his department who truly understood how it worked. Part of his duty was to convert Canadian investment amounts to US dollar amounts. When companies with foreign subsidiaries need to reconcile their financial statements into their local or functional currency, they engage in a process called foreign currency translation, which is a legitimate business process.[16] Only problem was, Nathan's currency translations were fraudulent.

To steal more money, Nathan purposely "weakened" the Canadian dollar in order to understate the US dollar value of the income. He took those offsetting debits, directed them into his fake company's account, and embezzled the money. "Losses" can happen when foreign currency translations are involved because you're restating the financial statements in the currency in which a company presents its financial statements. The process results in accounting foreign exchange gains and losses. The gains that were created ended up being future monies Nathan would embezzle.

Foreign currency translations are hard to detect because currencies constantly fluctuate. Nathan's supervisor would expect differences and the amounts to never balance, so he would detect nothing abnormal. Nathan would then route the stolen money through shell companies he set up.

During this time, Nathan spiraled deeper into his new world. He regretted never having any fun during college and decided to make up for some lost time.

The Las Vegas Strip became his second home, and his purpose was twofold: not only would he get to have the party lifestyle that he missed in college, but he'd also be able to tell his family and friends that this flood of cash was from gambling winnings. The plan was relatively simple. He would wire stolen money before he left. When the weekend was over, he'd bring back the wired cash and report it as a windfall.

Between May 2003 and August 2007, Nathan cut ninety-nine checks totaling $8,455,767.55. About $6 million of that went toward gambling, $1 million toward a new home in an affluent neighborhood, and the rest toward cars, jewelry, and clothes. He spent his cash on parties and picking up bar tabs.[17]

He admits that he did all this because he had low self-esteem. He also felt underappreciated. He had found out the salaries of other colleagues, who were out-earning him, and he got angry. He felt like he was a better worker and should be making more money than some of his colleagues. He started to feel resentful . . . so he took what he believed was owed to him. He coined his own term: "social laundering."[18]

Nathan probably would still be socially laundering if an accidental whistleblower hadn't piped up.

One afternoon, Nathan's ex-wife went to lunch with one of his close colleagues. His ex-wife talked about how erratic his behavior had been during their marriage, and how he had been traveling back and forth to Las Vegas and spending large sums of his money. The colleague's ears perked up. Where had Nathan gotten so much money, his ex-wife wondered? Something seemed off. Her gut, that second brain in her stomach, started whirring.

Nathan's accidental whistleblower colleague went back to the office and logged into her system. She knew that everyone shared passwords. It was an agreed-upon workaround so that if someone were out sick or on vacation, another person could still log in to the system and get the necessary information and reports submitted timely. When she logged in, she noticed that her password had been used to approve checks that she had never authorized. She investigated further . . . and all roads led to Nathan. She didn't want to be implicated, so she immediately alerted their internal fraud department.

I looked over at my students while Nathan was speaking. They were hanging on to his every word and furiously taking notes. After the interview, they asked him questions, specifically about ethics and ethical behavior, and how he had felt when he was their age. Nathan spoke candidly.

"I didn't think any of those ethics lectures applied to me," he recalled.

Later that night, my students and I went to dinner at a Benihana's in the Mall of America in Minneapolis. Over our hibachi dinner, they talked about how angry they were at the woman who turned him in.

"I would never have snitched on a friend!" Miguel said.

"Me neither," said Tanya.

"I would have just pretended like I didn't know. It's none of my business," Evan added.

"Who are you willing to go to jail for?" I said, "Make your list now because had this accidental whistleblower stayed quiet, she probably would have been sent to prison alongside Nathan. Her colleague had stolen her password and made it look like she had committed a crime. If she had stayed quiet, she would have had to save her own name."

Mic drop.

They got the message. We had a wonderful dinner and boarded our 9 p.m. flight back to Chicago. All in a day's work.

$$\bullet \quad \bullet \quad \bullet$$

Nathan and I have presented at conferences together over the years and I've always been intrigued by two things: how the audience reacts when they find out his colleague (our accidental whistleblower) turned him in. And that Nathan has always protected her identity.

"Her whistleblowing on me helped me turn my life around," he said. "I'm grateful to her."

As we know, employees play a critical role in fraud discovery. But I wanted to know what happens when one colleague confronts another about a potential fraud. So two colleagues and I conducted a study. We found that when people directly confront an alleged perpetrator, and the perpetrator does not stop the fraud, the whistleblower feels more comfortable reporting internally than reporting externally like to an auditor, the SEC, law enforcement, or the media.

These findings further support how accidental whistleblowers typically behave. They're not seeking fame and fortune; they just want the issue resolved. They never want to be implicated in the crime, so they tend to follow all of the appropriate procedures to ensure that their name is clear.

Five years ago, I developed an e-case based on Nathan's story, and I use it in corporate workshops and with my students.[19] Both students and professionals are shocked when they learn that Nathan was caught because a colleague blew the whistle on him. Some audiences see it as a betrayal of friendship. Others see it as a "snitch" (a word I loathe, remember). According to the Global Banking Fraud Survey conducted by KPMG International, 68 percent of frauds are discovered by a whistleblower.[20] And I would argue that many of these whistleblowers are accidental.

The fairness-loyalty trade-off is known as the *whistleblower's dilemma*.[21] The term refers to the conflict one faces when confronted with two options: either speaking up when something is ethically unsound or remaining loyal to the group.

You're Fired!

How do I teach my students to come forward and do the right thing if they might face serious retaliation? I grapple with this question each time I work on my annual whistleblowing lecture. Just like they tell you at the airport, in subways, and in New York's Times Square, if you see something, you should say something. Right?

I was working on this lecture during the 2016 Wells Fargo debacle, and I was unsure how to tell my students to say something when saying something could get them fired. People new in an organization are often the first ones to notice something out of place, and there was a very good chance that my students would be that person. If they were watching or reading the news, I feared they would never take my whistleblowing advice, which is to speak up if you notice something.

When I struggle with an issue, I tend to write about it, so I decided to post a column on my *Forbes.com* blog about how educators can encourage more millennials to become whistleblowers.[22]

Within twelve hours, a millennial reached out with her own story. Her name was Lynn, and she was a former Wells Fargo employee in Virginia who lost her job after speaking out against her higher-ups.

Wells Fargo, you might recall, was involved in a major scandal in 2016 when it opened millions of sham accounts that customers didn't ask for. Some customers were wrongly charged with overdraft and other fees that hurt their credit scores.[23]

"We were told to say, 'Oh, it must have been sent by accident—I'll go ahead and fix that for you,'" Lynn told me. But the company was banking on customers *not* discovering the extra accounts. In fact, Wells Fargo encouraged this behavior.

"You got high fives for opening up ten credit cards a week, whether people wanted them or not," she said.

Employees had a quota to meet. To meet this quota and prevent detection by the customers, employees used a process called "pinning," which sets the customers' PIN number to 0000 so that the banker can control the account without the customer knowing.

Employees were accused of creating fraudulent checking and savings accounts by moving money out of existing accounts into new ones.

Lynn was caught up in the middle of it.

Lynn had been working at Wells Fargo in southern New Jersey for nearly a decade before transferring to help manage a Virginia Beach branch in September 2013. It was a disaster pretty much from the start.

The first day she walked into her branch, she was told that two bankers and three tellers had quit and that the actual branch manager was out on family leave. So Lynn would be running the show on her own, essentially with a bunch of strangers, until further notice. Welcome, Lynn!

She ended up as a teller, working directly with customers, which wasn't what she had been hired to do. But she liked it well enough, even if it wasn't her primary job.

Several customers began coming to her and telling her that they'd been receiving credit cards in the mail that they hadn't requested. Lynn decided to run a duplicate social security number report to find accounts linked to the same social security number. Her findings were appalling.

"When I ran the report, which should have had nothing in it, it was actually a very, very large file," she said. So large, in fact, that it froze her computer. She'd never seen anything like it.

She found the last four digits of social security numbers and the addresses they were linked to. She did a duplicate address search, searched the bank branch address, and found fifteen hundred accounts with the branch address.

She found credit and debit cards as well as checking accounts, none of which should have been linked to the branch address. She began scribbling down the account numbers.

Lynn contacted Wells Fargo's ethics department on September 23 to let them know that she had found and recorded 150 fake accounts. Although none of the accounts had money in them or had ever been used, they were under social security numbers that did exist, tied to fake names like Jane Doe.

"They asked me to send an email to them with a file of all the accounts and there would be an investigation," she said.

She heard nothing for about a week, when the district manager came into her branch and asked to speak with her. "She proceeded to tell me that she did not transfer me from three hundred miles away to cause issues in her district," Lynn recalled. "Her district was now under investigation because I was 'nosy,' and I should really learn to mind my business."

Lynn walked out of the room, sat at her desk, and put her head in her hands. She had a sinking feeling that things were not going to turn out well for her. She was right.

On November 9, 2013, two months after she started working in this branch, the district manager showed up at the bank and darted into an empty office in the back. She beckoned Lynn over, shut the door, and handed her the phone. On the other line was an investigator from Wells Fargo, who began babbling about federal laws and illegal activities.

Lynn had no clue what she was talking about, but the upshot was straightforward: she was being accused of forging someone's signature on a bank document.

Lynn protested vehemently; it wasn't even her handwriting.

Lynn didn't get what was happening. She'd been working for the bank for eight and a half years and had been promoted seven times. She had never had any problems other than in the last two months, *after* she noticed some illegal activities. Was that really just a coincidence? She didn't think so. She felt like she was being set up.

She was done. She handed over her keys and quit.

• • •

Lynn understands how easy it was for the fraud to take place: it was sanctioned from the top down. "The shareholders were expecting so many sales and everything was considered a sale," she said. "A checking account. A savings account. Student credit card. Home equity line. The more of them you've got, the bigger the bonus everybody else got. A banker would only get maybe a $5,000 bonus, but a district manager who had successful bankers can end up with like $20,000. And the regional manager would get a $50,000 bonus. So all the stress and pressure for people to do that came from the top because they wanted those bonuses."

According to Bloomberg, fifty-three hundred Wells Fargo employees were fired for signing up customers for fake accounts that started as early as 2011. About eighty-five thousand of those accounts incurred nearly $2 million in fees. What's more, employees submitted unauthorized applications for 565,443 credit card accounts. This raked in about $403,145 in fees from approximately fourteen thousand unauthorized credit cards.[24]

It gets better. Employees opened 1,534,280 unauthorized deposit accounts by transferring money from consumers' existing accounts. This is why it's important to read your bank statements and understand all of the fees. The bank customers were innocent bystanders (chapter 4) victimized by their bank organizational targets (chapter 5).

Lynn was part of a class-action lawsuit set up by former Wells Fargo employees, who said the company had retaliated against them after they reported unethical behavior. Many ex-employees said they were fired after reporting wrongdoing to the bank's ethics hotline. The bank eventually paid $250 million in penalties and has since apologized.

"They ruined my life," Bill Bado, a former Wells Fargo banker also in New Jersey, told *CNN Money* in 2016. Three years earlier, after refusing to open phony credit and bank accounts, he emailed human resources and called the company ethics hotline. A little over a week later, he was fired for "tardiness." Apparently, this was a frequent occurrence at Wells Fargo among people who spoke out.[25]

Heather Brock, a senior business banker from Round Rock, Texas, was let go when she contacted the ethics hotline. Wells Fargo accused her of fabricating documents, which she denied. (She claimed the company bullied her into admitting she did.)[26]

"I endured harsh bullying . . . defamation of character, and eventually being pinned for something I didn't do," said Brock, a twenty-six-year-old single mother of two young sons.

These are all common occurrences in the world of accidental whistleblowers. And it's a shame because they *should* be supported. Remember, accidental whistleblowers are trying to do the right thing but are operating in corrupt environments. We need them. What would life be without them? I'm not certain we want to find out.

CHAPTER TAKEAWAYS

- Accidental whistleblowers are the biggest category of whistleblowers and they're often the ones who discover fraud. We could all become one at any moment.

- Accidental whistleblowers are people who are doing their jobs, minding their business, when something lands in their laps.

- This category can be challenging because we must assume a percentage of accidental whistleblowers don't come forward and a significant amount of fraud goes unreported.

- Depending on the environment, accidental whistleblowers can be supported, but in many settings, they are still fearful of coming forward due to retaliation.

- Proper internal training, effective hotlines, and corporate whistleblowing awards are several examples of mechanisms that can be implemented to support accidental whistleblowers.

Accidental whistleblower quick facts

Description	Characteristics
• Largest whistleblower category	• Committed
• Often find fraud in the normal course of doing their job	• Strong moral compass
• Not seeking attention/fame but fairness	• "Good soldiers"
	• Compassionate
• Don't organically agree with being a whistleblower	• Ambivalent

Chapter 7

Noble Whistleblowers

Just as we all have varied reactions toward accidental whistleblowers, we can also have a wide range of feelings about *noble whistleblowers*. The main difference between the two groups is that accidentals are observers. While minding their own business, they see something, and then they say something. But they're usually not directly involved in the transgression. Kathe Swanson, for example, wasn't told to do something illegal. She stumbled upon Rita Crundwell's lies. That's why she is accidental. Nobles, on the other hand, are usually asked to participate in the scheme themselves. So they really are risking something—their job, say, or their standing in the company or community—to not take part and blow the whistle.

Head of the Class

I had a personal encounter with a noble whistleblower in one of my classes.

It was the final exam for the winter quarter of 2018, and everyone was tense. This was our last hurrah before we could take off for the holidays and everyone, including me, was ready to be done. Exam time is stressful for everyone, including the professor who has to grade all those papers. For most of my students, the grade they got in this class would mean the difference between a plum internship at a swanky firm, graduation, or a prerequisite for another class. So the grade mattered.

After handing out the exam (on paper, no less!) I left the room for a bathroom break. When I returned, everyone was diligently writing. Heads down, pens moving swiftly, no one seemed to notice that I'd been gone.

About fifteen minutes after class ended, I got a text from one of my students, Jenna, wanting to talk. She called me later that afternoon, clearly nervous. She made a lot of excuses about what she was about to say. "I'm not trying to be a tattletale, or not be a team player," she said. "But there's something you should know."

I thought she wanted to talk about the fact that she thought she failed the exam. Instead, she wanted to discuss the cheaters in the class.

Turns out half the class had used my break as an opportunity to share answers with each other. The student sitting beside her asked her directly: "What did you get for question 13? I wrote B."

This isn't allowed, and my students know it. Students everywhere know this! *Duh.*

Jenna ignored him.

Jenna did not partake in the sharing of the answers; however, she was asked to participate. Jenna was a rule follower and was fully aware of the university honor code. I thought I had established a classroom culture in which students didn't need to cheat. Apparently, I was misinformed.

This is what makes her a noble whistleblower. What some people might call a classic "snitch" (a word I loathe, as you know).

To be clear, she *could* have gone along with the crowd and shared her answers. She also could have kept quiet and said nothing. Instead, she declined and decided to follow the university honor code, which states, in effect, "Don't cheat." (Yes. I paraphrased.)

Jenna was gobsmacked. So was I. I was also grateful. She's the kind of person I need in my class and society needs in general—even, or especially, accounting firms. In 2022, accounting giant PwC Canada was fined more than $900,000 by Canadian and US accounting regulators after eleven hundred of its auditors were caught cheating on an exam.[1] In 2019, the US Public Company Accounting Oversight Board fined KPMG $50 million, in part because its auditors had shared answers.[2]

Noble whistleblowers aren't angry, nor are they trying to prove a point. They're rule followers, and they believe everyone else should be, too. They're deeply moral and see the world as black and white, right and wrong. They're observers of fraud. Eyewitnesses that receive an invitation to participate in the fraud but choose not to. They're not seeking fame; they're seeking fairness.

As did the late Roger Boisjoly. Boisjoly was a booster rocket engineer who raised serious objections to the launch of the Space Shuttle *Challenger*, which exploded in January 1986.[3] I was in the sixth grade in Mrs. Crabtree's social studies class; I remember her wheeling in the TV so we could watch the *Challenger* take off. All of the students gathered around as if we were at a campfire, and we waited breathlessly for liftoff. Seventy-three seconds after launch, the space shuttle blew up, killing all seven of its crew members.

We were speechless. Mrs. Crabtree immediately switched off the television. But the event stuck with me all these years. Why did it happen? Could it have been prevented? I thought about when I was writing a Ted Talk I gave on whistleblowers' impact on history, and I remembered Roger Boisjoly.

Months after TED highlighted my talk on its website, I received a LinkedIn message from Carl McNair, the brother of the late Dr. Ronald McNair, the only Black astronaut on the *Challenger* and the second Black man in space. Both McNairs went to my alma mater, North Carolina A & T State University, where I gave the fall commencement speech in 2019.[4] Carl McNair watched both my TED talk and graduation speech recording and called me. An hour into our call, he said, "If they had only listened to the whistleblower, my brother would still be here."

McNair was referring to Roger Boisjoly, who thought the explosion definitely could have been prevented. Based on earlier flight data, Boisjoly correctly predicted that the O-rings on the rocket boosters would fail if the shuttle launched in cold weather (an O-ring blocks the passage of liquids and gases and if not working properly would allow hot combustion gases to leak and burn through the external fuel tank).[5] His employer, NASA contractor Morton Thiokol, ignored Boisjoly's analysis (the O-rings were never tested for cold weather) and launched the rocket anyway.

Initially, after he spoke up, Boisjoly's life was a living hell. Morton Thiokol cut him off from space work, and he was shunned by colleagues, managers, and his neighbors. Morton Thiokol had lost the NASA contract when Boisjoly blew the whistle, which eradicated jobs in the community. People held Boisjoly responsible for the high level of unemployment.

The stress took its toll on him. He had headaches and double vision. He was depressed. He filed two lawsuits against his former employer, but both were dismissed. Yet he continued to share his experience, despite how he was treated.

Boisjoly eventually became a hero of sorts. He was awarded the Prize for Scientific Freedom and Responsibility by the American Association for the Advancement of Science and began a lucrative speaking career on corporate ethics.[6] He became a sought-after expert in forensic engineering.

Boisjoly died in 2012, but his legacy lives on. Business and engineering schools and ethicists have written cases about Roger Boisjoly and his courage, resilience, and willingness to face a hugely difficult choice. To me, he embodies the word *hero*.

Whistle While You Work

Roger Boisjoly's determination and concern for others, and willingness to go against the grain, remind me of Jackie McLaughlin, a noble whistleblower I met through a mutual friend. She and Boisjoly were both fighters in different industries, and both had a huge impact on the larger culture.

Jackie McLaughlin and I were kindred spirits. I understood her passion for people and her love and knowledge of accounting. She was a CPA like me. Unlike me, she followed a corporate track and rose to the rank of controller at her manufacturing firm, reporting to the CFO.[7]

"As the controller, I was responsible for the day-to-day accounting operations as well as the month-end financial statements and the annual audit," she said. "Although I was young, I was ready for the challenge. I had spent some time working in public accounting, so I was confident that I could handle the demands of my new job."[8]

Her bosses were non-accountants who didn't really care about the ins and outs of financial statements. But they were single-minded in their desire to grow sales. In less than five years, they increased the size of the company from four locations to nine, from $20 million in sales to $120 million, and from one hundred employees to four hundred.

Since inventory was the company's largest asset, Jackie's bosses tasked her with developing systems and procedures to handle the inventory procurement process. Each month-end, the company experienced large inventory adjustments, but her bosses didn't seem to care.

"This should have been my first red flag about my boss's cavalier management philosophy, but I did not let the inventory adjustment issue impact me," she said.

Jackie soon realized that even though sales were increasing, net income was decreasing, and no one appeared to be watching the companywide bottom line. Poor expense control, bad inventory purchases, and increasing accounts receivable put a constant strain on cash flow, which all pointed directly back to her boss's sales strategy.

One day, the CFO asked Jackie to overstate the amount of inventory the company showed on its books. In that same conversation, the CFO also asked her to understate accounts receivable. Although this was not called "earnings management" during that time, this is essentially what it was. Earnings management really should be called earnings *manipulation* because it's what happens when a company alters financial reports to mislead people.[9]

Additionally, the CFO wanted Jackie to hide this action from the external auditors. This is a colossal no-no.

This wasn't the first time her CFO had asked her to manipulate earnings; he had asked her to do it on at least three other occasions during her audit preparation work. But this time, the audit was just around the corner. The CFO was running out of time, and the pressure was on.

Every time her CFO asked her to "cook the books," as we say in the industry, he methodically talked her through reasonable explanations as to why the accounts receivable were collectible and how the old inventory was saleable. "My CFO was trying to rationalize his actions and pull me into his scheme to justify his decisions," she said.

A *Journal of Business Ethics* study by J. H. Amernic and R. J. Craig proposed that accounting is a choice for narcissistic CEOs because it allows them to "construct a narrative about the corporation using financial accounting measures.[10] Despite people thinking that accounting is a rigid set of rules, there exists a significant level of subjectivity around reporting choices and decisions." In actuality, there are no rules. Accounting is a loose grouping of principles, not rules. That is what explains the "principles" in the Generally Accepted Accounting Principles (or GAAP), the accounting standards that corporate America must adhere to.[11]

Jackie didn't know what to do. She was early into her career and didn't want to make waves. "Standing up to your boss is not something that you are necessarily taught in college, so I was very nervous about which steps to take next," she said.

Her CFO's rationalizations were very believable, especially to a newly minted controller. He explained that delinquent customers would *eventually* pay their bills because competitors had long since stopped shipping orders to those same customers. Since the customers needed supplies to stay in business, they had no choice but to make payments at some point in time.

He went on to explain that old inventory was saleable because much of it was no longer manufactured. So if customers needed a replacement part for their clients, eventually, it would get sold.

"He was convinced that his strategy was correct," she said.

After every conversation, Jackie walked away thinking how wrong it all was. But her CFO convinced her that his strategy was better than hers. She left the conversations doubting herself and questioning her knowledge of accounting principles. She'd go home and think about their conversations further. She ultimately concluded that he was wrong and she was right.

After hours of rehearsing in her mind, she went back to work to argue her position. But her boss wouldn't back down. "My CFO told his story so many times that he truly came to believe it himself," she said.

This is highly possible. Renowned behavioral economist Dan Ariely coauthored a study in the journal *Nature Neuroscience* found that the brain adapts to lying.[12] The first time you fabricate a story, the amygdala and insula, two areas in the brain associated with emotion, light up. But by the twelfth time you do it, the brain has acclimated and so the response is less potent. You stop feeling any negative emotions or guilt (assuming you did in the first place).

"Once he realized that he wasn't convincing me to agree with his non-GAAP rationalizations, he finally made the statement that I still hear in my head when I close my eyes, just like it was yesterday," she said.[13] "He looked me in the eyes and said, 'Four hundred of your fellow friends and coworkers will lose their jobs if you don't do what I want you to do.'"[14]

Jackie had two options: she could misstate the financials and save four hundred jobs or do the right thing and cause hardship to so many people.

"Since I was part of the management team in a small to midsize company, I developed relationships with many of our employees," she said. "To me, they weren't names on a page. They were people with drama and dreams. They were lunchmates, gym buddies, colleagues, teammates, and friends. The thought of them being out of work for even a day filled me with dread. You can read about layoffs in a newspaper and gloss right over the numbers. But when you know each face, have heard each story, it becomes nearly impossible to agree with a layoff, let alone engineer one."[15]

Her bosses had offered stock to their "key" employees, but Jackie had refused to receive any. She didn't want to be compromised in any way—a noble whistleblower in the making. They tried to persuade her, but she wouldn't budge.

"I paid for that decision by being excluded more and more from critical management meetings," she said. "As confused and horrible as I felt, I was also angry that I had been put into this position," she added. "I ended up in this position because I had ignored so many red flags along the way. I think back to how things were in the early days of the company. In the beginning, everything seemed great, but things quickly changed."[16]

Figuring out how to report the overvalued assets without being discovered was not going to be easy. Jackie's company wasn't publicly traded, so she couldn't have gone to the SEC. So she went to the next best thing: her external auditor.

Luckily, she had a fairly good relationship with the external audit manager assigned to their audit. Before the audit began, Jackie asked her to lunch and told her the whole story. "I let her know where to look, what to ask for, what reports to examine and who to speak with," she said. "I provided her with all the information she would need to uncover the evidence for herself."

Jackie's tip-off helped the auditor discover the fraudulent transactions that her higher-ups had sanctioned. Ultimately, the company restated the financial statements, her bosses were furious, and Jackie quit.

She was concerned about post-whistle-blow retaliation.

And rightly so, her concerns were valid. A survey done by the Ethics Resource Center reported that one out of five people experiences retaliation after whistleblowing.[17]

A 2019 study in the *DePaul Business & Commercial Law Journal* reported that nearly two-thirds of whistleblowers had experienced the following forms of retaliation. Of these two-thirds:

- 69% lost their jobs or were forced to retire.

- 64% received negative employment performance evaluations.

- 68% had their work more closely monitored by supervisors.

- 69% were criticized or ostracized by coworkers.

- 64% were blacklisted from getting another job in their field.[18]

As a result of Jackie's coming forward, the bank adjusted her company's loan covenants (the agreements that lay out the terms and conditions of a loan between a lender and a borrower), lowering its access to cash.

The adjustment impacted the company's cash flow, yet no one went to jail. Jackie had stopped the ruse before it became a criminal offense.

Jackie's actions were noble, period. She could have easily accepted the stock and gone along with the group. This would have made it harder for her to blow the whistle. The fraud most likely wouldn't have gotten discovered. But she wouldn't have been able to live with herself.

And unlike accidental whistleblowers like Kathe Swanson, Jackie was directly involved and could have been implicated in the scheme.

It's worth noting that whistleblowing doesn't just refer to fraud cases. Anyone can be a whistleblower, in any industry. Although I've been talking about financial fraud, other types of whistleblowers clearly exist, in every industry and sector of society.

Pump the Brakes

Several years ago, I had the pleasure of meeting attorney Mary Inman, a partner from Constantine Cannon's San Francisco office. Constantine Cannon has extensive experience representing whistleblowers under the *qui tam* provisions of the False Claims Act, the Dodd-Frank Act, the IRS Whistleblower Law, and an array of other federal and state whistleblower laws.

We met on Twitter over a discussion about Theranos whistleblower and ex-employee Tyler Shultz, whose grandfather, former US Secretary of State George Shultz, introduced him to now-disgraced founder Elizabeth Holmes. After a few tweet exchanges, I wanted to meet her in person.

"I've been reading about your background and your firm," I said. "The work you do is amazing and so needed. I know you're based in London, but I wish you could speak to my students."

"Well, I'm actually in Washington, DC, at the moment, and I could stop through Chicago on my way back to London," she replied.

That was the start of a wonderful relationship. From speaking on panels together to learning about various whistleblowing cases from her many tweets, she has been an outstanding resource. When I learned that Constantine Cannon was the law firm representing Kim Gwang-ho (hereafter Mr. Kim), the Hyundai whistleblower who was awarded a record $24 million from his lawsuit against Hyundai's failure to report potentially fatal engine defects, Attorney Inman was my first email.[19]

She introduced me to her colleague Ari Yampolsky, who's also a partner in Constantine Cannon's San Francisco office. I sent over a list of interview questions to both attorneys to share with their client.

Mr. Kim was an engineer for Hyundai and Kia's quality strategy team. He was based in Korea and had worked at the company for twenty years. His job was to review engine seizures for Hyundai Theta II engines, the automaker's most popular engine. Based on his and his department's analysis, the Theta II engine was prone to seize and could potentially catch fire. In the worst case, a fire might start in the engine compartment and put the passengers at extreme risk. Although the Theta II engine was more powerful, the parts that surrounded it were not powerful enough to support it. Under more strain, those engine parts were failing, which led to seizure.[20]

Mr. Kim and his department drafted a report sharing their findings with senior leadership, explicitly describing this situation. Mr. Kim assumed that Hyundai would immediately address the problem due to the potential danger it caused the public.

During the summer of 2015, US regulators called in Hyundai because they were seeing problems with the Theta II engine. Mr. Kim produced the team's findings along with the recommendation to recall over 1 million vehicles.

Unfortunately, Hyundai ignored the safety team's analysis and said that debris entered the Alabama plant, causing manufacturing issues.[21] Hyundai also claimed the engine issues impacted only a few vehicles.

Mr. Kim's concerns grew. He believed that Hyundai and Kia moved too slowly to recall the vehicles.

In the summer of 2016, he flew from Korea to Washington, DC, with the goal of meeting key officials at the Department of Transportation (DOT). With internal documents in hand and no scheduled appointment, he arrived at the DOT and somehow landed a meeting with one of the key people at the National Highway Traffic Safety Administration (NHTSA).

He convinced the NHTSA that Hyundai was not telling the truth. The two automakers "inaccurately reported crucial information to NHTSA about serious defects in the engines," according to a statement from NHTSA.[22] Not only did Mr. Kim not speak English, but the documents were also in Korean, and he paid for his entire US trip out of his own pocket.

"He's fearing for his life," Attorney Yampolsky said. "He was speaking out against a large conglomerate. Hyundai is the second-largest company in Korea."

When Mr. Kim returned from the United States, Hyundai immediately fired him. Hyundai alleged that Mr. Kim took internal documents so that he could start his own company to compete with Hyundai.

Hyundai then filed a criminal complaint against Mr. Kim.[23] His home was ransacked on his birthday by local prosecutors. His wife and two college-aged daughters were there at the time. Authorities took records, computers, and files.

Mr. Kim went to the Korean Anti-Corruption and Civil Rights Commission (ACRC) for assistance.[24] He said he was a whistleblower.

"The agency found Mr. Kim's story to be true. He's vindicated," said Attorney Inman. In 2019, Mr. Kim settled with Hyundai.[25] The company effectively paid him money not to come back to work. He got a payout of his pension, but the experience took a tremendous toll on his life.

"You see, with Mr. Kim's story, he bore enormous consequences because he was involved in it and was asked to look the other way," Attorney Inman said. "He did not, and that's where blacklisting happens. If you're a quality assurance engineer, like Mr. Kim, you're never going to go on to be a quality assurance engineer anywhere else, once the industry figures out [that] Mr. Kim won't look the other way."

Congress passed the US Motor Vehicle Safety Whistleblower Act in 2015.[26] Similar to the False Claims Act, the law creates a program where automotive whistleblowers can be rewarded for providing information to safety regulators about defects in vehicles.

Mr. Kim's whistleblower journey lasted three years, and like most accidental whistleblowers, he knows he did the right thing. In November 2021, US Motor Vehicle Safety Whistleblower Act awarded him the largest whistleblower payment in the automotive industry.[27]

Mr. Kim has still not been paid.

"A lot of our clients don't consider themselves to be whistleblowers; they're just doing their job," Attorney Inman said. "Noble corporate whistleblowing can be challenging, however; members of law enforcement often face very different obstacles when they break away from the ranks."

Best-Kept Secrets

In 2017, my friend Dee and I went to see the film *Jackie*, which is about the assassination of President John F. Kennedy seen through the eyes of First Lady Jacqueline Kennedy. There was a scene in the movie where President Kennedy (played by Peter Sarsgaard) and Mrs. Kennedy (played by Natalie Portman) walk into the White House. A Black Secret Service agent stands at the door.

"Who's that Black man?" I asked Dee. I had no idea there were any Black Secret Service agents at that time.

"That's probably Abraham Bolden," she said.

I had never heard his name before. At dinner after the film, she told me more about him, what he tried to do, and where he ended up. When I found out he lived on the south side of Chicago, I was all over it.

I wanted to interview him for my *Nothing but the Truth* podcast. I found his number on WhitePages.com and called him out of the blue.

The phone rang three times before someone answered. I politely introduced myself but before I could get the second sentence out of my mouth, he promptly slammed down the phone. So I called back.

"Please don't hang up on me," I said quickly. "I want to talk to you about your story, I want to tell you how I learned about you and would really just like to meet you."

I must have sounded sincere, because he stayed on with me. He even came to my class to share his story with my students. They were blown away.

My sound engineer friend, Tim, and I drove to Mr. Bolden's bungalow in Englewood, a lower-income section of Chicago with a very high homicide rate. He welcomed us into his modest home, despite the fact that he could barely stand up. He was eighty-two at the time and used a walker and brace. I was excited to meet this man who had a front seat to history.

Bolden was born in East St. Louis, Illinois, and graduated from Lincoln University in Jefferson City, Missouri, with a degree in music before joining the Illinois State Police. He eventually joined the US Secret Service—formerly a division of the Treasury Department—for which he sometimes went undercover to bust counterfeiting rings. He was the first African American assigned to a presidential detail and worked on John F. Kennedy's detail for a short time.[28]

"While some agents got the coveted spots inside the McCormick Place banquet room near the president, my assignment was to guard a basement restroom that had been set aside for Kennedy's exclusive use," Bolden wrote in his memoir, *The Echo from Dealey Plaza*.[29]

According to Bolden, on a visit to Chicago on April 28, 1961, Kennedy stopped in front of the bathroom where Bolden was stationed and asked Bolden if a Black Secret Service agent had ever been at the White House. Bolden said no. Within a month, Bolden got the gig and moved to Washington, DC.[30]

It wasn't an easy job. He was discriminated against for his skin color. And he didn't like that his colleagues used Secret Service cars to transport women around and drank heavily on the job. He alleged that they often missed work shifts or came to work drunk. Bolden said that he had told the head of the Secret Service about the drinking but that he didn't do anything.[31]

After Kennedy's assassination on November 22, 1963, Bolden became even more vocal and had plans to testify in front of the Warren Commission while he was visiting DC. But he never made it to the Warren Commission. Instead, he was arraigned in Chicago on May 20, 1964, on federal charges that he had solicited a $50,000 bribe in exchange for a government file. He was tried twice, convicted, and sentenced to fifteen years in prison. He served thirty-nine months with two and a half years' probation.[32]

After being fired from the Secret Service in August 1964, he served three and a half years in federal prison and then worked as a quality control supervisor in the automotive industry.[33]

In 1977, the House Select Committee on Assassinations, established in 1976 to investigate the murders of both Kennedy and Martin Luther King, Jr., released its final report in 1979.[34] It read in part:

> In addition [to the threat by Thomas Arthur Vallee], the committee obtained the testimony of a former Secret Service agent, Abraham Bolden, who had been assigned to the Chicago office in 1963. He alleged that shortly before November 2, the FBI sent a teletype message to the Chicago Secret Service office stating that an attempt to assassinate the President would be made on November 2 by a four-man team using high-powered rifles, and that at least one member of the team had a Spanish-sounding name. Bolden claimed that while he did not personally participate in surveillance of the subjects, he learned about a surveillance of the four by monitoring Secret Service radio channels in his automobile and by observing one of the subjects being detained in his Chicago office.
>
> According to Bolden's account, the Secret Service succeeded in locating and surveilling two of the threat subjects who, when they discovered they were being watched, were arrested and detained on the evening of November 1 in the Chicago Secret Service office.
>
> The committee was unable to document the existence of the alleged assassination team. Specifically, no agent who had been assigned to Chicago confirmed any aspect of Bolden's

version. One agent did state there had been a threat in Chicago during that period, but he was unable to recall details. Bolden did not link Vallee to the supposed four-man assassination team, although he claimed to remember Vallee's name in connection with a 1963 Chicago case. He did not recognize Vallee's photograph when shown it by the committee.

The questionable authenticity of the Bolden account notwithstanding, the committee believed the Secret Service failed to make appropriate use of the information supplied by the Chicago threat in early November 1963.

Bolden had been trying to clear his name for the past fifty years.[35] He twice appealed to the US Supreme Court and asked presidents Nixon and Clinton to grant him clemency. In March 2016, he applied for a pardon from President Barack Obama. After a more than forty-year fight, President Joe Biden pardoned Abraham Bolden on April 26, 2022.[36] Finally, his voice was heard.

The War on Whistleblowing

Other noble whistleblowers, like Lieutenant Kimberly Young-McLear, PhD, have had a bit more success.[37] Young-McLear is a cybersecurity professional and engineer in the Coast Guard, who currently works at the Department of Homeland Security's Cybersecurity and Infrastructure Security Agency (CISA). CISA is responsible for protecting the Nation's critical infrastructure from physical and cyber threats.

Lieutenant Young-McLear was raised by immigrant parents from Trinidad and Tobago, each of whom served almost thirty years in the US Air Force. As a young adult, she spent a lot of time learning about civil rights and social movements, and she was passionate about social justice.

She was the first Black lesbian in the Coast Guard. She was proud of her accomplishments. But during her tenure between 2014 and 2019, she experienced on-the-job bullying, harassment, discrimination, and intimidation.

She decided to come forward when she discovered that two admirals in the Coast Guard were intentionally protecting bullies.[38] "It's a culture that impacts thousands of people in the Coast Guard, and many serve in silence, many suffer a severe psychological toll, or they are otherwise pushed out of the service, and the cycle continues," she said.

The day after she filed a complaint, the department head sent out an email to everyone about a whistleblower who died. However, he modified the online article to add the term *obituary* and changed the title in the email subject line. "I believe it was meant to send a message to me to intimidate me," she said.

After every stage of the complaint process or filing a new complaint, Lieutenant Young-McLear said she endured retaliation. The longer she persisted, the more intense the retaliation became, and from higher-ranking executives.

"I knew that I had to focus instead on how I could use my voice to show others that they always matter, even if the culture within the Coast Guard mistreated them like I was mistreated," she said.

Her case inspired new legislation to prevent sexual assault and develop cultural competency in the Coast Guard. In 2021, the National Defense Authorization Act was reformed to protect how members of the military report sexual assault and harassment.[39] These reforms removed the prosecution of sexual assault and related crimes from the military chain of command; preserved the independence of judges, juries, and proceedings; and made sure that prosecutors are equipped to take on sexual assault cases.[40] If you decide to blow the whistle, "reflect on who you are at your core and stay absolutely grounded on why you are coming forward," she told me. "Know that how your organization may be mistreating you is their problem. Make sure you also have strong emotional support and necessary financial support at home or amongst your closest relationships."

Silent Hero

For a few months, I was covering the journey of whistleblowers on my *Forbes* blog. Remember, so many people reached out after the Ted Talk launch that I wanted to help whistleblowers get their stories out on a larger platform. One of those people was Ben Dobson.

Ben was a nurse in the Sterile Processes Department at a Veterans Administration (hereafter the VA) hospital in Clarksville, Indiana, cleaning, assembling, and sterilizing medical instrument sets. When he noticed unsanitary health-care practices, he brought his concerns to his higher-ups. "My moral and ethical values did not allow me to condone the things I saw at the VA," said Ben, who saw over nine hundred patients a year there.[41]

Ben made numerous improvements to the Sterile Process department over the years. He believed he was protecting and advocating for his patients.

His bosses disagreed. Instead of taking action, they made his life hell.

"I was punished for complaining about things that I knew were either harming people or wasting essential dollars," he said. "These were often severe issues—sometimes life-threatening matters—and I was punished for trying to address these."[42]

For eight years, he complained about dirty dental instruments. "I had spoken to dental techs that told me they had to scrape the 'white stuff' off the instruments as they were laying them out for use," he said. "That 'white stuff' was the scrapings off the last patient's teeth. Although the package was labeled 'clean' instruments, they smelled like bad breath."[43] They used them anyway.

Another time, he was sent out to retrieve "scopes" for inventory. Scopes are short for various types of flexible endoscopes that enter through the nose and can extend to your lungs. One day, Ben picked up ten "processed" ready-to-use scopes. It was not a pretty sight. "All ten were grossly soiled, bloody, often covered with mucus, and some had caustic cleaning fluid in them," he recalled. He complained. Loudly. A few days later, he was removed from his department and investigated. He was then shuffled over to a job in the Health Tech Department, where he stayed for two more years. It was just as gross.

"I identified 290 critical lab errors per month," he said. This time, he assembled a team and tried to correct the errors. Once again, his life was a living hell."[44]

He eventually resigned, filed a case with the Office of Accountability and Whistleblower Protection, and filed a claim with the Joint Commission on Hospital Accreditation and the Office of Special Counsel.[45] "Veterans deserve the highest-quality care we can give them, and VA employees should not be subject to the type of retaliation I experienced," he said.

And then he said something that made me smile. "I look back now and wonder if I would do it again," he said. "I think I would."

Now *that's* a true noble whistleblower.

CHAPTER TAKEAWAYS

- Noble whistleblowers work inside a company and are often asked to take part in or turn a blind eye to an unethical scheme. They often don't ignore questionable behavior they've witnessed.

- Noble whistleblowers who shine a spotlight on unethical or illegal dealings in corporations are frequently punished rather than rewarded.

- Be sure to create an environment where a noble whistleblower feels comfortable standing up and speaking. You want employees who have the gumption to speak up when they don't have to.

Noble whistleblower quick facts

Description	Characteristics
• Internal employees approached to participate in an unethical plot	• See the world as black and white
• Utilize internal whistleblowing channels to report fraud	• Arbiters of fairness
	• Not motivated by recognition
• Often choose to report anonymously	

Chapter 8

Vigilante Whistleblowers

Vigilante whistleblowers go against a large system. Think Erin Brockovich, who in 1993 helped build a case against Pacific Gas and Electric Company, which had contaminated drinking water in Hinkley, California. Or Jeffrey Wigand, who blew the whistle on tobacco tampering at Brown & Williamson, where he was a vice president, in 1996. Or former FBI agent Terry Albury, who leaked classified "national defense information" about post-9/11 surveillance tactics in 2021. Albury was sentenced to four years in prison. The story was a cause célèbre and got an enormous amount of attention.

Unlike noble whistleblowers, who tend to prefer anonymity, vigilantes are fine with publicity. The more attention, the better, especially when they're lobbying Congress for their cause. They often get a bad rap—we like to think they're contrarians. In truth, vigilantes are independent thinkers who don't stay quiet just because everyone else does. This category of whistleblower is where "snitch," "rat," and "tattletale" monikers come from. Vigilantes—the blabbermouth who tells on their siblings for stealing from the cookie jar.

Not surprisingly, there is an actual condition to describe this behavior: *workplace vigilante syndrome*. According to Katy DeCelles and Karl Aquino in *Vigilantes at Work: Examining the Frequency of Dark Knight Employees*, a vigilante is someone who "regularly brings claims to the attention of authorities, colleagues, or the general public that one or more persons in their organization has committed a moral violation, a breach of company policy, or an unjust act, and makes an effort to punish that person or persons directly or indirectly."[1]

Research has found that vigilantes typically skew female and are usually found in large organizations and in unionized workforces like education, public administration or government, and hospitality or food services. They're more likely to appear at companies with ethics hotlines and built-in mechanisms to report bad behavior, and a clear-cut ethics code.

Vigilantes are often threatened with legal action. Consequently, they have to take matters into their own hands, which is why I have such respect for them.

Big Little League

All of Chicago was obsessed with the Jackie Robinson West (JRW) Little League team debacle in 2014.

The JRW team comprised twelve- and thirteen-year-old African American kids from the south side of Chicago. Or at least, that's how old they were supposed to be. In reality, thanks to a bit of gerrymandering, a handful of older kids were on the team. Jackie Robinson West won the 2014 US Championship before being defeated by the South Korea team in the World Championship.[2] Still, a huge pep rally featuring several higher-ups from the Cubs and White Sox was held at Millennium Park for the team. They received over $300,000 in donations. President Barack Obama invited them to the White House.

But something smelled funny to Little League coach Chris Janes. Janes lived in the neighboring town of Evergreen Park; the team he coached had lost to JRW much earlier in the series.[3] When the Jackie Robinson kids won, Janes noticed that some suburban communities outside of the JRW boundaries had bragged about being the hometowns of some of the players. As the publicity increased, so did the number of communities claiming the kids to be from their areas. This didn't make sense to Janes, so he began investigating the players' backgrounds.

After the team won the 2014 Little League World Series, Janes approached Patrick Wilson, the Little League vice president of operations, and told him about the impropriety.[4] Wilson ignored him and later publicly humiliated Janes and his family. Janes received death threats. He sued Little League International.[5]

Three months later, Little League International took back the title, saying JRW and its administrator falsified a boundary map to place players on the team who shouldn't have been on the team because they "lived outside the team's boundaries."[6] Eventually, Little League International stripped the team of its US championship and kicked it off the Little League.[7]

As a parent of student-athletes, a whistleblower researcher, and a self-proclaimed vigilante (which you'll hear about further below), I couldn't stop thinking about this story.

I was torn. I was furious at the coaches and parents who perpetrated the scam. And I felt awful for Janes, who received death threats for speaking up. But who was really wrong here? Was Janes wrong for reporting what he saw? Or were the coaches wrong for bending the rules to build a more powerful team?

I understood the ire. All of Chicago had celebrated the JRW win. I was extremely proud of the win, but we can't lose sight of the actions of a few adult coaches that led us to this discussion in the first place. And I felt terrible that these kids—innocent bystanders!—were victims of a few adults' actions. But there's always collateral damage when fraud occurs. Innocent bystanders who either lose their jobs (like the thousands of Enron employees) or lose their life savings (like Mary West and the other victims in the James Bailey Ponzi scheme case, which I discussed in chapter 4) often suffer greatly due to other people's selfishness.

But it's real, and adults are at fault—and so is a larger culture that puts a misguided value on winning at all costs.

I wrote a blog about the case on *Forbes.com*.[8] I also talked about it with my students. I wrote on the chalkboard: "What does society think of whistleblowers versus what people think of whistleblowers?" Then I invited them to come to the board and write down the first words that came to mind (see table 8-1).

TABLE 8-1

Student feedback: How you view whistleblowers vs. how the world views whistleblowers

What do you think?	What does society think?
Ethical	Snitch
Moral person	Hater
Justice	Villain
Honest	Snitches
Needed	Rat
Righteous	Hero
Courageous	Self-interest
Fair to all	Taking the easy way out

There it was, the Whistleblower Dilemma in plain chalk. What made it even *more* interesting was that I had also invited a visitor: Chris Janes—the whistleblower himself—along with journalist Mark Konkol. Konkol had read my *Forbes* blog and contacted me.[9] He wanted to witness my students debating the issue in person. As an added bonus, he would bring Chris Janes.

Chris looked like a hard-nosed, no-nonsense coach: 6'2" with a buzz cut and athletic dad bod. He listened silently as I laid out the facts of the case, and my students debated with him. Half the class sided with him ("He was following the rules!"), and the other half thought he was a colossal snitch.

Finally, it was his turn to speak. He came to the front of the room and leaned against my desk. "What would *you* do if you lost a game to someone who was breaking the rules? All I did was raise the question."

My students tentatively raised their hands.

"I'm not sure!" said Venus.

"I'd report it to someone in charge," said Michael.

"I wouldn't be a sore loser," said James.

Chris took it all in and nodded. "Fair is fair," he said. He explained that he wasn't a racist, which several people accused him of being. He said his wife was African American and his children were interracial. He said that he'd had death threats and that his family had taken a lot of heat because of his actions. But he hadn't seen any other way. "Fair is fair," he said. Also, people were upset about the JRW kids being stripped of their title. But what about the kids who had lost unfairly?

The JRW parents filed a lawsuit against Little League International, claiming that officials should have figured out that the residency problems existed before the team became a national phenomenon. They also maintained that JRW treasurer Bill Haley submitted false documents to league officials after complaints from coaches of one of JRW's early-round opponents prompted an investigation.

The lawsuit argued that Little League officials should have ignored a complaint filed by Janes and other coaches from Evergreen Park in December 2014—months after JRW lost the international championship game to South Korea—because league rules stipulated that Evergreen Park had to make their challenge before JRW played their next game.[10] The lawsuit was settled for an undisclosed amount. Filmmaker Kevin Shaw (*Let the Little Light Shine, American to Me, City So Real*) is making a documentary entitled *One Golden Summer*, which chronicles the scandal.

March Madness

As a native of Durham, North Carolina, I grew up right in between the campus of Duke University and the University of North Carolina at Chapel Hill (UNC). Oddly, I root for both teams, and it's always a difficult choice when they play each other in basketball. When I heard about the UNC academic fraud scandal, I was fascinated.[11] But when I learned that the whole case came to light because of a vigilante whistleblower, I couldn't stop following the story. And that's one of the reasons I was so excited to meet vigilante extraordinaire Mary Willingham.

As reports filled the headlines about the UNC athletics academic scandal in 2012, one question quickly sprung into my head: "Who was the whistleblower?" After a little digging, Mary Willingham's name rose to the top of the list.

We agreed that an in-person interview at her home in Chapel Hill would be ideal. I was back home again in my Durham stomping grounds.

We pulled up to Mary's home, a beautiful brick colonial home surrounded by huge pine trees. Mary greeted us at the door with a smile and a hug.[12]

Born and raised on the south side of Chicago, Mary Willingham graduated from Loyola University in Chicago with a degree in psychology. After spending twenty years in corporate America working in human resources, she decided to follow her passion and pursue teaching. She earned a degree from the University of North Carolina at Greensboro. Her master's thesis, "Academics & Athletics—A Clash of Cultures: Division I Football Programs," argued that the goal of educating student-athletes had been overlooked for the pursuit of money.[13]

In 2003, she took a job at UNC in the Academic Support Program as a learning specialist. She began noticing that many of the student-athletes, especially those who played on the revenue-generating sports teams, weren't prepared for the academics. Mary was surprised that some student-athletes were admitted to the university despite having severely deficient academic abilities.

"Students were steered, or enrolled, by academic counselors to a lot of 'paper classes' that were offered in the African-American studies department," she said. ("No-show" or "fake classes" are classes in which students either aren't required to attend or do very little work and still earn high grades.[14] These fake classes were the primary way that struggling student-athletes could remain eligible.)

Mary was outraged when she discovered a system designed to keep student-athletes eligible to play sports and proceeded to tell her supervisor. But it should not have come as such a shock.

Collegiate sports are estimated to be a $100 million business.[15] The success of collegiate sports programs greatly depends on the academic advisers who oversee student-athletes' studies. More than 460,000 NCAA student-athletes compete in twenty-three sports every year. According to the NCAA website, member schools support their student-athletes' academic success by providing "state-of-the-art technology, tutoring, and access to academic [advisers]." Student-athletes look to these advisers to provide advice and guidance on academic majors and course selection.

A CNN investigation found public universities across the country where many student-athletes in basketball and football programs specifically could read only up to an eighth-grade level.[16] For ill-prepared student-athletes, juggling academics and sports to remain eligible to play can be difficult, which has led to an increase in fraudulent eligibility schemes.

Many schools have been reported as having disturbing trends of athletes clustering into certain courses and athletic-friendly professors who provide independent study courses too frequently to athletes.[17] At UNC, an academic fraud was exposed that experts argue is the most historic academic fraud case in collegiate athletics.

UNC enrolls more than 28,000 students, 5 percent of whom are student-athletes.[18] UNC is one of the fifteen member schools belonging to the Atlantic Coast Conference (ACC).[19] Its athletic programs have been hugely successful and, especially with basketball and football, huge revenue-generating programs.[20] In 2012, for example, the UNC basketball program earned a profit of $17 million. Several notable ballplayers went there, among them Michael Jordan. After three years playing at UNC under legendary Coach Dean Smith, Jordan joined the Chicago Bulls in 1984.

So big bucks were at stake. And UNC did not take kindly to someone trying to expose corruption in one of its biggest money-making sports.

From 1993 to 2011, UNC offered "independent study" courses within the Department of African and Afro-American Studies.[21] The professor consistently awarded high grades, regardless of the quality of the student's work. If the course required a final research paper, the papers weren't graded by faculty members but rather by the department administrator.

Some administrators and professors were aware of this arrangement, among them Jan Boxill, a philosophy instructor and director of the university's Center for Ethics. Boxill actually admitted that she had requested specific grades for her student players and written parts of their papers for them.[22] During the eighteen-year period these sham courses existed, thirty-one hundred students were enrolled, with almost half being student-athletes. The October 2014 "Wainstein report" found that many faculty and administrators, including some members of the athletic support department and the director of UNC's Parr Center for Ethics, had varying degrees of knowledge about the true nature of the courses.[23]

Mary was never asked to engage in the fraud (like noble whistleblowers), but as a good vigilante whistleblower, she felt that she needed to stop it. In January 2014, she released research showing that 60 percent of the 183 athletes from 2004 to 2012 could read at only a fourth- and eighth-grade reading level and that 8 percent to 10 percent read below a third-grade level.[24]

When speaking to her supervisor didn't work, Mary reached out to internal university administrators. No one did anything about it. She posted a blog, which attracted the attention of a reporter at the

News & Observer in Raleigh. The paper published a scathing story.[25] The story blew up.

The aftermath was hard. Mary was verbally attacked, isolated, and demoted. People accused her of plagiarizing her thesis. She received numerous death threats. In May 2014, she resigned and sued UNC, claiming she was discriminated against for being a whistleblower.[26] She also claimed that UNC had violated her whistleblower protection rights, which are defined in the North Carolina Whistleblower Act. UNC agreed to pay her $335,000 to settle the lawsuit.[27]

In June 2015, the board of the Southern Association of Colleges and Schools Commission on College (SACS) placed UNC on probation for failing to meet seven accreditation standards, including academic integrity and control of athletics.[28] Numerous officials left UNC in the wake of the scandal, including former Chancellor Holden Thorp, who resigned. Nine others resigned, were fired, or were placed under disciplinary review. A year later, in a surprise announcement to many, the NCAA announced that there would be no penalties against UNC because "no rules were broken."[29]

Mary had ideas about how to rectify the problem in the future. "If universities are going to continue to admit students who aren't ready to do the work," she told the *Times*, "the NCAA should pay for fifteen months' remediation, after which the athlete would have to pass a test."[30] In addition, she said, they should have five-year scholarships to help improve the odds of graduating.

"I want to see the NCAA machinery dismantled," she continued. "I want faculties to take back their universities from the athletic departments."[31]

She never worked at UNC again.

. . .

I've always wondered how the students felt about the UNC case. More specifically, how they felt knowing that coaches and professors, so-called "grown-ups," were behaving so terribly.

It's the same thing I wondered when I first heard about "Operation Varsity Blues," the 2019 college admission bribery scandal, in which super-wealthy parents and celebrities paid hundreds of thousands of dollars to get their kids into schools like Yale, University of Southern California, and the University of Texas.[32] Were the students aware of their parents' fraud schemes? Did they know what their parents were doing on their behalf?

I think a few probably did.

As a former child and current parent, I understand that we all want the best for our kids. But when I look back on my college application days, I recall very little parent involvement. My father was a college president and had a PhD in operations research from Purdue University; my mother was a school guidance counselor and had a master's in education from the University of Maryland. Of course, they reviewed my application, checking for typing errors and clarity, but I did the final sign-off.

So I was interested by a *New York Times* article that reported that many students said they were unaware of what their parents were up to.[33]

That's really hard for me to believe. Maybe initially the kids may not have known what their parents did, but eventually they did. It's terrible that the parents put their children in this position, but it speaks to the concept of privilege, power, and money.

Inflated test scores, falsified essays, photoshopped pictures, fabricated learning disabilities, doctored athletic records. I vividly remember the day I took the SAT. I was nervous and felt like the entire world hinged on this one test score. I would surely remember if I didn't take the SAT and mysteriously got accepted into a top-ranked school.

As we know, 40 percent of frauds are discovered by whistleblowers.[34] We also know that retaliation is real and painful. The students faced a no-win situation and had no easy way out.

When one of the Varsity Blues students was asked during orientation about being a member of the track team and a top athlete, he had no idea what the interviewer was talking about. When it was clear that someone lied on his behalf, what did he do? What *could* he do? The student had to know that he was not a top athlete (as did the coach when his time was 70 seconds in the 4×100). Did he tell the truth or let the lie continue because it would benefit him greatly? Since the student stayed enrolled in the college and on the track team, we partially know the answer to this question. But what we don't know is the lengths this student went through to attempt to mitigate the situation.

It raises an interesting ethical dilemma. What happens when children need to blow the whistle on their parents?[35]

In my graduate forensic accounting class, we spend a lot of time discussing corporate culture and how a sound corporate culture leads to an ethical environment. The assumption is that morality and personal values have been established and nurtured at home. But if parents are going to such lengths to cheat for their children and children observe these behaviors and stay silent, we can expect to see daily headlines of fraud and corruption. These children are our future employees, business leaders, movie stars, fashion designers, and authors. If your home environment is threatened, how is your ethical safety protected?

• • •

I'm a vigilante. Self-proclaimed, yes, but when I look back over my own history of whistleblowing, it definitely falls in the vigilante category.

For example: Once I was defrauded by a Chicago-based moving company.[36] I hired them to move me into my new home, not to steal from me. But when my wedding ring came up missing, it was my word against the movers'.

Before you ask yourself why an intelligent person like me had her wedding rings lying around, ripe for the plucking, let me affirm: I didn't. I had taken them off to go to the gym, and deliberately hid them in the back of a drawer in my bathroom vanity.

I called the police, who told me I needed to file a report. I did. Then I found the moving company's CEO on LinkedIn and sent him a request to connect.

"One of your employees stole my wedding ring," I wrote. "How can you help me fix this problem?"

He put me in touch with the company's lawyer, whom I thought would listen and help me. But he didn't respond to emails or voice-mails. I posted stories about the situation on Twitter. I even mentioned the company by name. Vigilantes demand to be heard, and I must say: this got the lawyer's attention. He accused me of *defamation per se*, a false statement either spoken or written that injures someone's reputation. He said I had made up the whole story and threatened to sue me if I didn't remove my posts. In effect, he was accusing me of insurance fraud: if I told my insurance company that I had been robbed, then they'd cover some of the costs to replace the rings.

I didn't have money to fight, so I deleted the posts. But I needed to do something to defend my name. I also wanted to warn other customers about this company. I decided to take a polygraph test. I'd seen this over and over on *Law and Order*. Now it was my turn to sit in the hot seat to prove my innocence. It may seem a little extreme, but hey—that's how we vigilante whistleblowers can respond when threatened. We believe in justice, and we never stop until justice is served.

I googled "Where to take a polygraph test in Chicago" and found a retired FBI agent to administer it. As the polygrapher placed sticky patches around my body to monitor my heart rate, sweat glands, and pulse, I kept thinking, "How cool this would be to share with my students!" But then I worried. What if my emotions got the best of me and I failed the test? (Polygraphs don't actually detect lies; they detect your autonomic responses to a series of questions. So the machines are not lie detectors; they're really nerve detectors. And nothing's more nerve-wracking than being connected to a contraption that's supposed to discern how truthful a person is.)

The retired agent began the inquisition. He asked me to answer either yes or no.

Are you 43 years old? (Yes. At the time, I was).

Have you ever stolen something? (Yes. A piece of gum from my mom's purse when I was eight; my mother's car to visit a friend when I was seventeen . . . you get the point.)

Did you make a fraudulent claim about those rings? (No!)

He must have asked this same question seventy-two different times and ways. As the second hour approached, I became slightly annoyed. Why had I subjected myself to this? Oh yes. I needed to clear my name. I wasn't willing to let my life's work and reputation get tarnished by a false accusation from a moving company *that had stolen my wedding ring.*

COMMON REASONS COMPANIES DON'T OFFER FRAUD-REPORTING PLATFORMS

Unfortunately, not all companies offer reporting options. According to Juliette Gust and Tricia Fratto, cofounders of Ethics Suite, a Phoenix-based employee incident-reporting platform, these reasons include some common myths.

- "We don't have fraud in my company."
- "A hotline will breed a culture of negativity and paranoia."
- "A hotline will just encourage people to avoid talking to their supervisor about workplace problems."
- "I have an open-door policy; if there's a problem, someone would tell me."
- "My employee will abuse the hotline and report frivolous workplace issues."

None of these myths should prevent any organization from establishing a whistleblowing reporting mechanism or program.

Two hours later, the test was complete. I breathed a sigh of relief and exited the building.

Two weeks later, the results flew into my in-box: I had lied through the roof. Kidding! I passed with flying colors. Of course, I was telling the truth. I reached back out to the moving company's CEO and lawyer and explained how disappointed I was in how they handled the situation, and let them know my polygraph results. They never responded, so I wrote about it in my *Forbes* blog. This time I didn't mention the company by name (but I may have told people who wrote to me privately).

This was the first time I'd experienced life as a vigilante whistleblower, and I got to see firsthand how hard it is to get people to believe you.

CHAPTER TAKEAWAYS

- Vigilantes are the Mohammed Ali of whistleblowers.

- Vigilantes won't back down until they're heard, even if they're bloodied and their teeth are knocked out. They'll fight to the end for whatever cause they believe in.

- Vigilantes are willing to risk it all as long as justice prevails.

- You want a vigilante in your organization.

Vigilante whistleblower quick facts

Description	Characteristics
• Often embody the negative characteristics of whistleblower (*snitch, rat, traitor*, etc.)	• Independent thinkers
	• Ethically minded
• Visible and willing to bring to the attention of the media/authorities	• Vocal
• Typically take a personal hit to fight for justice	• Perseverant
• Often speak up about an injustice that may or may not involve them	• Determined
	• Fair-minded

Chapter 9

Crossovers

Some vigilantes are known as *crossovers*, transitioning from perp to whistleblower status. Feeling guilty about their bad behavior, they decide to work for the other team. Yes, obviously some of them are also incentivized to become whistleblowers—they're getting themselves out of a tight spot.

I met Weston Smith when I was working on my first documentary, *Crossing the Line: Ordinary People Committing Extraordinary Crimes.* I was looking for white-collar offenders who would be willing to share their fraud stories on camera.[1] I emailed Weston, explained the project, and invited him to Chicago.[2]

Weston was born and raised in Alabama and was a Southern gentleman from head to toe. About fifteen minutes into our interview, I realized that his fraud story was a little different from the others because he was the first person I interviewed who outed his colleagues and himself. He was an intentional perpetrator turned noble whistleblower, placing him in the crossover category.

Weston was the fifth of six CFOs at HealthSouth, the nation's largest operator of rehabilitation hospitals (now Encompass Health Corporation). The hospital was also committing massive fraud.

Between 1998 and 2002, HealthSouth overstated its income by transferring expenses such as depreciation on property, plant, and equipment, reclassifying those expenses as capital assets. This allowed expenses to move from the income statement to the balance sheet, which slowed down the amount of expenses that appeared on the income statement. Capitalizing these expenses allowed the company to defer recognizing over $200 million in expenses.[3]

Senior management at HealthSouth took full advantage of the company's massive internal control deficiencies. They filled the ranks of senior management with employees they could manipulate, people without the appropriate experience, educational background, or training. This allowed a series of CFOs to launch and maintain fraudulent and aggressive policies without objections from senior management. Fraudulent accounting techniques became standard operating procedure.

HealthSouth was hiding a $2.7 billion accounting fraud. Weston, who was once involved in the fraud, crossed over and became a whistleblower. The feds came in with investigators.

The investigators had to restate the financial statements between 2000 and 2003, a job that entailed analyzing 1.4 million accounts and required more than 1 million hours of outside help. Ninety-two percent of the accounts required adjustment because HealthSouth aggressively overstated revenues and understated expenses. Additionally, over five hundred business combination transactions had to be reviewed and corrected.[4]

Nearly a dozen HealthSouth executives, including five former chief financial officers, pleaded guilty to criminal violations of the federal securities laws and related statutes. In July 2006, Weston was ordered to pay $6.9 million in restitution and sentenced to twenty-seven months in jail.[5] Investigators credited him with opening up a can of worms.

As former Assistant US Attorney Mike Rasmussen said at Weston's sentencing, "I think it's fair to say that Mr. Smith coming into us is what started the HealthSouth fraud investigation."[6]

Disguising Fraud

Hiding financial statement fraud is pretty difficult. As we know from the accounting equation (Assets = Liabilities + Owner's Equity), entries that affect income statement accounts should result in a corresponding balance sheet account. So, it takes a lot of effort to conceal fraudulent transactions.

At HealthSouth, fictitious assets had to be added to the fixed asset list in order to balance the overstatement of revenue. Those nonexistent assets were not entered into the general ledger system in the normal fashion and had no accompanying documentation. Employees in the fixed asset department created more than $1 billion of fictitious assets in order to conceal the income statement fraud.

Weston's primary motive for perpetrating the fraud may have been to build a successful company, not to accumulate personal wealth, but there is no doubt that he benefited, at least temporarily, from the illegal activity. Unfortunately, his desire for his company's success led him to federal prison.

This was post-Enron and immediately after the passage of the Sarbanes-Oxley Act in 2002, which, if you recall, mandates certain practices in financial record keeping and reporting for corporations. With SOX's passage, Weston became increasingly concerned about certifying the legitimacy of HealthSouth's financial statements. His conscience wouldn't allow him to sign his name to verify that the financial statements were truthful; he could no longer be involved in a massive fraud scheme orchestrated by his colleagues. In early 2003, he blew the whistle on the company in a meeting with the FBI. And just like that, he was a crossover (an intentional perp to a noble whistleblower).

The government encourages people with "unclean hands" to come forward because of the "often dynamite evidence that they have," said Ari Yampolsy, an attorney and partner in Constantine Cannon's Whistleblower Representation practice. "Government prosecutors and law enforcement love whistleblowers as a general matter and see them as a force multiplier that allows them to do their jobs more efficiently and with fewer resources."

A Star Is Born

Weston Smith blew the whistle and the fraud stopped cold. Mark Whitacre blew the whistle and became an FBI informant, passing intel to the FBI. Mark Whitacre is a crossover (an intentional perp turned vigilante whistleblower). The film *The Informant*, starring Matt Damon, is based on his case. It's a fascinating story and definitely movie-worthy. I was especially interested in how he moved from perp to whistleblower.

Mark grew up in Morrow, Ohio, about an hour north of Cincinnati. "I'm convinced that white-collar criminals are made, not born," he said. "The background I have is really even further proof of that. There was no criminality at all in my background."

He met his now-wife, Ginger, when she was in seventh grade and he was in eighth. She was class treasurer and he was senior class president. He went to Ohio State University and then received a full scholarship to Cornell University, where he got his PhD in nutritional biochemistry.

In 1989, at thirty-two, he joined Archer Daniels Midland (ADM), one of the largest food additive companies in the world, with about thirty thousand employees and about $85 billion in revenues (as of February 2022). He became divisional president of the BioProducts division and was soon promoted to corporate vice president of the whole company, the youngest corporate vice president in its hundred-year history. His base salary was $350,000, with tens of thousands of shares of stock options worth millions.

"There was a big incentive to get the company to grow as fast as you could, to get the stock price to go up as quickly as you could," he said. "We were watching the stock price quarter to quarter because the quicker the stock price went up, the quicker our own personal stock options went up."

One of his responsibilities was to oversee the building of a $300 million lysine plant. (Lysine is an essential amino acid added to food.) It was one of the biggest investments in the division, and it was losing about $7 million a month. "We just couldn't get it right," he said. The CEO was talking about closing that plant down, which would be embarrassing to Mark.

"My pride at age thirty-two was definitely in my way," he admitted. "It was an obstacle. It would have been embarrassing to me to close down the plant, being president of the division; it would have been a slap in my face. If they closed the plant down, I would have to leave the company, and I wasn't willing to leave the company without a fight. And I was at a stage in my life I was willing, at that point, to win at all costs."

So Mark told his manager that someone was "sabotaging that plant." This wasn't true, but he wanted to buy time to figure out how to keep it open.

When Mark first joined the company, he had heard from other employees that price-fixing was rampant throughout the corporation. In the spring of 1992, the vice president he reported to told him that he was going to have Mark work with the president of the Corn division. He said, "Not to work *for* him, to work *with* him as a 'mentor' but only for a few months for him to teach me the way ADM does business."

"That's when I knew how ADM does business and price-fixing was going to be introduced to the division that I was president of," Mark said. "I had to make a decision. Do I stay with the company, or do I leave?"

"I was all about moving up the corporate ladder," he said. "I lost my moral compass during that time, and my focus was definitely on how far can I get in that company? How much money can I make? Greed became the priority."

. . .

Price-fixing affects every consumer in the world, and no one benefits from it except the fixers. It is an arrangement, either spoken, written, or inferred, between competitors to lower, raise, or maintain prices. In the United States, it's a federal offense under Section 1 of the Sherman Antitrust Act. ADM, along with Japanese companies Ajinomoto and Kyowa Hakko Kogyo and Korean companies Sewon America Inc. and Cheil Jedang Ltd., artificially inflated the price of lysine.

The so-called international cartel stole almost one billion dollars a year from its own customers, which included Coca-Cola, Pepsi, Kraft, General Foods, Procter & Gamble, and Tyson Foods.[7] And since it was a more expensive ingredient, consumers purchased a more expensive product. If it's more expensive for them, then it's more expensive for you, the consumer. Consumers have no idea why their Kraft macaroni and cheese has increased in price.

Mark didn't realize that the "sabotage" excuse he gave would lead to an FBI investigation. But his bosses had contacted them to investigate the claims. On November 5, 1992, Mark met with the FBI and ADM's head of security.[8] Mark had been coached on what to say and what not to say; he was instructed not to mention anything about price-fixing. The FBI wanted to put a tape recorder in his house so they could record him talking to his colleagues. The crossover process had begun.

An hour before the FBI arrived at his house, Mark told Ginger about the price-fixing. She was aghast. She, like many other innocent bystanders, didn't even know what price-fixing was. When he explained it to her, she wasn't happy.

She gave him an ultimatum: "Either you tell the FBI, or I will."

"We could lose our home, our cars," Mark stammered. "The kids will have to leave their private schools. We'll lose our standard of living."

Ginger didn't care. "I'd rather be homeless than have my husband involved with illegal activity," she said firmly.

So the FBI came to his house, and Mark told them everything about the international cartel and the price-fixing scheme.

It was liberating. "Prior to that, I felt dirty," he said. "I wasn't sleeping at night, and I didn't feel good about myself. I felt like I had taken a thousand pounds off my shoulders."

Mark became an FBI informant. For the next three years, he kept a tape recorder in his jacket, one in a briefcase, and one in a notebook. He taped his supervisors and coworkers every day for almost three years. "During the day, I was a very loyal executive, building one of the largest divisions in biotechnology in the world. At night, I was tearing down the very company that I was building." He met with the FBI a couple of nights a week, turning over tapes and debriefing them. The pressure was intense and not uncommon for a vigilante whistleblower.

"There were times I would be in our driveway blowing leaves during thunderstorms at three in the morning because I lost my identity," he said. "I didn't know who I worked for—ADM during the day and FBI during the night. I definitely lost who I was." He attempted suicide twice.

About a year before he met the FBI, Mark and three other vice presidents lost money in an investment and reimbursed themselves about $200,000 with funds from ADM.

"We sat around and talked about it," he said. "That if our management found out about it and they said, 'Look, you four guys just stole $200,000 from us,' our reply was going to be 'You guys are stealing $100 million a month, every month, $1 billion a year from every consumer in the world with this international cartel.' So it was our security at that point that they really couldn't turn us in for a small crime because they were conducting a much larger crime. It doesn't make it right. That's just what our thinking was back then when we made that decision."

One night in late June, about eighty FBI agents descended on Decatur, Illinois, and seized company computers and paperwork. "They had enough evidence, both video and audiotape," he said.

They had that evidence because of him.

The company found out that Mark was the mole (a company lawyer exposed him). One night a friend in the accounting department called him up and said that the executives were going to charge him with embezzlement.

He made an appointment to meet with federal agents at a Chinese restaurant and confessed everything, including $9 million he had taken while he was working with the FBI.

He told my students that he did this because he was trying to secure enough money to maintain his lifestyle, because once it came out that he was an informant, he was pretty sure he'd never get a job again. He admitted that for the past three years he hadn't been as up-front with them as they may have liked.

He found a lawyer and received a nine-year sentence.

And something else happened. Coca-Cola, Pepsi, Kraft, General Foods, Procter & Gamble, and Tyson Foods sued ADM civilly and won large settlements. (Coca-Cola alone got $400 million.) "Those companies recognized they would have never won those settlements without me wearing a wire, without my wife blowing the whistle," he said.

Shortly after he went to prison, Ginger and the kids moved in with Ginger's parents. Out of nowhere, a lawyer that represented a class-action lawsuit from the customers contacted Ginger. According to Mark, they said they wanted to support her financially while Mark was locked up.

"They put my wife back in college to become a schoolteacher. They put my kids through college. They paid our house bills. They paid our car payments," he said. "And even when my wife became a teacher and had two children in college and she could not afford that, they made up the difference to make sure that my family could make it financially until I got out."

EPILOGUE

One afternoon in late 2021, an email appeared on my computer screen. The writer had big news: Rita Crundwell was getting out of prison.

"No way!" I said aloud.

It was true. Dixon, Illinois, was another pandemic casualty.

Here's how it went down. On April 22, 2020, Rita had written a letter to Judge Phillip Reinhard requesting compassionate release from the Federal Prison Camp in Pekin, Illinois, where she had spent the last few years.

A district court can reduce a defendant's sentence and release him or her when "extraordinary and compelling reasons warrant such a reduction" or when a defendant with a mandatory life sentence reaches at least seventy years of age, has served at least thirty years, and is not a danger to the safety of the community.[1] In Rita's case, the pandemic presented an opportunity to request early release to home confinement.

In Rita's letter to the judge, she said that she believed that she met all of the criteria laid out by then-Attorney General William Barr, after he issued a memo in March 2020 directing the Bureau of Prisons to prioritize releasing inmates who were deemed to have especially serious health issues that put them at higher risk for severe illness caused by Covid-19.[2]

TABLE E-1

CARES Act early-release factors: How did Rita Crundwell do?

Age and vulnerability	At the time of the letter, Rita was sixty-seven years old and had health issues.
Security level	The Pekin, Illinois, federal prison camp is a low-security prison camp.
Conduct in prison	Rita was a model inmate and had earlier received a five-month reduction for good behavior.
Female PATTERN score*	Rita had a minimum score for both the general and violent categories. Her PATTERN score reflects her minimal risk of recidivism.
Demonstrated and verifiable reentry plan	She planned to return to Dixon and live with her brother, Richard.
Inmate's crime of conviction and danger posed	Rita said that her crime did not pose a danger to the community (side-eye on that one).

Source: K. R. Pope, "Will Jailed Dixon Embezzler Be Released from Federal Prison? Maybe," *Forbes*, May 9, 2022, https://www.forbes.com/sites/kellypope/2020/05/09/will-jailed-dixon-embezzler-be-released-from-federal-prison-maybe/be-released-from-federal-prison-maybe/.

*PATTERN = the Prisoner Assessment Tool Targeting Estimated Risk and Needs.

Table E-1 shows some of the criteria for early release and how Rita matched up.

"My conduct during my over seven years of incarceration has been exemplary," she wrote. "I have never had any infractions and have been referred to as a 'model inmate.'" Never mind that she would have served less than half of her sentence at that point.

When I got wind of Rita's request, I was one of the first (if not the first) to break the news on my *Forbes* blog.[3] Word spread quickly. Rita's letter was soon reprinted in full in numerous outlets. People were outraged.

"Despite monetary recovery from multiple sources, the residents of Dixon will never fully recover the financial loss from this unprecedented betrayal of trust," Brad Cole, the Executive Director of the Illinois Municipal League, wrote in a letter to Judge Reinhard.

Apparently, the message got to Rita, and she withdrew her request.

Fast forward to 2021. This year, Rita met all the requirements for compassionate release. She reapplied and got it. By then, she had served more than half of her sentence.

My phone blew up. One of the first people to call me was Kathe Swanson, the innocent bystander/accidental whistleblower who discovered Rita's crime.

"I just heard from Dan Langloss at the city of Dixon that Rita was released from prison this morning," she said. (Langloss was the Dixon city manager.) "We have no further info as of now."

"Are you serious?" I asked.

"She only served eight and a half years. Even if she were gravely ill, I can't believe they released her."

Once again, the public was livid. So was I. Here I was, trying to teach my students to do the right thing, and Rita Crundwell got eight years knocked off her sentence. Why should anyone follow the law if the law isn't going to follow itself?

Rita was heading back to Dixon to live with her brother, Richard. She would be relegated to home confinement and monitored by the Bureau of Prisons. But still. Richard's home was a far cry from a depressing jail cell.

A few days after Rita was released, I held a webinar with Jason Wojdylo, a retired chief inspector of Asset Forfeiture from the US Marshals Service, to analyze Rita's release and to help answer any questions people had. Jason had been assigned to Rita's case and had given me access to all things Rita during the filming of *All the Queen's Horses*.

"There is no parole in the federal system, so when a judge sentences you to nineteen years and seven months, you are required to serve no less than 85 percent of your sentence," he said. "You're also entitled to fifty-four days a year of good time if you behave, are not a problem for the correctional officers, comply with the rules and you take certain training programs."

The innocent bystanders of Dixon, Illinois were confused. A handful of people thought justice was served, but most believed it emphatically was not.

"The general public consensus is that white-collar public official criminals get a slap on the wrist," said current Dixon Mayor Liandro Arellano, Jr. "She got the book thrown at her and didn't even serve half of her sentence!"

I shared the same sentiments until I met with attorney Doug Passon, who forced me to think about Rita's early release from a different perspective.

I was reacquainted with Doug when I posted the news of Rita's early release on LinkedIn. The online conversation had gone viral. Many responses reflected disappointment with the criminal justice system, but Doug felt otherwise.

Doug is a successful defense attorney based in Phoenix, Arizona, with expertise in sentencing mitigation. He creates videos that he uses for clients during the sentencing phase of their trials, so I knew he would break this down so I could see a new perspective. As he said, "Every client has a story to tell. How we tell it can mean the difference between victory and defeat."

One Saturday evening, Doug and I logged on to Zoom to discuss Rita's early release. I fully expected him to be as angry as I was, but he had a different take.

"I just can't believe that she was released early!" I said. "It seems so unfair. Don't you agree?"

"Well, actually, I don't agree," he said. "Let me explain to you a little about sentencing guidelines, and maybe you will see things a little differently. Eight and a half years for a white-collar case even involving $53 million is very significant. I think people are stuck on the fact that she got sentenced to almost twenty years, and so the fact that she didn't have to serve that entire sentence was what was so outrageous to people."

As a result of the Rita Crundwell affair, Doug decided to do some research on sentencing statistics, which can be analyzed by jurisdiction, by judge, and by county.

He pointed me in the direction of Mark Allenbaugh, who runs SentencingStats.com, a website that provides attorneys an easy way to access and analyze federal sentencing statistics. Mark's research showed that from 2010 to 2020, four defendants had been sentenced under the exact same federal guidelines as Rita Crundwell. SentencingStats.com data goes back to 1992 and consists of over several billion data points, so I felt very comfortable that Mark's research was both accurate and thorough and that Doug's explanation would be sound.

According to SentencingStats.com data, the average sentence imposed for an offender who committed a similar offense to Rita's was 96.6 months, not the 235 months Rita received.

The sentencing guidelines recommendation for offenders in a position like Rita's ranged from 151 months to 188 on the high end.

"The judge has the discretion to go lower or higher in most cases, so the judge went high all the way to what was the statutory maximum of twenty years, or 235 months," Doug explained on our Zoom call. "Rita had received the highest sentence out of all four offenders in her category. "The eight and a half years that she ended up serving is basically a ten-year sentence, because in the federal system you earn good time credits," he said. "So she essentially served an ordinary ten-year sentence for this crime, which in and of itself is still way higher."

I asked Mark to explain more about the process he used to reach his conclusion that Rita's early release was just. He sent me the raw data set (table E-2). As table E-2 indicates, Rita's sentence was well above other inmates with similar crime profiles.

"As far as the guidelines are concerned, all eighty-four cases are 'similarly situated' to Rita's inasmuch as they all match her guidelines calculations and were not subject to any mandatory minimums/consecutive sentences," Mark said.

"Take a look at the spreadsheet. Look at the 'No5K' tab in the attached," he said. "I eliminated all sentences that resulted from a government motion for a [downward] departure or variance. That left 56. The average sentence was 115.2 months, and the median was 120 months. Arguably, these sentences are even more similarly situated inasmuch as none received a government-sponsored departure/variance. Rita's was far and away the highest. The next-highest sentence was only 188 months. I also forgot to add that Rita received the only upward variance for this group of offenders."

He added, "Rita's sentence literally is sui generis."

This *disturbingly* made sense. As I always say in class, numbers tell stories, but this time, I'm not sure I was ready to hear the story these numbers were telling me.

But the numbers didn't lie. Rita's sentence was an outlier compared with the others in her sentencing class.

Wow. Just wow.

TABLE E-2

Crundwell sentencing guidelines

Year	Months in prison	District	Total restitution
2018	4	New York, Southern	$0
2018	8	New York, Southern	$0
2010	36	Virginia, Eastern	$4,252,751
2012	48	Florida, Southern	$0
2011	60	South Carolina	$0
2010	60	South Carolina	$0
2011	60	Virginia, Eastern	$2,709,238
2016	60	Florida, Middle	$3,200,636
2012	66	Florida, Southern	$0
2014	66	Ohio, Southern	$9,644,602
2019	70	California, Central	$0
2011	72	Tennessee, Middle	$2,661,811
2012	72	Florida, Southern	$0
2012	72	Florida, Southern	$0
2012	78	Florida, Southern	$0
2012	84	Florida, Southern	$2,200,000
2017	84	New York, Eastern	$29,336,497
2017	84	New York, Southern	$0
2011	90	Minnesota	$32,886,849
2014	100	Mississippi, Southern	$0
2010	108	Puerto Rico	$0
2012	108	Florida, Middle	$26,911,074
2011	120	Oklahoma, Western	$9,045,451
2013	120	North Carolina, Western	$3,170,739
2011	120	Mississippi, Southern	$18,068,448
2011	120	Mississippi, Southern	$18,068,448
2012	120	Hawaii	$11,586,335
2014	120	Washington, Western	$18,321,209
2016	120	Virginia, Eastern	$705,500
2019	120	North Carolina, Western	$27,366,774
2016	121	Indiana, Northern	$1,400,000
2014	126	Tennessee, Eastern	$3,091,651
2010	151	Georgia, Northern	$0

(continued)

TABLE E-2 *(continued)*

Crundwell sentencing guidelines

Year	Months in prison	District	Total restitution
2011	151	California, Northern	$2,488,613
2011	151	Iowa, Northern	$10,927,063
2012	151	California, Central	$39,590,212
2013	151	Texas, Western	$0
2013	151	Maryland	$42,196,090
2015	151	California, Central	$3,468,934
2018	151	California, Northern	$0
2018	151	Texas, Southern	$8,970,396
2020	151	California, Central	$0
2020	151	Virginia, Eastern	$23,233,803
2015	156	Alabama, Southern	$0
2014	160	Kentucky, Eastern	$0
2018	165	Texas, Southern	$8,970,396
2013	170	Illinois, Northern	$17,646,084
2016	170	Texas, Western	$25,434,940
2020	170	Utah	$45,258,892
2011	180	Maryland	$9,830,111
2013	188	Florida, Middle	$2,060,621
2019	188	Texas, Southern	$0
2013	235	Illinois, Northern	$53,740,394

Source: SentencingStats.com

In the end, I guess Rita had the last laugh. She stole over $53 million, lived like a queen for decades, and after being caught, served fewer than nine years on an almost twenty-year sentence.

About forty-five thousand inmates were released to home confinement under the Coronavirus Aid, Relief and Economic Security Act (CARES) Act during Covid as of July 2022.[4] None of them are required to report back to prison, though they do remain in the custody of the Bureau of Prisons until they reach probation status.

Righteous perp Keila Ravelo (chapter 3) and intentional perp Bob Lattas (chapter 1) were also released, although Keila was closer to completing her sentence than Bob. Intentional perp Robert Courtney (chapter 1) also applied for early release but was thankfully rejected.[5]

Yep. Rita got the last laugh.

. . .

Dixon, Illinois, has still not fully come back from the wake of the Rita disaster. She stole $54 million, about $40 million of which was returned. That's actually a high number; most people typically only recover pennies on the dollar. But no dollar amount could make up for the emotional betrayal that Dixon residents felt.

"Have we recouped all of the lost trust in government? Of course not," Arellano said. "That is a very long process."

Arellano was a businessman and never really interested in politics, but he ran for office in 2015 precisely because of the Rita fiasco. He watched it unfold and realized just how much corruption was happening in his own backyard. He wanted to do something about it. To his surprise, he won. He was even elected for a second term in 2019.

Although the city has hardly recovered—a word "I'm always careful of," Arellano said—things are slowly moving forward. But one detail in the Rita debacle was a huge kick in the teeth: her 2021 release from prison. This old wound never truly healed. Mayor Arellano announced his bid for the Republican candidacy for State Representative in January 2022.

. . .

While I know that all perps aren't bad, I'm conflicted about Rita Crundwell. I don't have the same empathy for her that I have for other perps, even the intentional ones.

I'm sure Kathe feels betrayed by the system, which was put in place supposedly to protect her and other victims. I'm not a Dix-onite, but I teach consequences: *If you commit X crime, then Y will happen to you.* The ending of Rita's story threw a big wrench into my teaching plans. Would Kathe have blown the whistle if she thought that a little more than eight years later, she'd once again be living in the same town as her former boss? I don't think so.

• • •

While I've never met Rita Crundwell in person, many of the white-collar offenders I've encountered over the years have since become my friends. They've taught me some of the most valuable lessons in fraud detection. Thanks to them, I understand the *why* for every archetype category.

When we hear stories, our brains allow us to see ourselves in the story. These fraud archetypes have helped me better understand my varied reactions to the many fraud cases and individuals who visit my forensic accounting classes. These archetypes help me understand why I can empathize with some white-collar felons and understand how their fraud started and feel angry with others.

Understanding the *Fool Me Once* archetypes could help you identify potential flaws within your systems and develop more effective training programs. Intentional perps can find the weaknesses in a system and use those for personal gain. Scenario-based training opportunities can expose potential intentional perpetrators' thought processes and help you identify internal control weaknesses so that you can thwart future fraud attacks. Accidental perps often develop in high-pressure environments where unattainable goals are set. Righteous perps can also develop when we don't spend enough time getting to know our colleagues and understanding their passions and or personal pressures they may face.

As for prey, the innocent bystander category should terrify all of us. The best piece of advice is to remember that you're always a sitting duck. There are some situations in which we're vulnerable, and we can't protect ourselves from them. Organizational targets, however, always know who has access to their most important intellectual property. The person or the system that has this coveted access will always be a target.

The presence of whistleblowers is a sign of a healthy organization. A study conducted by Stephen Stubben and Kyle Welch found that the more employees use internal whistleblowing hotlines, the fewer lawsuits companies face, and the less money firms pay out in settlements.[6] The increased use of internal hotlines tends to signal improved communication between employees and management. Accidental whistleblowers, noble whistleblowers and even vigilantes should be protected and celebrated. Accidentals and noble whistleblowers are not looking for the fraud they find, but their information is valuable. And although vigilante whistleblowers can appear like organizational troublemakers, take a deep breath and a step back and closely analyze what they're trying to show and tell you.

Perhaps my most shocking realization is my evolved understanding of Rita Crundwell's sentencing. Though I was initially outraged, the data has informed me that Rita is an intentional perp outlier who could one day join the crossover category to help us understand fraud from her point of view. It's unlikely, but stranger things have happened.

One thing to remember is that the fraud schemes don't really change. The schemes have stayed pretty constant for eons; what has significantly changed is who is engaging in fraud. No longer are the players con artists and career criminals, but employees, doctors, and government officials (well, that may not be new). In other words, the people who commit fraud are the people you least suspect.

This new breed of white-collar offender is the reason why implementing sound internal controls and utilizing scenario-based learning when developing ethics training programs and during quarterly (not annual) compliance training is so critical.

• • •

When you began reading this book, you may have thought that all perpetrators of fraud were the same. Prosecutors would agree with that, arguing that they all do it for greed, to live lavish lifestyles. Some people do things for the good of others, even if it means breaking the law. But there are nuances to each category, and those nuances humanize us all.

Even if you thought you understood intentional perps, the most ubiquitous type of perp, I hope I've helped you see how and why they ended up doing what they did. That's not to say you would do the same thing, but at least you can see how their crime started and the circumstances that led to the crime.

While you might never identify with the intentional perps— they're the people movies are made about—you may become an accidental perp without even knowing it. Just as clearly, you could become an innocent bystander without knowing it until it's way too late. Your company, in turn, could easily be an organizational target.

I remember when Cheryl Obermiller (chapter 5) told me that simply "opening the mail" could have prevented her accountant's million-dollar embezzlement. That would have shown Tammie that Cheryl was paying attention to her business.

"What an easy, cost-effective strategy," I thought at the time. It's such an important and valuable lesson for business owners and organizations.

Innocent bystanders must always remember to pay attention to the red flags that wave around them (and remember my personal red flag list from chapter 4), especially the ones we typically ignore. Our natural instinct is to trust. Still, it's better, certainly in business, to assume that someone shouldn't be trusted, and then you will be prepared when fraud happens.

Targeted organizations may consider hiring a "white hat" hacker—that is, an ethical computer security company like Social-Proof Security.

SocialProof Security helps people and organizations understand how they could get hacked. This, in turn, helps them stay safe from cybercriminals. "No one is immune from hacking," said CEO and cofounder Rachel Tobac. With the right pretext and timing, anyone can get hacked. It's essential that every organization understands how hacking happens and what specific tools and protocols to implement to reduce their risk as much as possible.

Not long ago, a well-known bank hired SocialProof to hack it and understand how a cybercriminal could bypass its identity verification systems in its customer support flows to take over customer accounts. "We were able to take over two accounts within one day," Rachel told me. "The bank was very thankful that we were able to do a controlled hack and train them before the bad folks got there first."

You must also train staff and employees in best practices and establish a chief information officer to oversee your systems.

Please use the *Fool Me Once* archetypes to remind yourself of the various categories. These archetypes have allowed me to better analyze and understand the roller-coaster of emotions I feel when I encounter a fraud case (and remember: cross-pollination happens). This could be a vital resource in protecting your organization when fraud happens. As the Civil War taught us, *it takes a rogue to catch a rogue*. My hope is that this book has helped you reflect on ways you can prevent fraud from spreading within your organization and stop yourself from ever being fooled again.

What's Next for Me?

Since I started studying this topic back in 1998, I've had some pretty wild adventures, but none as amazing as the one I'm about to share.

One afternoon I received a LinkedIn message. *"We're making a film on the most controversial figure in crypto and exploring whether his token is real or a scam,"* it said. *"Would you be up for a discussion about the project, your potential role and see if there could be a fit?"*

The message was from filmmaker Patrick Moreau of Muse Storytelling. I didn't know him, but I was interested in the topic. I knew nothing about cryptocurrency and have always had some yellow flags about the subject, but I wanted to learn more.

Patrick and I set up a call, thinking we would just continue to meet over Zoom. But he surprised me.

"We'd love to fly out to Chicago and meet with you to share more about the film," he said.

"Fly to Chicago? Really?"

Red flags waved in my face. This sounded fishy. So I googled this man and tried to find out everything I could about him. He seemed legit, so we set a date to meet.

Four days later, Patrick and his partner Grant Peele appeared in Chicago for a Saturday meeting. Patrick was wearing a blazer with a pocket square (he's Canadian). Grant wore a sleeveless tech vest. They looked harmless. These were real people not looking to steal my identity. My red flags slowly began to lower.

We met for a little over an hour, and the film sounded exciting.

"We're going to Spain next week to meet the founder of this crypto coin," Patrick said. Then he invited me to join.

My mind was blown. Go to Spain to investigate a potential crypto scam with a film team I met on LinkedIn?

I started doing hours of research on bitcoin, cryptocurrency, de-financing, Ethereum, and, of course, the controversial founder. People were making billions of dollars investing in cryptocurrency. Was this the fastest-appreciating asset ever or a total scam? It sounded way too good to be true, and I was more than intrigued.

Within a matter of days, a business-class ticket to Spain was sitting in my inbox. Equipped with my fraud archetypes, tons of questions about cryptocurrency, and pump-and-dump schemes (artificially inflating the price through misleading statements in order to sell the cheaper stock at a higher price), I was ready to start my investigation.

I packed my bags and headed to the south of Spain.

Interview day arrived, and I was ready to meet the founder. At this point, I've interviewed tons of white-collar felons, but speaking to a *potential* scam artist requires a different set of skills.

A car picked me up and we arrived on set. A white Ferrari and black McLaren were parked in front of a modern, white Mediterranean mansion on a mountain cliff. The front door seemed to be made of thick Brazilian wood and was about thirty feet tall.

The founder was waiting for me, dressed in a full Gucci jump-suit, Gucci tennis shoes, Rolex watch, and diamond-embossed medallion. He wore his wealth like skin.

"Ohhhh boyyyyy," I thought. "What have I gotten myself into?"

He welcomed me into the dining room to begin the interview.

My first question was for him to explain his crypto coin. He responded with a slew of the most difficult, four-syllable technical words that you could imagine. My first red flag shot up. As the late P. J. O'Rourke wrote in the April 2002 issue of *The Atlantic*, "Beyond a certain point complexity *is* fraud."[1] I was beyond that point. My head began pounding so hard that I had to ask for an aspirin. For real.

The more we talked, the more questions I had. The more questions I asked, the more convoluted the responses. None of it made sense. And it was exactly my kind of story . . .

NOTES

Introduction

1. D. Carozza, "Dixon's Quiet Hero," *Fraud Magazine*, November–December 2018, https://www.fraud-magazine.com/cover-article.aspx?id=4295003585.

2. A. Grimm, M. Jenco, and *Chicago Tribune* reporters, "Small Town Rocked by $30 Million Theft Case," *Chicago Tribune*, August 23, 2021. Retrieved July 29, 2022, from https://www.chicagotribune.com/news/ct-xpm-2012-04-18-ct-met-dixon-comptroller-embezzle-charges-20120418-story.html; M. Jenco, "Dixon CFO Fired Following Misconduct Scandal," *Chicago Tribune*, August 23, 2021, https://www.chicagotribune.com/news/ct-xpm-2012-04-23-chi-dixon-cfo-fired-following-misconduct-scandal-20120423-story.html.

3. T. A. Press, "NCCU Chancellor under Pressure\Richmond May Resign, Trustee Says," *Greensboro News and Record*, January 25, 2015). Retrieved July 29, 2022, from https://greensboro.com/nccu-chancellor-under-pressure-richmond-may-resign-trustee-says/article_568d275a-b5b6-5473-9e95-08ca53a43dcd.html.

4. Marc Vitali, "All the Queen's Horses' Tells the Story of Rita Crundwell," *WTTW News*, November 13, 2017. Retrieved July 29, 2022, from https://news.wttw.com/2017/11/13/all-queen-s-horses-tells-story-rita-crundwell; N. Metz, "Chicago Professor Turns Filmmaker in Quest to Unravel Dixon Embezzlement," *Chicago Tribune*, December 17, 2018. Retrieved July 29, 2022, from https://www.chicagotribune.com/entertainment/movies/ct-mov-all-the-queens-horses-kelly-pope-interview-20171106-story.html.

5. K. R. Pope, "What 20 Film Festival Rejections Taught Me about Resilience," *Forbes*, August 8, 2017. Retrieved July 29, 2022, from https://www.forbes.com/sites/kellypope/2017/08/08/what-20-film-festival-rejections-taught-me-about-resilience/?sh=4f5fd9e94476.

6. PwC, *Fighting Fraud: A Never-Ending Battle*, PwC's Global Economic Crime and Fraud Survey 2020. Retrieved February 15, 2022, from https://www.pwc.com/gx/en/forensics/gecs-2020/pdf/global-economic-crime-and-fraud-survey-2020.pdf.

7. L. Daly, "Covid-19 Fraud Statistics: $100 Million in Losses and Counting," The Ascent, *The Motley Fool*, October 27, 2021. Retrieved February 14, 2022, from https://www.fool.com/the-ascent/research/covid-19-stimulus-check-fraud-statistics/.

8. N. Chilingerian, "Digital Fraud Attempts Up 46% Globally Since Pandemic Began: TransUnion," *Credit Union Times*, March 25, 2021. Retrieved July 27, 2022, from https://www.cutimes.com/2021/03/25/digital-fraud-attempts-up-46-globally-since-pandemic-began-transunion/?slreturn=20220627230149.

9. TransUnion, "Global Fraud Trends: Device Insights Highlight Increased Threats Since Onset of Pandemic," *TransUnion* blog, March 22, 2021. Retrieved July 28, 2022, from https://www.transunion.com/blog/global-fraud-trends-Q1-2021.

10. TransUnion, "Global Fraud Trends."

11. "30 Million People Across 10 Countries Were Victims of Cybercrime in 2020," Help Net Security, April 14, 2021. Retrieved June 17, 2022, from https://www.helpnetsecurity.com/2021/04/14/victims-of-cybercrime/.

12. Daly, "Covid-19 Fraud Statistics."

13. Chilingerian, "Digital Fraud Attempts Up 46 Percent."

14. Association of Certified Fraud Examiners, "ACFE Report to the Nations," press release, April 16, 2020. Retrieved February 14, 2022, from https://www.acfe.com/press-release.aspx?id=4295010563.

15. Association of Certified Fraud Examiners, *Occupational Fraud 2022: A Report to the Nations*, ACFE, 2022. Retrieved June 5, 2022, from https://acfepublic.s3.us-west-2.amazonaws.com/2022+Report+to+the+Nations.pdf.

16. R. Rubin, "High-Income Tax Avoidance Far Larger Than Thought, New Paper Estimates," *Wall Street Journal*, March 22, 2021. Retrieved February 14, 2022, from https://www.wsj.com/articles/high-income-tax-avoidance-far-larger-than-thought-new-paper-estimates-11616364001?mod=itp_wsj&ru=yahoo.

17. SEC, "SEC Expands the Scope of Smaller Public Companies That Qualify for Scaled Disclosures," press release, June 28, 2018. Retrieved July 27, 2022, from https://www.sec.gov/news/press-release/2018-116.

18. SEC press release.

19. E. Bumiller, "Bush Signs Bill Aimed at Fraud In Corporations," *New York Times*, July 31, 2002. Retrieved July 28, 2022, from https://www.nytimes.com/2002/07/31/business/corporate-conduct-the-president-bush-signs-bill-aimed-at-fraud-in-corporations.html.

20. SEC, "SEC Expands the Scope of Smaller Public Companies That Qualify for Scaled Disclosures," press release, June 28, 2018. Retrieved July 27, 2022, from https://www.sec.gov/news/press-release/2018-116.

21. B. Carmody, "Only 0.04 Percent of Companies Reach $100 Million in Annual Revenue. Here's the 1 Thing Driving YapStone's Explosive Growth," *Inc.com*, December 24, 2015. Retrieved July 27, 2022, from https://www.inc.com/bill-carmody/only-0-04-reach-100-million-in-annual-revenue-here-s-the-one-thing-driving-yapst.html.

22. PwC, *Protecting the Perimeter: The Rise of External Fraud*, PWC's Global Economic Crime and Fraud Survey 2022. Retrieved July 28, 2022, from https://www.pwc.com/gx/en/services/forensics/economic-crime-survey.html.

23. "Ford Says Charges Against Pinto Are 'Rehash' of 1977 Allegations," *New York Times*. October 15, 1979. Retrieved July 28, 2022, from https://www.nytimes.com/1979/10/15/archives/ford-says-charges-against-pinto-are-rehash-of-1977-allegations.html.

24. Andrew Gordon, *Integrity in the Spotlight: The Future of Compliance*, 15th Global Fraud Survey. EY, June 10, 2019. Retrieved July 28, 2022, from https://assets .ey.com/content/dam/ey-sites/ey-com/en_gl/topics/assurance/assurance-pdfs /ey-integrity-in-spotlight.pdf.

25. J. Ewing, "Volkswagen and BMW Are Fined Nearly $1 Billion for Colluding on Emissions Technology," *New York Times*, July 8, 2021. Retrieved February 14, 2022, from https://www.nytimes.com/2021/07/08/business/volkswagen-bmw -daimler-emissions-scandal.html.

26. S. Mathis, "Harriette Walters Sentenced to 17.5 Years in Prison," *DCist*, June 30, 2009. Retrieved February 14, 2022, from https://dcist.com/story/09/06/30 /harriette-walters-sentenced-to-175/.

27. D. Nosowitz, "The Inside Story of One of the Biggest Organic Farm Scams in History," *Modern Farmer*, January 22, 2020. Retrieved February 14, 2022, from https://modernfarmer.com/2020/01/the-inside-story-of-one-of-the-biggest -organic-farm-scams-in-history/.

28. E. Griffith and E. Woo, "Elizabeth Holmes Is Found Guilty of Four Counts of Fraud," *New York Times*. January 4, 2022. Retrieved July 28, 2022, from https://www.nytimes.com/2022/01/03/technology/elizabeth-holmes -guilty.html.

29. P. Reilly, Cash Injection: NY Nurses Busted for Forging VAX Cards in $1.5M Scheme," *New York Post*, January 29, 2022. Retrieved February 14, 2022, from https://nypost.com/2022/01/29/long-island-nurses-julie-devuono-marissa -urraro-busted-in-900k-fake-vax-card-scheme/.

30. E. Javers and S. Zamost, "Criminals Have Stolen Nearly $100 Billion in Covid Relief Funds, Secret Service Says," *CNBC*, December 21, 2021. Retrieved February 14, 2022, from https://www.cnbc.com/2021/12/21/criminals-have-stolen -nearly-100-billion-in-covid-relief-funds-secret-service.html.

31. Association of Certified Fraud Examiners, *Occupational Fraud 2022: A Report to the Nations,* ACFE. Retrieved July 28, 2022, from https://legacy.acfe.com /report-to-the-nations/2022/.

32. Whistleblower Protection Act of 1989, S. 20, 101st Congress (1989).

33. "Jeffrey Wigand," National Whistleblower Center. Retrieved July 28, 2022, from https://www.whistleblowers.org/whistleblowers/jeffrey-wigand/.

34. D. Kerr and M. Rivero, *Whistleblower Peter Buxtun and the Tuskegee Syphilis Study,* Government Accountability Project, April 30, 2014. Retrieved July 28, 2022, from https://whistleblower.org/uncategorized/whistleblower -peter-buxtun-and-the-tuskegee-syphilis-study/.

35. J. L. Albini, "Donald Cressey's Contribution to the Study of Organized Crime: An Evaluation," *Crime and Delinquency* 34, no. 3 (July 1988): 338–354. Retrieved July 28, 2022, from https://www.ojp.gov/ncjrs/virtual-library /abstracts/donald-cresseys-contribution-study-organized-crime-evaluation.

Section One

1. Kelly Richmond Pope, dir. *All the Queen's Horses*. Kartemquin Films/Helios Digital Learning, 2017.

Chapter 1

1. N. Cowan et al. "Foundations of Arrogance: A Broad Survey and Framework for Research," *Qualitative Inquiry* 23, no. 4 (2019): 147–150. Retrieved July 29, 2022, from https://journals.sagepub.com/doi/10.1177/1089268019877138.

2. D. L. Paulhus and K. M. Williams, "The Dark Triad of Personality: Narcissism, Machiavellianism, and Psychopathy," *Journal of Research in Personality* 36, no. 6 (2002): 556–563, https://doi.org/10.1016/S0092-6566(02)00505-6.

3. R. Rogoza et al., "The Bright, the Dark, and the Blue Face of Narcissism: The Spectrum of Narcissism in Its Relations to the Meta Traits of Personality, Self-Esteem, and the Nomological Network of Shyness, Loneliness, and Empathy," *Frontiers in Psychology*, March 14, 2018. Retrieved February 15, 2022, from https://www.frontiersin.org/articles/10.3389/fpsyg.2018.00343/full.

4. E. Patterson, "What Is Grandiose Narcissism?" *Choosing Therapy*, August 13, 2021. Retrieved February 15, 2022, from https://www.choosingtherapy.com /grandiose-narcissism/.

5. PwC, *Fighting Fraud: A Never-Ending Battle*, PwC's Global Economic Crime and Fraud Survey 2020. Retrieved February 15, 2022, from https://www.pwc.com /gx/en/forensics/gecs-2020/pdf/global-economic-crime-and-fraud-survey-2020.pdf.

6. Miles & Stockbridge, P.C., "The Stark Law and Anti-Kickback Statute Final Rules: Value-Based Arrangements," *JD Supra*, April 9, 2021. Retrieved February 15, 2022, from https://www.jdsupra.com/legalnews/the-stark-law -and-anti-kickback-statute-5189041/; LLP, "The Anti-Kickback Statute and Stark Law," Constantine Cannon, July 20, 2021. Retrieved February 15, 2022, from https://constantinecannon.com/practice/whistleblower/whistleblower-types /healthcare-fraud/anti-kickback-stark/.

7. N. Cowan et al. "Foundations of Arrogance: A Broad Survey and Framework for Research.

8. J. A. Shepperd et al., "A Primer on Unrealistic Optimism," *Current Directions in Psychological Science* 24, no. 3 (June 2015): 232–237, doi: 10.1177/0963721414568341.

9. T. Sharot, "The Optimism Bias," *Time*, May 28, 2011. Retrieved February 15, 2022, from http://content.time.com/time/health/article/0,8599,2074067,00.html.

10. Sharot, "The Optimism Bias."

11. *United States v. Chez*, Crim. No. 07-00546 (ND Ill.) (GWL). Indictment filed August 23, 2007.

12. *United States of America v. Robert D. Lattas*, No. 13 CR 463-2 (January 11, 2021).

13. *United States v. Lattas.*

14. *United States v. Lattas.*

15. J. Bilyk, "Illinois Supreme Court Disbars 13 Attorneys, Suspends 16 Others, in September," *Cook County Record*, September 30, 2016. Retrieved February 15, 2022, from https://cookcountyrecord.com/stories/511014172-illinois-supreme -court-disbars-13-attorneys-suspends-16 others-in-september.

16. Bilyk, "Illinois Supreme Court Disbars."

17. *United States v. Lattas.*

18. M. Poteet, "What Exactly Is a Compounding Pharmacist?" Compounding Pharmacy of America, June 30, 2014. Retrieved February 15, 2022 from https://compoundingrxusa.com/blog/exactly-compounding-pharmacist/.

19. K. Gaines, "Nursing Ranked as the Most Trusted Profession for 20th Year in a Row," *Nurse.org*. Retrieved February 15, 2022, from https://nurse.org/articles /nursing-ranked-most-honest-profession/.

20. R. E. Pierre, "Pharmacist Admits He Diluted Drugs," *Washington Post*, February 27, 2002. Retrieved July 28, 2022, from https://www.washingtonpost .com/archive/politics/2002/02/27/pharmacist-admits-he-diluted-drugs/d1e95b42 -a058-4df1-a41f-bb50665fd0ee/.

21. D. Collins, "Drug-Diluting Pharmacist Gets 30 Years," *CBS News*, December 6, 2002. Retrieved July 28, 2022, from https://www.cbsnews.com/news/drug-diluting -pharmacist-gets-30-years/.

22. Pierre, "Pharmacist Admits He Diluted Drugs."

23. Based on a one-on-one interview between Tom Hughes and Kelly Richmond Pope and class notes from ACC 635: Principles of Forensic Accounting on or around February 2013.

24. E. Primeaux, "How a Fraudster's First Stolen Dollar Turned into Much More," *Fraud Conference News*, July 1, 2019. Retrieved July 29, 2022, from https://www.fraudconferencenews.com/home/2019/6/29/stealing-will-turn-you -into-a-thief.

Chapter 2

1. "People-Pleasing," *Psychology Today* website, (n.d.). Retrieved February 15, 2022, from https://www.psychologytoday.com/us/basics/people-pleasing/.

2. J. Dean, "*Asch Conformity Experiment: The Power of Social Pressure*," *PsyBlog*, September 14. 2021. Retrieved July 28, 2022, from https://www.spring.org.uk/2021 /06/asch-conformity-experiment.php.

3. S. E. Asch, "Effects of Group Pressure upon the Modification and Distortion of Judgment," in *Groups, Leadership and Men*, ed. H. Guetzkow (Pittsburgh: Carnegie Press, 1951); "Asch Conformity Experiment Explained," *Modern Therapy*, July 17, 2019. Retrieved July 28, 2022, from https://moderntherapy.online/blog-2 /asch-conformity-experiment-explained.

4. L. Borreli, "People-Pleaser: Brain Scans Show Pushovers Agree with Others to Avoid Mental Stress," *Medical Daily*, March 2, 2016. Retrieved July 28, 2022, from https://www.medicaldaily.com/people-pleaser-brain-activity-mental-stress-376139.

5. *United States v. Johnson*, Crim. No. 03-1153 (D Ill.) (JBZ). Indictment filed 12/10/03.

6. Based on a one-on-one interview between Andrew Johnson and Kelly Richmond Pope, filmed at DePaul University School of Accounting and Management Information Systems on or around July 27, 2016.

7. T. Segal, "Enron Scandal: The Fall of a Wall Street Darling," *Investopedia*, November 26, 2021. Retrieved February 15, 2022, from https://www.investopedia .com/updates/enron-scandal-summary/.

8. I. Suh, et al., "Boiling the Frog Slowly: The Immersion of C-Suite Financial Executives into Fraud," *Journal of Business Ethics*, July 19, 2018. Retrieved February 15, 2022, from https://www.thecaq.org/wp-content/uploads/2018/03 /Suh-et-al-Journal-of-Business-Ethics-published-20181.pdf.

9. *Crossing the Line: Ordinary People Committing Extraordinary Crimes*, directed and produced by Kelly Richmond Pope in 2013.

10. Based on a one-on-one interview between Diann Cattani and Kelly Richmond Pope on or around May 2013, filmed in Atlanta, Georgia.

11. S. Israelsen-Hartley, "Greed Is No Respecter of Persons; Y Grad., Convicted Felon Shares Her Cautionary Tale," *Deseret News*, March 5, 2011. Retrieved February 15, 2022, from https://www.deseret.com/2011/3/6/20177489 /greed-is-no-respecter-of-persons-y-grad-convicted-felon-shares-her-cautionary -tale#diann-cattani-lectures-to-college-students-about-how-to-avoid-moral-gray -areas-and-keep-themselves-away-from-rationalizing.

12. N. Garrett, "The Brain Adapts to Dishonesty," *Nature Neuroscience* 19, 1727–1732 (2016). https://doi.org/10.1038/nn.4426. Retrieved February 15, 2022.

13. L. ten Brinke, J. J. Lee, and D. R. Carney, "The Physiology of (Dis)Honesty: Does It Impact Health?" *Current Opinion in Psychology* 6 (December 2015): 177–182. Retrieved February 15, 2022, from https://www.sciencedirect.com /science/article/pii/S2352250X15001980.

14. T. Wheatcroft, "Expense Fraud Costs U.S. Employers $2.8 Billion per Year, Shows Chrome River Survey," *BusinessWire*, March 29, 2016. Retrieved February 15, 2022, from https://www.businesswire.com/news/home /20160329005218/en/Expense-Fraud-Costs-U.S.-Employers-2.8-Billion -per-Year-Shows-Chrome-River-Survey.

15. Association of Certified Fraud Examiners, *Occupational Fraud 2022: A Report to the Nations*, ACFE, 2022. Retrieved June 5, 2022, from https://acfepublic .s3.us-west-2.amazonaws.com/2022+Report+to+the+Nations.pdf.

16. S. Ball, "How to Tackle the UK Scourge of Expenses Fraud," GPA, November 23, 2021. Retrieved June 17, 2022, from https://globalpayrollassociation .com/blogs/regional-focus/how-to-tackle-the-uk-scourge-of-expenses-fraud.

17. Wheatcroft, "Expense Fraud Costs U.S. Employers."

18. "The Unusual Suspect," *Course Hero* (n.d.). Retrieved July 28, 2022, from https://www.coursehero.com/file/60305881/The-Unusual-Suspectdocx/; "Preview: The Unusual Suspect: Understanding Employee Embezzlement: Forensic Accounting" (n.d.), *Helios Online Catalog*. Retrieved July 29, 2022, from https:// store.heliosdigital.com/product?catalog=preview-0001-tus.

19. D. Inman, "$428 Billion in Merchandise Returned in 2020," National Retail Federation, January 11, 2021. Retrieved February 15, 2022, from https://nrf.com /media-center/press-releases/428-billion-merchandise-returned-2020.

20. T. Rittman, "Nine Tactics Consumers Use to Make Fraudulent Returns," *Chain Store Age*, December 3, 2012. Retrieved February 15, 2022, from https://chainstoreage.com/news/nine-tactics-consumers-use-make -fraudulent-returns.

Chapter 3

1. J. Gordon, "Robin Hood Effect (Economics)—Explained," *The Business Professor*, July 1, 2021. Retrieved February 15, 2022, from https:// thebusinessprofessor.com/en_US/economic-analysis-monetary-policy /robin-hood-effect-definition.

2. J. Paonessa, "Robin Hoods: A Myth in Flux," *Western Illinois Historical Review* V (Spring 2013). Retrieved February 15, 2022, from http://www.wiu.edu /cas/history/wihr/pdfs/Paoness-RobinHoodVol5.pdf.

3. J. Williams, "Billionaire Who Said He Would Pay Off Morehouse Student Debt Admits to Tax Fraud," *The Hill*, October 16, 2020. Retrieved February 15, 2022, from https://thehill.com/policy/finance/521389-billionaire-who-said-he -would-pay-off-morehouse-student-debt-admits-to-tax.

4. "The Good Will," *Kant's Philosophy* (Immanuel Kant blog), February 24, 2012. Retrieved February 15, 2022, from https://kantphilosophy.wordpress.com /kants-ethics/the-good-will/#:~:text=Happiness%20is%20not%20intrinsically %20good,unconditional%20good%20despite%20all%20encroachments.

5. C. Morgan, "Is Corruption Ever Ethically Permissible?" *Arkansas Journal of Social Change and Public Service* (February 7, 2017). Retrieved February 15, 2022, from https://ualr.edu/socialchange/2013/10/09/is-corruption-ever -ethically-permissible/.

6. "Ezekiel 18:7b—The Righteous Man Does Not Steal, but Instead Feeds the Hungry and Clothes the Naked," *Theology of Work Project*, (n.d.). Retrieved February 15, 2022, from https://www.theologyofwork.org/old-testament/ezekiel /ezekiel-18/he-commits-no-robbery-gives-his-bread-to-the-hungry-and-covers -the naked.

7. University of Texas McCombs School of Business, "Edward Snowden: Traitor or Hero?" *Ethics Unwrapped* (blog) September 11, 2017. Retrieved February 15, 2022, from https://ethicsunwrapped.utexas.edu/case-study/edward-snowden -traitor-hero.

8. "U.S. Congress Passes Espionage Act," History.com, A&E Television Networks, November 5, 2009. Retrieved February 15, 2022, from https://www .history.com/this-day-in-history/u-s-congress-passes-espionage-act.

9. L. Dishman, "Scientific Proof That Your Gut Is Best at Making Decisions," *Fast Company*, July 31, 2015. Retrieved February 15, 2022, from https://www .fastcompany.com/3049248/scientific-proof-that-your-gut-is-best-at-making -decisions.

10. J. Ovia, "You Already Know the Answer: Learn to Trust and Follow Your Instincts," *Forbes* Books Author Post, *Forbes*, September 19, 2018. Retrieved July 28, 2022, from https://www.forbes.com/sites/forbesbooksauthors/2018/09/19/you -already-know-the-answer-learn-to-trust-and-follow-your-instincts/.

11. S. M. Müller et al., "Decision Making—a Neural Psychological Perspective," Somatic Marker Hypothesis, *ScienceDirect*, September 17, .2021, Retrieved February 15, 2022, from https://www.sciencedirect.com/topics/neuroscience /somatic-marker-hypothesis.

12. "What Does 'Possession: Close of Escrow' Mean?" Real Estate Glossary, *Redfin*, January 2020. Retrieved February 15, 2022, from https://www.redfin.com /definition/possession-closeof-escrow.

13. FBI: Chicago Division, "Attorney Among Four Defendants Indicted in Alleged $16.2 Million Mortgage Fraud Scheme Involving at Least 35 Residential Loans," FBI, June 4, 2012. Retrieved February 15, 2022, from https://archives .fbi.gov/archives/chicago/press-releases/2012/attorney-among-four-defendants -indicted-in-alleged-16.2-million-mortgage-fraud-scheme-involving-at-least -35-residential-loans.

14. *United States of America v. Hakeem Rashid, Kareem Broughton, Marguerite Elise Dixon-Roper, Jada Elaine Lucas* (United States District Court Northern District of Illinois Eastern Division January 2012).

15. FBI: Chicago Division, "Attorney Among Four Defendants Indicted."

16. *United States of America vs. Hakeem Rashid*. Indictment June 2012.

17. *United States v. Ravelo*, Crim. No.15-57, (D. NJ) (KM). Criminal Complaint filed 12/19/14.

Section Two

1. M. Hendrickson, "$5M Ticket Reselling Scheme's Victims Included Economist at U. of C.," *Chicago Sun-Times*, December 4, 2018. Retrieved February 16, 2022, from https://chicago.suntimes.com/2018/12/4/18314941/5m -ticket-reselling-scheme-s-victims-included-economist-at-u-of-c.

2. Kelly Richmond Pope, dir. *All the Queen's Horses*. Kartemquin Films/Helios Digital Learning, 2017.

Chapter 4

1. GAO, "Identity Theft and Tax Fraud: Enhanced Authentication Could Combat Refund fraud, but IRS Lacks an Estimate of Costs, Benefits and Risks," GAO-15-119, US GAO, February 19, 2015. Retrieved February 16, 2022, from https://www.gao.gov/products/gao-15-119.

2. N. Faulkner, *The Multi-Faceted Threat of Fraud: Are Banks up to the Challenge?*. KPMG, May 2019. Retrieved February 16, 2022, from https://home .kpmg/xx/en/home/insights/2019/05/the-multi-faceted-threat-of-fraud-are-banks -up-to-the-challenge-fs.html.

3. *Treasury Inspector General for Tax Administration*, "TIGTA Releases Public Service Announcements Warning Taxpayers of the Ongoing Threat of IRS Impersonation Scams," press release, June 10, 2022, retrieved July 28, 2022, from https://www.treasury.gov/tigta/press/press_tigta-2022-01.htm.

4. R. Reber and N. Schwarz, "Effects of Perceptual Fluency on Judgments of Truth," *Consciousness and Cognition* 8, no. 3 (1999): 338–342, https://doi .org/10.1006/ccog.1999.0386.

5. K. R. Pope, "Even the Best of Us Get Duped, Professors Included," *Forbes*, December 14, 2018. Retrieved July 9, 2022, from https://www.forbes.com/sites /kellypope/2018/12/07/even-the-best-of-us-get-duped-even-professors/.

6. Oracle and KPMG, *Keeping Pace at Scale: The Impact of the Cloud-Enabled Workplace on Cybersecurity Strategies,* Oracle and KPMG Cloud Threat Report, 2018, https://www.oracle.com/a/ocom/docs/cloud/oracle-cloud-threat-report-2018 .pdf.

7. G. Topham, "Boeing Admits Full Responsibility for 737 MAX Plane Crash in Ethiopia," *The Guardian*, November 11, 2021. Retrieved February 16, 2022, from https://www.theguardian.com/business/2021/nov/11/boeing-full -responsibility-737-max-plane-crash-ethiopia-compensation.

8. D. Gates and M. Baker, "The Inside Story of MCAS: How Boeing's 737 Max System Gained Power and Lost Safeguards," *Seattle Times*, June 24, 2019. Retrieved February 16, 2022, from https://www.seattletimes.com/seattle-news/times -watchdog/the-inside-story-of-mcas-how-boeings-737-max-system-gained -power-and-lost-safeguards/.

9. "Boeing Commercial Airplanes: A Better Way to Fly," Boeing website. Retrieved February 16, 2022, from https://www.boeing.com/commercial /#:~:text=Today%2C%20there%20are%20more%20than,bottom%2Dline %20performance%20to%20operators.

10. *Downfall: The Case Against Boeing*, directed by Rory Kennedy, written by M. Bailey and K. McAlester, Netflix, February 18, 2022, https://www.google .com/url?sa=t&rct=j&q=&esrc=s&source=web&cd=&cad=rja&uact=8&ved =2ahUKEwiQkJGh4t35AhXdFFkFHQmrDhYQFnoECBUQAQ&url =https%3A%2F%2Fwww.netflix.com%2Ftitle%2F81272421&usg =AOvVaw3CSSsbMZpxvie5HD6N85Nq.

11. History.com editors, "Kitty Genovese," History.com. A&E Television Networks, May 20, 2021. Retrieved February 16, 2022, from https://www.history .com/topics/crime/kitty-genovese.

12. I. Hussain et al., "The Voice Bystander Effect: How Information Redundancy Inhibits Employee Voice," *Academy of Management Journal* 62, no. 3 (2019): 828–849, https://doi.org/10.5465/amj.2017.0245.

13. "The U.S. Public Health Service Syphilis Study at Tuskegee," Centers for Disease Control and Prevention, *Tuskegee Study and Health Benefit Program,* Centers for Disease Control and Prevention, April 22, 2021. Retrieved July 27, 2022, from https://www.cdc.gov/tuskegee/index.html.

14. "Tuskegee Dispute Near Settlement," *New York Times*, December 15, 1974. Retrieved July 29, 2022, from https://www.nytimes.com/1974/12/15/archives /tuskegee-dispute-near-settlement.html; J. Heller, "AP Was There: Black Men Untreated in Tuskegee Syphilis Study," *AP News,* May 10, 2017. Retrieved February 16, 2022, from https://apnews.com/article/business-science-health-race -and-ethnicity-syphilis-e9dd07eaa4e74052878a68132cd3803a.

15. US National Archives, "Remarks by the President in Apology for Study Done in Tuskegee," May 16, 1997. Retrieved February 16, 2022, from https:// clintonwhitehouse4.archives.gov/textonly/New/Remarks/Fri/19970516-898.html.

16. A. Gill, A. Rivas, and K. Walker, "Family of Tuskegee Syphilis Study Participant Say They'll Take COVID-19 Vaccine but Understand the Distrust," *ABC News*, December 17, 2020. Retrieved February 16, 2022, from https://abcnews .go.com/Health/family-tuskegee-syphilis-study-participant-theyll-covid-19 /story?id=74787123.

17. R. E. Pierre, "Pharmacist Admits He Diluted Drugs," *Washington Post*, February 27, 2002. Retrieved July 28, 2022, from https://www.washingtonpost .com/archive/politics/2002/02/27/pharmacist-admits-he-diluted-drugs/d1e95b42 -a058-4df1-a41f-bb50665fd0ee/.

18. K. T. Higgins, "Industry Hardens Defenses Against Food Fraud, Counterfeiting Threats," *Foodprocessing.com*, May 4, 2017. Retrieved February 16, 2022, from https://www.foodprocessing.com/articles/2017/defenses-against -food-fraud/.

19. A. Silvio and L. Orlando, "Don't Fall Victim to Olive Oil Fraud," *CBS News*, January 4, 2016. Retrieved February 16, 2022, from https://www.cbsnews.com /news/60-minutes-overtime-how-to-buy-olive-oil/.

20. Centers for Disease Control and Prevention, "Foodborne Germs and Illnesses," Centers for Disease Control and Prevention, March 18, 2020. Retrieved February 16, 2022, from https://www.cdc.gov/foodsafety/foodborne-germs.html.

21. World Health Organization, "Estimating the Burden of Foodborne Diseases," WHO, (n.d.). Retrieved July 29, 2022, from https://www.who.int /activities/estimating-the-burden-of-foodborne-diseases.

22. M. Basu, "28 years for Salmonella: Peanut Exec Gets Groundbreaking Sentence," September 22, 2015, CNN. Retrieved February 16, 2022, from https://www .cnn.com/2015/09/21/us/salmonella-peanut-exec-sentenced/index.html.

23. D. Flynn, "Parnell Brothers Finally in Prison for Deadly Peanut Butter Outbreak," *Food Safety News*, July 31, 2018. Retrieved February 16, 2022, from https://www.foodsafetynews.com/2016/02/123674/.

24. L. Buder, "Beech-Nut Is Fined $2 Million for Sale of Fake Apple Juice," *New York Times*, November 14, 1987. Retrieved February 16, 2022, from https://www.nytimes.com/1987/11/14/business/beech-nut-is-fined-2-million -for-sale-of-fake-apple-juice.html.

25. "2008 Chinese Milk Scandal," Wikimedia Foundation, modified January 19, 2022. Retrieved February 16, 2022, from https://en.wikipedia.org/wiki/2008 _Chinese_milk_scandal#:~:text=The%202008%20Chinese%20milk %20scandal,components%20being%20adulterated%20with%20melamine .&text=The%20scandal%20was%20first%20exposed,were%20diagnosed%20with %20kidney%20stones.

26. T. E. Holmes, "Fraud by a Fiduciary Can Be Especially Costly," AARP, January 26, 2022. Retrieved February 16, 2022, from https://www.aarp .org/money/scams-fraud/info-2021/financial-advisor.html?intcmp=AE -FRDSC-MOR-R2-POS3.

27. Based on an interview between the late Mary West and Kelly Richmond Pope on or around June 2015, filmed in Asheville, NC.

28. R. W. Wood, "What is 1031 Exchange? Know the Rules,"*Investopedia*, November 7, 2021, https://www.investopedia.com/financial-edge/0110/10-things -to-know-about-1031-exchanges.aspx.

Chapter 5

1. PwC, *Fighting Fraud: A Never-Ending Battle*, PwC's Global Economic Crime and Fraud Survey 2020. Retrieved February 15, 2022, from https://www.pwc.com /gx/en/forensics/gecs-2020/pdf/global-economic-crime-and-fraud-survey-2020.pdf.

2. T. Ziezulewicz and *Tribune* reporter, "Romeoville Church Copes with Volunteer's Theft," *Chicago Tribune*, November 4, 2021. Retrieved July 29, 2022, from https://www.chicagotribune.com/suburbs/ct-xpm-2014-06-10-ct-church -embezzlement-romeoville-tl-0612-20140610-story.html.

3. Association of Certified Fraud Examiners, *ACFE Report to the Nations: 2018 Global Fraud Study*, ACFE, 2018. Retrieved February 16, 2022, from https://s3 -us-west-2.amazonaws.com/acfepublic/2018-report-to-the-nations.pdf; Association of Certified Fraud Examiners, "The Average Fraud Costs Companies More Than $1.5 Million," *ACFE Report to the Nations* press release, April 15, 2020. Retrieved February 14, 2022, from https://www.acfe.com/about-the-acfe/newsroom-for -media/press-releases/press-release-detail?s=report-to-the-nations-2020; Association of Certified Fraud Examiners, *Occupational Fraud 2022: A Report to the Nations*, ACFE, 2022. Retrieved July 28, 2022, from https://legacy.acfe.com /report-to-the-nations/2022/.

4. ACFE, "The Average Fraud Costs Companies More Than $1.5 Million."

5. ACFE, "The Average Fraud Costs Companies More Than $1.5 Million."

6. ACFE, *Occupational Fraud 2022*.

7. "How Much Money Do ATMs Hold? And How Much Money Is in an ATM?" fxski.com. https://fxski.com/how-much-money-do-atms-hold-how-much-money -is-in-an-atm/#:~:text=ATMs%20hold%20anywhere%20from%20%2450%2C000 %20to%20%2480%2C000%20in,their%20ATMs%20to%20accommodate %20increased%20demand%20from%20consumers. June 8, 2022.

8. FBI, "Bank Robbery," "What We Investigate," FBI. Retrieved July 29, 2022, from https://www.fbi.gov/investigate/violent-crime/bank-robbery.

9. Based on a one-on-one interview between Cheryl Obermiller and Kelly Richmond Pope on or around May 2015, filmed in Harrisonville, Missouri, at Obermiller Construction; "Beauty & the Beast: Understanding the Importance of Internal Controls," Helios Digital Learning (n.d.). Retrieved July 29, 2022, from https://helios.remote-learner.net/course/info.php?id=1117.

10. ACFE, *Occupational Fraud 2022*.

11. ACFE, *Occupational Fraud 2022*.

12. ACFE, *Occupational Fraud 2022*.

13. U.S. Attorney's Office Western District of Missouri, "Overland Park Woman Pleads Guilty to Embezzling $400,000 from Employer in Bank Fraud Scheme," FBI, March 8, 2011. Retrieved February 17, 2022, from https://archives .fbi.gov/archives/kansascity/press-releases/2011/kc030811.htm.

14. J. A. Luna, "The Toxic Effects of Branding Your Workplace a 'Family,'" *Harvard Business Review*, October 27, 2021. Retrieved February 17, 2022, from https://hbr.org/2021/10/the-toxic-effects-of-branding-your-workplace-a -family.

15. "Because Who Has Better Security Tips Than a Former Identity Thief?" *NBCNews.com* (January 14, 2018). Retrieved July 29, 2022, from https://www .nbcnews.com/business/consumer/former-identity-thief-now-fights-crimes -he-helped-perfect-n837166.

16. N. Vardi, *Criminal Outbreak, Forbes*, June 6, 2013. Retrieved July 29, 2022, from https://www.forbes.com/forbes/2004/1227/116.html?sh=1c63dda61072.

17. E. Prey, "The Life of a Cybercriminal with Brett Johnson," *Easy Prey*, podcast. March 18, 2021. Retrieved July 30, 2022, from https://www.easyprey .com/the-life-of-a-cybercriminal-with-brett-johnson/.

18. J. Howarth, "The Ultimate List of Cyber Attack Stats (2022)," *Exploding Topics*, February 12, 2022. Retrieved July 29, 2022, from https://explodingtopics .com/blog/cybersecurity-stats#covid-and-cybercrime.

19. C. Stokel-Walker, "More Than 40 Billion Records Were Exposed in 2021," *Cybernews*, January 28, 2022. Retrieved July 29, 2022, from https://cybernews.com /security/more-than-40-billion-records-were-exposed-in-2021/.

20. "COVID-19 Pandemic Leaves Consumers Vulnerable to Cybercrime," *Bloomberg.com*, April 13, 2021. Retrieved July 29, 2022, from https://www .bloomberg.com/press-releases/2021-04-13/covid-19-pandemic-leaves-consumers -vulnerable-to-cybercrime.

21. "330 Million People Across 10 Countries Were Victims of Cybercrime in 2020," Help Net Security, April 14, 2021. Retrieved June 17, 2022, from https://www.helpnetsecurity.com/2021/04/14/victims-of-cybercrime/.

22. C. Pete, "Question: What Is the Budapest Convention on Cybercrime?" Absolute Tours, Budapest, May 13, 2021. Retrieved July 29, 2022, from https://absolutebudapest.com/faq/question-what-is-the-budapest-convention-on-cybercrime.html.

23. N. Schwellenbach and R. Summers, *Red Flags: The First Year of COVID-19 Loan Fraud Cases*, Project on Government Oversight (n.d.). Retrieved July 29, 2022, from https://www.pogo.org/investigation/2021/04/red-flags-the-first-year-of-covid-19-loan-fraud-cases.

24. Schwellenbach and Summers, *Red Flags.*

25. M. LaCrosse, "Former Owner of Beverly Pizzeria Charged with Covid-relief Fraud," CBS Boston, May 4, 2021. Retrieved February 17, 2022, from https://boston.cbslocal.com/2021/05/04/dana-mcintyre-ppp-loan-fraud-rasta-pasta-pizzeria/.

26. "Coppell Man Pleads Guilty to $24 Million Covid-Relief Fraud Scheme," The United States Department of Justice, March 24, (2021. Retrieved July 29, 2022, from https://www.justice.gov/usao-ndtx/pr/coppell-man-pleads-guilty-24-million-covid-relief-fraud-scheme.

27. Office of Public Affairs, "Texas Man Pleads Guilty to $24 Million COVID-Relief Fraud Scheme," US Department of Justice, March 24, 2021. Retrieved February 17, 2022, from https://www.justice.gov/opa/pr/texas-man-pleads-guilty-24-million-covid-relief-fraud-scheme.

28. U.S. Attorney's Office, "Issaquah, Washington Man Pleads Guilty to COVID-19 Relief Fraud Scheme." US Department of Justice, January 21, 2021. Retrieved February 17, 2022, from https://www.justice.gov/usao-wdwa/pr/issaquah-washington-man-pleads-guilty-covid-19-relief-fraud-scheme.

29. "Phases of Unemployment Fraud After COVID-19," Thomson Reuters (n.d.). Retrieved July 29, 2022, from https://legal.thomsonreuters.com/en/insights/articles/phases-of-unemployment-after-covid.

30. "Phases of Unemployment Fraud After COVID-19.

31. "Justice Department Announces Director for Covid-19 Fraud Enforcement," US Department of Justice, March 10, 2022. Retrieved July 29, 2022, from https://www.justice.gov/opa/pr/justice-department-announces-director-covid-19-fraud-enforcement.

Section Three

1. K. R. Pope, "How Whistle-Blowers Shape History," TED Talk (n.d.). https://www.ted.com/talks/kelly_richmond_pope_how_whistle_blowers_shape_history.

2. N. Fandos, and M. Haberman, "White House Whistle-Blower Tells Congress of Irregularities in Security Clearances," *New York Times*, April 1, 2019. Retrieved February 19, 2022, from https://www.nytimes.com/2019/04/01/us/politics/trump-security-clearances.html.

3. "What Is Moral Injury?" The Moral Injury Project, Syracuse University (n.d.). Retrieved February 19, 2022, from https://moralinjuryproject.syr.edu/about-moral-injury/.

4. N. Walsh, "How to Encourage Employees to Speak Up When They See Wrongdoing," *Harvard Business Review*, February 4, 2021. Retrieved July 29, 2022, from https://hbr.org/2021/02/how-to-encourage-employees-to-speak-up-when-they-see-wrongdoing.

5. K. R. Pope, "How Whistle-Blowers Shape History," *Forbes*, December 26, 2018. Retrieved July 29, 2022, from https://www.forbes.com/sites/kellypope/2018/12/26/the-truth-about-whistle-blowers/?sh=467a2cf6a9b3.

6. Piacentile, Stefanowski, Gonzalez & Associates LLP, "Whistleblowing History Overview," Whistleblowers International, September 2, 2021. Retrieved February 19, 2022, from https://www.whistleblowersinternational.com/what-is-whistleblowing/history/.

7. T. Agovino, "Whistleblowers: An Early Detection System," SHRM, February 1, 2020. Retrieved February 19, 2022, from https://www.shrm.org/hr-today/news/all-things-work/pages/whistleblowers-an-early-detection-system.aspx.

8. The Hesch Firm LLC, "The Definition of the Term 'Relator' Under the Qui Tam Provisions of the False Claims Act," The Hesch Firm LLC. March 27, 2019. Retrieved February 19, 2022, from https://www.howtoreportfraud.com/the-definition-of-the-term-relator-under-the-qui-tam-provisions-of-the-false-claims-act/.

9. The False Claims Act of 1863. 1 U.S.C. §§ 3729–3733. Retrieved July 29, 2022, from https://www.justice.gov/civil/false-claims-act.

10. A. Hayes, "Dodd-Frank Wall Street Reform And Consumer Protection Act," *Investopedia*, February 11, 2022. Retrieved February 19, 2022, from https://www.investopedia.com/terms/d/dodd-frank-financial-regulatory-reform-bill.asp.

11. Office of Public Affairs, "Justice Department Recovers Over $2.2 Billion from False Claims Act Cases in Fiscal Year 2020," US Department of Justice, January 14, 2021. Retrieved February 19, 2022, from https://www.justice.gov/opa/pr/justice-department-recovers-over-22-billion-false-claims-act-cases-fiscal-year-2020.

12. *United Nations Convention Against Corruption,* United Nations Office on Drugs and Crime—National Whistleblower Center, 2004. Retrieved July 29, 2022, from https://www.whistleblowers.org/wp-content/uploads/2018/10/un-convention-against-corruption.pdf.

13. *United Nations Convention Against Corruption*, United Nations Office on Drugs and Crime, n.d. Retrieved June 29, 2022, from https://www.unodc.org/unodc/en/treaties/CAC/.

14. H. Latan et al., "'Whistleblowing Triangle': Framework and Empirical Evidence," *Journal of Business Ethics* 160 (2019): 189–204, https://doi.org/10.1007/s10551-018-3862-x.

Chapter 6

1. Kelly Richmond Pope, dir. *All the Queen's Horses*. Kartemquin Films/Helios Digital Learning, 2017.

2. D. Carozza, "Dixon's Quiet Hero," *Fraud Magazine*, November/December 2018. https://www.fraud-magazine.com/cover-article.aspx?id=4295003585; Pope, *All the Queen's Horses*.

3. Pope, *All the Queen's Horses*.

4. Carozza, "Dixon's Quiet Hero."

5. Pope, *All the Queen's Horses*.

6. S. Stephens, "Former Dixon City Clerk Honored for Whistleblowing in Rita Crundwell Case," Northern Public Radio: WNIJ and WNIU, October 30, 2017. Retrieved July 29, 2022, from https://www.northernpublicradio.org/government /2017-10-30/former-dixon-city-clerk-honored-for-whistleblowing-in-rita-crundwell -case.

7. *United States v. Mueller*, Crim. No. 08-00206 (D. Minn.) (PJS). Indictment filed 7/7/08.

8. *Mood in the Middle*. Helios Digital Learning. Retrieved July 29, 2022, from http://helioscpe.com/; Based on a class interview with students enrolled in ACC 635 Principles of Forensic Accounting at DePaul University on or around March 20, 2013 filmed at the home of Nathan Mueller in the suburbs of Minneapolis, MN.

9. J. Pritchard, "ING Direct History & Merger with Capital One," *The Balance*, May 1, 2021. Retrieved February 19, 2022, from https://www.thebalance.com /ing-direct-banking-reviews-315149.

10. *Mood in the Middle*.

11. *Mood in the Middle*.

12. M. Nigrini and N. Mueller, "Lessons from an $8 Million Fraud," *Journal of Accountancy*, August 1, 2014. Retrieved February 19, 2022, from https://www .journalofaccountancy.com/issues/2014/aug/fraud-20149862.html.

13. *Mood in the Middle*.

14. *Mood in the Middle*.

15. American Bankers Association, *Deposit Account Fraud Survey*, ABA, January 1, 2020. Retrieved February 19, 2022, from https://www.aba.com/news -research/research-analysis/deposit-account-fraud-survey-report.

16. Nigrini and Mueller, "Lessons from an $8 Million Fraud."

17. *United States v. Mueller*, Crim. No. 08-00206 (D. Minn.) (PJS). Indictment filed July 7, 2008.

18. *Mood in the Middle*.

19. *Mood in the Middle*.

20. "Global Banking Fraud Survey: The Multi-Faceted Threat of Fraud: Are banks up to the challenge," KPMG. May 2019, Retrieved February 16, 2022, from https://home.kpmg/xx/en/home/insights/2019/05/the-multi-faceted-threat-of -fraud-are-banks-up-to-the-challenge-fs.html.

21. A. Waytz, J. Dungan, and L. Young, "The Whistleblower's Dilemma and the Fairness-Loyalty Tradeoff," Northwestern Scholars, March 19, 2016. Retrieved July 29, 2022, from https://www.scholars.northwestern.edu/en/publications /the-whistleblowers-dilemma-and-the-fairness-loyalty-tradeoff.

22. K. R. Pope, "Wells Fargo and Millennial Whistle-Blowing? What Do We Tell Them?" *Forbes*, September 24, 2016. Retrieved July 29, 2022, from https://www .forbes.com/sites/kellypope/2016/09/23/wells-fargo-and-millenial-whistle-blowing -what-do-we-tell-them/?sh=6cb22ab1ece9.

23. M. Levine, "Wells Fargo Opened a Couple Million Fake Accounts," Bloomberg.com, September 9, 2016. Retrieved February 19, 2022, from https:// www.bloomberg.com/opinion/articles/2016-09-09/wells-fargo-opened-a-couple -million-fake-accounts.

24. M. Levine, "Wells Fargo Opened a Couple Million Fake Accounts."

25. M. Egan, "Wells Fargo Workers: I Called the Ethics Line and Was Fired," *CNNMoney*, September 21, 2016. Retrieved February 19, 2022, from https://money .cnn.com/2016/09/21/investing/wells-fargo-fired-workers-retaliation-fake-accounts /index.html.

26. Egan, "Wells Fargo Workers."

Chapter 7

1. M. O'Dwyer, "PWC Fined over Exam Cheating Involving 1,100 of Its Auditors," *Financial Times*, February 25, 2022. Retrieved July 29, 2022, from https://www.ft.com/content/2e246b48-a6a9-4dc6-b4fb-136b62ab3a3a.

2. O'Dwyer, "PWC Fined over Exam Cheating."

3. H. Berkes, "Remembering Roger Boisjoly: He Tried to Stop Shuttle Challenger Launch," NPR, February 6, 2012. Retrieved February 19, 2022, from https://www.npr.org/sections/thetwo-way/2012/02/06/146490064/remembering -roger-boisjoly-he-tried-to-stop-shuttle-challenger-launch.

4. "N.C. A&T Taps Alumna, Professor and Filmmaker as Fall Commencement Speaker," North Carolina Agricultural and Technical State University (November 6, 2019). Retrieved July 29, 2022, from https://www.ncat.edu/news/2019/11/fall -commencement-2019.php#:~:text=EAST%20GREENSBORO%2C%20N.C. %20%28Nov.%206%2C%202019%29%20%E2%80%93%20Professor%2C,at %20Greensboro%20Coliseum%2C%201921%20W.%20Gate%20City%20Blvd/.

5. Berkes, "Remembering Roger Boisjoly."

6. Berkes, "Remembering Roger Boisjoly"; Associated Press, "Engineer to Get Award for Warning on Shuttle," *New York Times*, January 28, 1988. Retrieved July 29, 2022, from https://www.nytimes.com/1988/01/28/us/engineer-to-get-award -for-warning-on-shuttle.html.

7. Based on a one-on-one interview with Jackie McLaughlin and Kelly Richmond Pope on or around May 2013, filmed at Wake Forest University.

8. "Preview: Whistling While You Work: The Story of One Controller," Helios Online Catalog (n.d.). Retrieved July 29, 2022, from https://store.heliosdigital.com /product?catalog=preview-0006-WWYW.

9. E. L. Hamilton et al., "The Naughty List or the Nice List? Earnings Management in the Days of Corporate Watchdog Lists," Institute of Management Accountants, August 2018. Retrieved February 19, 2022, from https://www.imanet .org/-/media/f133e24fca9645d49bc157faaad30c13.ashx.

10. J. H. Amernic and R. J. Craig, "Accounting as a Facilitator of Extreme Narcissism," *Journal of Business Ethics* 96 (2010); 79–93. Retrieved February 19, 2022, from https://link.springer.com/article/10.1007/s10551-010-0450-0.

11. R. Downie, "GAAP vs. Non-GAAP: What's the Difference?" *Investopedia*, May 19, 2021. Retrieved February 19, 2022, from https://www.investopedia.com /articles/financial-analysis/062716/gaap-vs-nongaap-which-should-you-consider -evaluation.asp.

12. N. Garrett et al., "The Brain Adapts to Dishonesty," *Nature Neuroscience* 19 (2016): 1727–1732. Retrieved February 19, 2022, from https://www.nature.com /articles/nn.4426.

13. Downie, "GAAP vs. Non-GAAP."

14. "Preview: Whistling While You Work."

15. "Preview: Whistling While You Work."

16. "Preview: Whistling While You Work."

17. Ethics Resource Center, *Retaliation: When Whistleblowers Become Victims*, 2012. Retrieved July 30, 2022, from https://www.bozeman.net/home/showdocument?id=502.

18. T. M. Marcum, J. D. Young, and J. Young, *Blowing the Whistle in the Digital Age* (2019). Retrieved February 19, 2022, from https://www.whistleblowers.org/wp-content/uploads/2019/10/Marcum-Young-2019-Blowing-the-Whistle-in-the-Digital-Age.pdf.

19. Reuters, "Whistleblower Gets Record $24 Million for Exposing Hyundai and Kia's Safety Lapses," CNN, November 9, 2021. Retrieved February 19, 2022, from https://edition.cnn.com/2021/11/09/cars/nhtsa-whistleblower-award-hyundai/index.html.

20. Reuters, "Whistleblower Gets Record $24 Million."

21. See, for example, Associated Press, "Hyundai, Kia Recall 1.4m v=Vehicles; Engines Can Fail. WINK NEWS. Retrieved July 30, 2022, from https://www.winknews.com/2017/04/07/hyundai-kia-recall-1-4m-vehicles-engines-can-fail/.

22. Z. Strozewski, "Whistleblower Who Reported That Hyundai-Kia Moved Too Slowly on Major Recall Awarded $24M," *Newsweek*, November 9, 2021, https://www.newsweek.com/whistleblower-who-reported-that-hyundai-kia-moved-too-slowly-major-recall-awarded-24m-1647630.

23. J. S. Kwaak, "Hyundai Whistle-Blower, in Rarity for South Korea, Prompts Recall," *New York Times*, May 16, 2017. Retrieved July 30, 2022, from https://www.nytimes.com/2017/05/16/business/hyundai-south-korea-whistle-blower-recall.html.

24. Kwaak, "Hyundai Whistle-Blower."

25. Reuters, "Whistleblower Gets Record $24 Million."'

26. "Auto Safety—Motor Vehicle Safety Whistleblower Act," Constantine Cannon, November 9, 2021, Retrieved July 30, 2022, from https://constantinecannon.com/practice/whistleblower/whistleblower-types/auto-safety/.

27. Reuters, "Whistleblower Gets Record $24 Million."

28. R. L. Nave, "Abraham Bolden: A Betrayed Pioneer Still Trying to Clear His Name," *Ebony*, November 11, 2016. Retrieved February 19, 2022, from https://www.ebony.com/news/abraham-bolden-secret-service/.

29. A. Bolden, *The Echo from Dealey Plaza: The True Story of the First African American on the White House Secret Service Detail and His Quest for Justice After the Assassination of JFK* (New York: Three Rivers Press, 2008).

30. Nave, "Abraham Bolden."

31. Nave, "Abraham Bolden."

32. M. Mitchell, "First White House Black Secret Service Agent Still Trying to Clear His Name," *Chicago Sun-Times*, April 23, 2021. Retrieved February 19, 2022, from https://chicago.suntimes.com/columnists/2021/4/23/22400324/abraham bolden first black secret service agent pardon efforts.

33. "Secret Service Agent Accused," *Reading Eagle*, May 20, 1964. Retrieved February 19, 2022, from https://news.google.com/newspapers?id=aSArAAAAIBAJ&pg=5240%2C2208206.

34. *JFK Assassination Records,* National Archives and Records Administration, October 29, 2018. Retrieved February 19, 2022, from https://www.archives.gov /research/jfk/select-committee-report.

35. F. Chideya, "Secret Service Agent Tells True-Life Tale of Intrigue," NPR, March 24, 2008. Retrieved February 19, 2022, from https://www.npr.org/transcripts /88965136.

36. "Clemency Recipient List," The White House, April 26, 2022. Retrieved July 30, 2022, from https://www.whitehouse.gov/briefing-room/statements-releases /2022/04/26/clemency-recipient-list/.

37. K. R. Pope, "Conversations with a Coast Guard Whistleblower," *Forbes,* April 14, 2020. Retrieved July 9, 2022, from https://www.forbes.com/sites/kellypope /2020/04/13/conversations-with-a-coast-guard-whistleblower/?sh=5120366a678c/; K. R. Pope, "Conversations with a Coast Guard Whistleblower: Part 2," *Forbes,* April 27, 2020. Retrieved July 9, 2022, from https://www.forbes.com/sites /kellypope/2020/04/26/conversations-with-a-coast-guard-whistleblower-part-2/.

38. *Testimony of Lieutenant Commander Kimberly C. Young-McLear, Ph.D. (USCG) to the Civil Rights and Civil Liberties Subcommittee Transportation and Maritime Security Subcommittee U.S. House of Representatives,* December 11, 2019.

39. William M. (Mac) Thornberry National Defense Authorization Act for Fiscal Year 2021. GovInfo (n.d.). Retrieved July 30, 2022, from https://www.govinfo .gov/content/pkg/PLAW-116publ283/html/PLAW-116publ283.htm.

40. House Armed Services Committee, "The Facts: Delivering Real Reforms to Address the Military Sexual Assault Crisis," December 13, 2021. Retrieved July 30, 2022, from https://armedservices.house.gov/2021/12/the-facts-delivering-real -reforms-to-address-the-military-sexual-assault-crisis.

41. K. R. Pope, "Conversations with a Hospital Whistleblower," *Forbes,* May 1, 2020. Retrieved July 30, 2022, from https://www.forbes.com/sites/kellypope /2020/04/27/conversations-with-a-hospital-whistleblower/?sh=2f4341bd5323.

42. Pope, "Conversations with a Hospital Whistleblower."

43. Pope, "Conversations with a Hospital Whistleblower."

44. Pope, "Conversations with a Hospital Whistleblower."

45. Pope, "Conversations with a Hospital Whistleblower."

Chapter 8

1. K. DeCelles and K. Aquino, *Vigilantes at Work: Examining the Frequency of Dark Knight Employees,* SSRN, May 2, 2017. Retrieved February 24, 2022, from https://papers.ssrn.com/sol3/papers.cfm?abstract_id=296094.

2. P. Skrbina, "Jackie Robinson West Wins U.S. Championship at Little League World Series," *Chicago Tribune,* August 19, 2019. Retrieved July 30, 2022, from https://www.chicagotribune.com/sports/breaking/ct-chicago-little-league-world -series-spt-0824-20140824-story.html.

3. K. R. Pope, "Who Really Blew It? Jackie Robinson West Coaches or Chris Janes?" *Forbes,* February 25, 2015. Retrieved July 30, 2022, from https://www .forbes.com/sites/kellypope/2015/02/13/who-really-blew-it-jackie-robinson-west -coaches-or-chris-janis/?sh=79444f733d79.

4. CBS Interactive, "Coach Who Accused JRW of Cheating Sues Little League," *CBS News*, September 20, 2016. Retrieved July 30, 2022, from https://www.cbsnews .com/chicago/news/jackie-robinson-west-chris-janes-lawsuit/.

5. CBS Interactive, "Coach Who Accused JRW of Cheating Sues."

6. M. Evans, "Jackie Robinson West Won't Get 2014 National Title Back, but Coaches Say They're Vindicated After Little League Drops Fraud Suit," *Block Club Chicago*, April 28, 2021. Retrieved July 30, 2022, from https://blockclubchicago .org/2021/04/28/jackie-robinson-west-wont-get-2014-national-title-back-but -coaches-say-theyre-vindicated-after-little-league-drops-fraud-suit/.

7. SI Wire, "Little League: Jackie Robinson West Title Stripped Due to Fraud, Cover-Up," *Sports Illustrated*, August 12, 2015. Retrieved July 30, 2022, from https://www.si.com/more-sports/2015/08/12/little-league-jackie-robinson-west -fraud-cover-up-world-series-title-stripped.

8. M. Konkol, "Jackie Robinson West Whistleblower Faces Depaul Ethics Class," *DNAinfo Chicago*, February 18, 2015. Retrieved July 30, 2022, from https:// www.dnainfo.com/chicago/20150218/morgan-park/jackie-robinson-west -whistleblower-faces-depaul-ethics-class/.

9. K. R. Pope, "Wells Fargo and Millennial Whistle-Blowing? What Do We Tell Them?" *Forbes*, September 24,2016. Retrieved July 29, 2022, from https://www .forbes.com/sites/kellypope/2016/09/23/wells-fargo-and-millenial-whistle-blowing -what-do-we-tell-them/?sh=6cb22ab1ece9.

10. T. Daniels, "Jackie Robinson West Parents Sue ESPN, Little League over Ineligible Players," *Bleacher Report*, September 22, 2017. Retrieved February 24, 2022, from https://bleacherreport.com/articles/2616118-jackie-robinson-west -parents-sue-espn-little-league-over-ineligible-players.

11. S. Ganim and D. Sayers, "UNC Athletics Report Finds 18 Years of Academic Fraud," CNN, October 23, 2014. Retrieved February 24, 2022, from https://www .cnn.com/2014/10/22/us/unc-report-academic-fraud/index.html.

12. Based on a one-on-one interview between Mary Willingham and Kelly Richmond Pope on or around June 2015, filmed at the home of Mary Willingham in Chapel Hill, North Carolina.

13. M. C. Willingham, "Academics & Athletics—A Clash of Cultures: Division I Football Programs," (master's thesis, University of North Carolina Greensboro, 2009). Retrieved July 30, 2022, from https://libres.uncg.edu/ir/uncg/f/Willingham _uncg_0154M_10097_updated.pdf.

14. *Gameday: A Whistle-Blower's Story of the UNC Academic Fraud Case*, The Helios Digital Library (n.d.). Retrieved July 30, 2022, from http://www .heliosdigital.com/library.html.

15. S. Gregory, "In College Sports, a New $100 Million Industry Emerges," *Time*, September 10, 2021. Retrieved February 24, 2022, from https://time.com /6094842/college-sports-nil-operndorse/.

16. S. Ganim, "CNN Analysis: Some College Athletes Play Like Adults, Read Like 5th-Graders," CNN, January 8, 2014. Retrieved July 30, 2022, from https://www.cnn.com/2014/01/07/us/ncaa-athletes-reading-scores.

17. "Athletes' Tendencies to 'Cluster' in Certain Academic Fields Problematic, Some Say," *Lawrence Journal-World*, June 15, 2012. Retrieved July 30, 2022, from https://www2.ljworld.com/news/2012/jun/15/athletes-tendencies-cluster -certain-academic-field/; Z. P. Square, "Why Student Athletes Continue to Fail,"

Time, April 20, 2015. Retrieved July 30, 2022, from https://time.com/3827196 /why-student-athletes-fail/.

18. *The Atlantic Coast Conference*. North Carolina–Atlantic Coast Conference (n.d.). Retrieved July 30, 2022, from https://theacc.com/index.aspx?path=north _carolina.

19. "By the Numbers," University of North Carolina at Chapel Hill website. Retrieved February 21, 2022, from https://www.unc.edu/about/by -the-numbers/.

20. B. N. Hayes, "UNC Athletics Surpasses $100 Million Mark," InsideCarolina .com (January, 18, 2019). Retrieved July 30, 2022, from https://247sports.com /college/north-carolina/Article/UNC-Athletics-Basketball-Football-100-Million -128024785/.

21. S. Ganim, "UNC 'Fake Classes' Whistleblower to Get $335k in Settlement," CNN, March 17, 2015. Retrieved February 25, 2022, from https://www.cnn.com/2015/03/17/us/north-carolina-willingham-unc -settlement/index.html.

22. A. Thomason, "The Confounding Case of Jan Boxill," *Chronicle of Higher Education,* September 22, 2021. Retrieved July 30, 2022, from https://www .chronicle.com/article/the-confounding-case-of-jan-boxill.

23. K. L. Wainstein, A. J. Jay, and C. D. Kukowski, *Investigation of Irregular Classes in the Department of African and Afro-American Studies at the University of North Carolina at Chapel Hill*, October 16, 2014.

24. S. Ganim, "CNN Analysis."

25. S. Lyall, "Reporter Digging into Scandal Hits a University's Raw Nerve," *New York Times*, April 26, 2014. Retrieved July 30, 2022, from https://www .nytimes.com/2014/04/27/sports/reporter-digging-into-scandal-hits-a-universitys -raw-nerve.html.

26. "Former UNC Advisor Mary Willingham Files Lawsuit Against University After NCAA Reopens Investigation," ABC11 Raleigh-Durham, July 1, 2014. Retrieved July 30, 2022, from https://abc11.com/unc-ncaa-investigation -scandal/149570/.

27. ESPN Internet Ventures, "UNC to Pay $335k in Settlement," ESPN, March 17, 2015. Retrieved July 30, 2022, from https://www.espn.com/college-sports/story/_/id/12498874/university-north-carolina-pay-335000-academic -fraud-whistleblower.

28. "Accreditors Place UNC on One Year of Probation," *Carolina Alumni Review*, posted June 11, 2015. Retrieved July 30, 2022, from https://alumni.unc.edu /news/accreditors-place-unc-on-one-year-of-probation/.

29. "SACS Restores UNC to Full Accreditation," *Carolina Alumni Review*, June 16, 2016. Retrieved July 30, 2022, from https://alumni.unc.edu/news/sacs -restores-unc-to-full-accreditation/.

30. J. Nocera, "She Had to Tell What She Knew," *New York Times*, May 6, 2014. Retrieved July 30, 2022, from https://www.nytimes.com/2014/05/06/opinion /nocera-she-had-to-tell-what-she-knew.html.

31. Nocera, "She Had to Tell What She Knew."

32. Mark J. Drozdowski, "The College Admissions Scandal That Shook Higher Ed," BestColleges.com, May 6, 2022. Retrieved July 30, 2022, from https://www .bestcolleges.com/blog/operation-varsity-blues-college-admissions-scandal/.

33. "Here's How the F.B.I. Says Parents Cheated to Get Their Kids into Elite Colleges," *New York Times*, March 12, 2019. Retrieved July 30, 2022, from https://www.nytimes.com/2019/03/12/us/admissions-scandal.html.

34. ACFE, *ACFE Report to the Nations: 2022 Global Fraud Study*, 2022. Retrieved July 28, 2022, from https://legacy.acfe.com/report-to-the-nations/2022/.

35. K. R. Pope, "When Children Need to Become Whistle-Blowers: A Response to the College Admissions Fraud Scandal," *Forbes*, March 14, 2019. Retrieved July 30, 2022, from https://www.forbes.com/sites/kellypope/2019/03/13/when-children-need-to-become-whistle-blowers-a-response-to-the-college-admissions-fraud-scandal/?sh=20bf37977ad2.

36. K. R. Pope, "Thou Shalt Not Lie . . . ," *Forbes*, September 8, 2017. Retrieved July 30, 2022, from https://www.forbes.com/sites/kellypope/2017/09/07/thou-shalt-not-lie-2/?sh=24521c3f5b03.

Chapter 9

1. *Crossing the Line: Ordinary People Committing Extraordinary Crimes* directed and produced by Kelly Richmond Pope in 2013.

2. Based on a one-on-one interview between Weston Smith and Kelly Richmond Pope on or around June 2016, filmed at DePaul University.

3. "Preview: Going South: Lessons Learned from the HealthSouth Fraud," Helios Online Catalog (n.d.). Retrieved July 30, 2022, from https://store.heliosdigital.com/product?catalog=preview-0002-gs.

4. "Preview: Going South."

5. S. Taub, "Ex-HealthSouth CFO to Pay $6.9 Million," *CFO*, July 24, 2006. Retrieved July 30, 2022, from https://www.cfo.com/risk-compliance/2006/07/ex-healthsouth-cfo-to-pay-6-9-million-3402/.

6. "Preview: Going South."

7. M. Cohn et al., "Informant Blew the Whistle on Price Fixing at ADM," *Accounting Today*, June 21, 2012. Retrieved July 30, 2022, from https://www.accountingtoday.com/opinion/informant-blew-the-whistle-on-price-fixing-at-adm.

8. H. Henderson, "Crime in the Suits," *Chicago Reader*, May 31, 2001. Retrieved July 30, 2022, from https://chicagoreader.com/news-politics/crime-in-the-suits/.

Epilogue

1. R. Waters, "Federal Compassionate Release in the Era of COVID-19: Practice Tips," Americanbar.org, December 11, 2020. Retrieved July 30, 2022, from https://www.americanbar.org/groups/litigation/committees/criminal/articles/2020/winter2021-federal-compassionate-release-in-the-era-of-covid-19-practice-tips/.

2. K. R. Pope, "Will Jailed Dixon Embezzler Be Released from Federal Prison? Maybe," *Forbes*, May 9, 2020. Retrieved July 9, 2022, from https://www.forbes.com/sites/kellypope/2020/05/09/will-jailed-dixon-embezzler-be-released-from-federal-prison-maybe/.

3. K. R. Pope, "Will Jailed Dixon Embezzler Be Released."

4. "Frequently Asked Questions Regarding Potential Inmate Home Confinement in Response to the COVID-19 Pandemic," *Federal Bureau of Prisons* (n.d.). Retrieved July 30, 2022, from https://www.bop.gov/coronavirus/faq.jsp.

5. S. Kaut, "Federal Judge Denies Robert Courtney's Attempt to Leave Federal Prison," KSHB. Retrieved February 15, 2022, from https://www.kshb.com/news /local-news/federal-judge-denies-robert-courtneys-attempt-to-leave-federal-prison.

6. S. Stubben and K. Welch, "Research: Whistleblowers Are a Sign of Healthy Companies," *Harvard Business Review*, November 14, 2018. Retrieved February 20, 2022, from https://hbr.org/2018/11/research-whistleblowers-are-a-sign-of-healthy -companies.

Coda

1. P. J. O'Rourke, "How to Stuff a Wild Enron," *The Atlantic Monthly,* April 1, 2002. Retrieved from https://www.theatlantic.com/magazine/archive/2002/04 /how-to-stuff-a-wild-enron/302468/Epilogue.

INDEX

ACKNOWLEDGMENTS

There are so many people who have made *Fool Me Once* possible, but I must start with Lorence Pope, aka Lon, my husband and biggest cheerleader. Lon, thank you for putting up with it all. I'm sure you've thought for years that I've been running in circles, but now, hopefully, you can see how a lifetime of work has culminated in this book. There have been a lot of late nights, long trips, missed vacations and games, but now you see why. To Evan and Vivien, you've only known Mom to be working on a research paper or presentation, but hopefully, you've learned that persistence and resilience are the keys to success.

When my TED Talk, "How Whistleblowers Shape History," was published on the TED website, a literary agent reached out to me about writing a book. I put the idea in the back of my mind. I had been busy writing cases for class content; conducting on-camera interviews with white-collar felons, whistleblowers, and victims of fraud and turning those interviews into content; and facilitating fraud seminars around the world. I had a lot of subject matter in many different places, but never all in one place. When my dear sister/friend Blair started working on her second book, she encouraged me to consider writing a book too. I remember telling her, "Accounting professors don't write books," and she replied, "Well, accounting professors don't do documentaries either, but you did that, so why not?"

She was right. Why not?

As the saying goes, it takes a village to raise a child; well, it takes a village to write a book! My next call was to my journalist/author friend, Abby Ellin, about the book-writing process, and she, too, encouraged me to pursue the book. What was once at the back of my mind was now at the forefront. Abby served as my development editor and mentor throughout the book-writing process. I started to think of her as the "book-writer whisperer." From brainstorming sessions, proposal writing, assistance in finding an agent (Michael "Sig" Signorelli at Aevitas Creative Management, thank you for believing in this project from the beginning) to rewrite after rewrite (after rewrite), her support and guidance were vital.

My students have always served as my constant inspiration. My desire to help them better understand how common ethical lapses occur was the main reason for my first on-camera interview with a white-collar felon over a decade ago. One interview turned into many, which led to directing and producing my first documentary, *Crossing the Line: Ordinary People Committing Extraordinary Crimes.* This film process led to me meeting several of the perps you will meet in *Fool Me Once.*

I love telling fraud stories, and when the largest municipal fraud in US history happened in the Chicagoland area, I knew this was the perfect fraud story for my next documentary. After five years of researching the case, interviewing relevant people, and editing the film, *All the Queen's Horses* was born. I will forever be indebted to my amazing *All the Queen's Horses* film team—especially, my talented editor and friend Lesley Kubistal and executive producer Gordon Quinn of Kartemquin Films. So much of what I learned from *All the Queen's Horses* serves as the foundation for *Fool Me Once.*

To the *Fool Me Once* perps, prey, and whistleblowers included in the book, thank you for trusting me with your stories and allowing me and others to gain valuable insights from your experiences. Without you, this book would not have been possible. Your vulnerability and transparency are commendable, and I thank you for your willingness to participate in an interview, visit my DePaul class, be interviewed for one of my documentaries or speak alongside me on a panel. This has truly been a life-changing experience, and I do hope all readers will learn how easy it is to become a perp, prey, or a whistleblower at any moment in time.

To my reviewers, Jason Wojdylo (retired deputy marshal for the US Marshal Service), Dr. Barry Jay Epstein, Natalie Thompson, Alexis Aldridge, and Ayanna King, thank you for sacrificing your time to read *Fool Me Once* in its early days.

To Alyssa Westring, my DePaul colleague and friend, thank you for introducing me to the Harvard Business Review Press team. I remember how nervous I was submitting the first *Fool Me Once* draft to HBR Press editor Kevin Evers, but when the first round of reviewer comments came back and the response was overwhelmingly positive, I was overjoyed. Thank you to the entire production team at Harvard Business Review Press for bringing something that existed only in my head to something that existed on paper. Special shout out to design director Stephani Finks on designing the dopest book cover on the planet, and Lindsey Dietrich from direct sales and Victoria Desmond from production for shepherding me through the process. See, it takes a village!

And to Keila Ravelo, thank you for stepping into the project when you did by offering your insight, research support, and copyediting expertise. Starting the race is one thing, but getting to the finish line often requires support you don't always know you need at the beginning. Thank you, Keila, for helping me cross the finish line with my Wonder Woman power pose (shout out to Amy Cuddy!). Vince LoRusso from TrueUpNow, thank you for creating the *Fool Me Once* interactive game to accompany the book.

Writing a book is definitely a labor of love, and as I reflect back on the process, I've been fortunate to be surrounded by creative minds that have supported me unconditionally along the journey.

We all get fooled from time to time, but my hope for everyone after reading this book is that you will only be fooled once.

ABOUT THE AUTHOR

Kelly Richmond Pope is the Dr. Barry Jay Epstein Endowed Professor of Forensic Accounting in the School of Accountancy and MIS at DePaul University in Chicago, Illinois, where she teaches forensic accounting and managerial accounting. She is also the Institute of Management Accountants (IMA) Research Fellow, leading research projects in corporate governance, ethics, and fraud. She is the coauthor of *A.B.C.'s of Behavioral Forensics: Applying Psychology to Financial Fraud Prevention and Detection* and *Managerial Accounting*, 1st edition. In 2020, Pope was recognized as one of the twenty-five top female leaders in the accounting profession with the Most Powerful Women in Accounting Award given by the American Institute of Certified Public Association and CPA Practice Advisors.

Pope is the director and producer of the award-winning documentary *All the Queen's Horses*, which explores the largest municipal fraud in US history. She has appeared on numerous true-crime shows such as CNBC's *Superheist* and VH1's *My True Crime Story*, and on media outlets such as WGN-TV and the BBC.

Pope is a popular keynote speaker to numerous companies and organizations such as KPMG, Deloitte, EY, RSM, RubinBrown, Microsoft, LinkedIn, Allstate, McDonald's, the Institute of Internal Auditors (IIA), the Institute of Management Accountants (IMA), the American Institute of Certified Public Accountants (AICPA), the Department of Justice, the Securities and Exchange Commission, the Public Company Accounting Oversight Board (PCAOB), the Internal Revenue Service-Criminal Investigations, and the Federal Bureau of Investigation.

Prior to joining the faculty at DePaul University, she worked in the forensic accounting practice at KPMG. She received her doctorate in accounting from Virginia Tech and is a licensed certified public accountant (CPA). Pope received her bachelor of science in accounting from North Carolina A&T State University and her MACCT and PhD in accounting from Virginia Tech.

She resides in the Chicagoland area with her family, but calls Durham, North Carolina, home.

INTERESTED IN MORE?

If you enjoyed this book, please check out my documentary, *All the Queen's Horses*. It goes into more detail about one of the largest municipal frauds committed in US history.

If you want to find out what type of perpetrator or whistleblower you'd be, check out the interactive assessment I created, called *Fool Me Once: A Fraud Experience*.

You can find information about both on my website at www.kellyrichmondpope.com.